ABOVE AND BEYOND

ABOVE AND BEYOND

By the Editors of Time-Life Books

TIME-LIFE BOOKS, ALEXANDRIA, VIRGINIA

CONTENTS

1
AUDACIOUS ADVENTURERS

Looking for trouble: Captain Adventure—Sir Richard Francis Burton . . . African trader . . . Polar knights . . . horse sense . . . open seas . . . riding the wind . . . underground divers

7

2
OUTRAGEOUS EXPLOITS

Dubious distinctions: Tomato taster . . . laughless barrel . . . bagging the Channel . . . boinnng . . . ultra long, ultra light flight . . . grape fun . . . surfing the sky

41

3
UNTO OTHERS

Selflessness and sacrifice: A nation's Darling . . . the mighty Midgetts . . . Shackleton and his men . . . bogus diplomat . . . nuclear infernos

71

4
AGAINST ALL ODDS

Press on regardless: The hero of the *Bounty* . . . blind in Buchenwald . . . a homemade tank . . . survival sacrament . . . endless war . . . death stalks a family at risk

101

Acknowledgments **134**

Picture Credits **134**

Bibliography **135**

Index **139**

AUDACIOUS ADVENTURERS

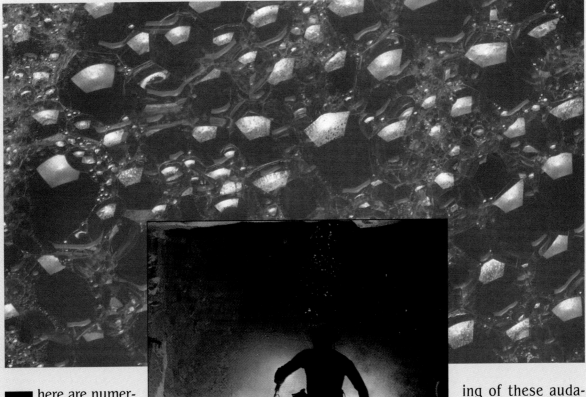

There are numerous motives for adventure. The nineteenth-century English explorer Captain Sir Richard Francis Burton, whose life fairly defined the term, was driven by an insatiable curiosity about the people whose lands he explored. Traveling alone, he took hostility and hospitality, kindness and cruelty, as they came, mapping the labyrinths of unfamiliar cultures. But Burton was more than a seeker of new knowledge. He was one of a rare breed of men and women who seem not to understand the full meaning of deadly peril or impossibility.

Some have been drawn to adventure by the gravitations of excitement; some have come for science or to verify an idea. But the questing of these audacious pilgrims is also an intensely personal journey of exploration through a hidden, largely mental geography within. They have *chosen* the panicking touch of suffocation in a submerged cave, the frightening sting of frostbite in a mountain gale, the leap of the heart when death stands in full view—precisely in order to confront the personal demons of fear, failure, and the dark corners of great souls. No matter what the motive that initially impelled these remarkable travelers, each adventure becomes a redemptive act. As one peerless mountaineer phrased it, using the understatement of the very brave: After the impossible achievement, "a new life begins."

Turkish Delight

Lady Hester Stanhope, niece of the eighteenth-century British prime minister William Pitt the Younger, cut a dashing figure wherever she went. Whether entertaining at Number 10 Downing Street at her uncle's behest or roving the Syrian desert, she placed a premium on her own iconoclastic style and savvy, which won her admirers of a powerful sort.

Egotistical, haughty, and heroically ambitious, Lady Hester had a fascination for all that was alien and strange—an appetite that helped shape her later travels in forbidden lands. When she was still a young woman, a religious zealot named Richard Brothers, then an inmate in Bedlam, London's infamous asylum, had begged to see her. This self-styled nephew of the Almighty claimed supernatural powers and wanted to tell her what he had seen. Against all advice and custom, she had gone to Bedlam to hear him. One day, the madman told her, she would make a pilgrimage to the Holy Land, spend seven years in the desert, be crowned queen of the Jews, and lead forth a chosen people. She believed him, at least to a degree.

The memorable encounter had taken place in 1795, when the young Lady Hester was sweeping London society before her, propelled by her father's wealth, her relationship to Pitt, and her own fearsome wit, towering egotism, and

A horsewoman much admired by the Arabs, Lady Hester Stanhope *(left)* adopted her own colorful version of Turkish pantaloons and turban and took up residence in the Lebanese hilltop home shown above.

domineering personality. Upon William Pitt's death in 1806, however, Lady Hester came to a difficult juncture. A quarrel over her lifestyle had alienated her father and his money; although Pitt's death left her with a handsome pension, the income was nothing like the wealth necessary to live in the style to which she had become accustomed. Her best bet, she decided, was to become an expatriate. In February 1810, now aged thirty-four, Lady Hester and her physician, Charles Meryon, sailed for Gibraltar and from there began a tour of the Mediterranean, shedding proper British conventions at every turn.

One of them was discretion. En route, she met a young Englishman, Michael Bruce, and shocked society by openly taking him as her lover. In Greece, among other highlights, Lady Hester met her heroic model, the brave, brooding poet Lord Byron, whose features she admired, but whose pursuit of the limelight she despised. She and her party narrowly survived a shipwreck en route to Alexandria, Egypt, and she lost most of her belongings. Undaunted, Lady Hester adopted the dress of Turkish men, with billowing pantaloons and vest. While her unconventional attire scandalized some compatriots, various Arab potentates found her androgeny and her renowned horsemanship intriguing.

Arriving in Jerusalem, Lady Hester sensed that she had fulfilled the first part of the Bedlam prophet's prediction. She then pressed on to Damascus, determined to visit the ruins of the ancient city of Palmyra, where only a few Europeans had succeeded in going. The desert surrounding Palmyra was dominated by belligerent Bedouins, who demanded baksheesh, a cash payoff, to allow passage when they did not simply rob and kill unprotected travelers. But Lady Hester—remembering the words of the demented prophet of Bedlam—was set on reaching the ancient city, where she would sit upon the throne of the exotic queen Zenobia. Striking an expensive bargain with the Bedouin leader Mahanna El Fadel, she gained safe passage.

Accompanied by Meryon, Bruce, Mahanna's son Emir Naser, and a retinue of seventy Arabs and forty camels, Lady Hester rode regally into the Syrian desert wearing a striped Bedouin robe, with a brightly colored kaffiyeh on her head. As always, the proud Englishwoman was unflappable, even when Naser staged a mock desertion in an attempt to lever more money out of her. Naser relented, and the party continued on its way.

Just inside Palmyra, they entered the valley of the tombs, littered with the fallen stones that were all that remained of the lost city. The unlikely party made its way through the site to the beat of kettledrums, and as Lady Hester reached a colonnade leading to a triumphal arch, inhabitants of a dusty village near the ruins began to appear. Maidens swathed in veils and bearing garlands posed like statues until the Englishwoman passed, then leaped into an unbridled dance. Under the arch, one girl placed a wreath on La-dy Hester's head, and the crowds greeted the Englishwoman as their *melika,* or "queen."

The remainder of Lady Hester's life served as a sorry footnote to her Palmyra triumph. On her return from the desert, she encouraged Bruce to go back to England while she stayed on in the Syrian town of Sidon. The plague, which had been raging throughout the Levant, attacked her there. She recovered from that illness, but not from frustration or penury. For the rest of her life she was wracked by bouts of depression; her money gone, she borrowed heavily from friends, who generously forgave the debts. However, Lady Hester, the woman who went unveiled into Damascus, the English noble in Turkish dress, remained a legendary figure to Arabs and Europeans alike until her death in 1839, at sixty-three.

Strangely, she left no written record of her accomplishments. Details of her exploits have survived due to the efforts of Charles Meryon, who kept extensive journals of their Near Eastern travels. After Lady Hester's death he published an account drawn from those diaries. The book sold well, and Meryon, who frequently had gone months without pay, was finally compensated for his lifelong loyalty to his colorful employer. □

Blind Chance

In 1819, James Holman embarked on a grand tour of the European continent, a fairly commonplace undertaking for a young English gentleman. But Holman, the son of an Exeter pharmacist, made the three-year junket more memorable than most. He braved the Mediterranean off the beach at Marseilles, climbed to the top of St. Peter's Basilica in Rome, and toured the smoking crater of Mount Vesuvius near Naples, fearlessly negotiating steep paths as his shoes filled with smoking cinders. Returning to England, Holman described his exploits in matter-of-fact prose that focused less on the sights than the detailed sounds of the exotic places he visited and the views of the scores of people he met. His narrative was immensely popular among British readers and went to four editions.

Holman's next undertaking—an effort to circumnavigate the earth from England eastward across Russia—began inauspiciously with a midnight collision between his ship and another on the Thames River. Groping his way on deck, clad only in a nightgown, the intrepid traveler discovered that the ship's helm was unattended. Holman, who had joined the British navy at the age of twelve and had attained the rank of lieutenant before his discharge in 1810, was in his element. He seized the wheel and, as the captain bellowed steering orders, safely guided the ship to a dock.

When the vessel had been repaired, Holman voyaged to St. Petersburg and Moscow, then climbed aboard a horse-drawn cart and lurched 3,500 miles across the Russian steppes into Siberia. There, in the far eastern city of Irkutsk, he enjoyed the attentions of local society until the czarist regime, no doubt suspicious of the foreigner's limitless curiousity, labeled Holman a spy and sent a secret-police officer to escort him back to Moscow. He returned through the howling Russian winter under guard, on a sled, and was ultimately deposited at the Polish border. Although this aborted his first effort to circle the world, the resulting two-volume description of the strange lands and people to the east enhanced his literary standing—and went through three printings.

James Holman's principal work, the four-volume *Voyage Round the World*, appeared in 1834 and described his most ambitious journey: a five-year odyssey comprising Africa, Asia, Australasia, and the Americas. It was, as one biographer wrote later, "one of the most extraordinary monuments of energy and perseverance extant in a literary shape."

Despite the breadth of his experience, the adventurous James Holman was, in a sense, just one more British traveler in an age when subjects of the empire—many far more venturesome than Holman—could be found in every corner of the globe. But Holman traveled with certain handicaps, financial and otherwise. Subsisting on a meager half-pay pension from the Royal Navy, he made his way across the world without servants, relying exclusively on public transportation. Unlike such linguists as Sir Richard Burton *(pages 11-13)*, he knew no language but English. Most remarkable, as a result of some nameless disease that had struck him in the navy, James Holman traveled without his sight. To those who wondered how he did it, Holman explained that constant motion, "by the succession of objects it presents, serves to fill up the deficiencies." Without vision, the Blind Traveler, as Holman came to be called, had truly seen the world. □

James Holman, an extraordinary British traveler of the early nineteenth century, posed for contemporary portraitist George Chinnery in 1830, between journeys to far corners of the earth.

The Amateur Barbarian

The palace of the emir of Harar, in the mountains of what is now Ethiopia, was a windowless mud-and-stone barn, not the kind of building that could, by itself, instill wonder in Lieutenant Richard Francis Burton of the Bombay Native Infantry. But the unfolding spectacle within and around the palace filled Burton with awe and forboding; he was the first European to see it—and live. Other white men had been killed approaching Harar, because the emir and his minions held to an ancient belief that the kingdom would fall with the entrance of the first Christian.

As it often would during his turbulent life of adventure, Burton's fate depended on the outcome of an audience with the person in power. Entering the palace, Burton saw the emir, a slight young man, seated at the far end of a 100-foot-long hall, the approaches to him flanked by a gauntlet of glowering warriors armed with spears whose heads, Burton later recalled, were the size of shovels. Containing his apprehension, Burton strode boldly forward, ready at any time to defend himself with the pistol that he carried in his sash. Two chamberlains forced him to bow. Then the two men faced each other. Why, asked the prince, had the Englishman come to Harar? "To see the light of His Highness's countenance," replied Burton, realizing that his answer, intended to flatter, could be taken as sarcasm. Instead, as Burton wrote later, "the Amir smiled graciously" at his intrepid visitor.

In fact, the rumpled infidel who stood before the emir of Harar was already a heroic figure back in England. Only thirty-three, the tall, powerfully built officer, with his darkly flashing eyes and calm demeanor, epitomized the Victorian explorer extraordinary. There seemed to be nothing he could not—or would not—do. Even in an age of colonial expansion and individualism, Richard Burton loomed large; rarely have the times been better tailored to the man.

Born in 1821, the son of a lieutenant colonel in the Royal Army, Burton grew up in the French city of Tours, where his father took the family after the army pensioned him off. Never easy, Burton was an aggressive boy who evidently welcomed combat with his French schoolmates but had little use for lessons. When the family returned to England a few years later, young Richard remained untutored and undisciplined. A biographer called him a juvenile delinquent, and Burton himself said he was a "resolute and unblushing" liar. Yet Burton's father wanted the boy to be a clergyman, like his grandfather. To that end, Richard attended Oxford University until being dismissed in his second year, then went into the army. Characteristically, he eschewed a commission with a prestigious home-based regiment in favor of one in the Indian army, a composite force of British and native soldiers then controlled by the British East India Company. It was there, in 1842, that Richard Burton's education and extraordinary life really began.

He had already shown an interest in the East while at Oxford. Now, immersed in that world, he studied the Koran, plunged himself into the mysteries of Islam, and became an adherent of the mystical, ascetic Sufi sect. He ventured into bazaars, brothels, and markets called suks, where over pipes of hashish and opium, he assimilated the language, religion, and cul- ◊

ture. Often, he moved in the guise of a native, costumed in flowing robes, his skin artificially darkened. Nearly killed by cholera in July 1846, Burton was given two years' convalescent leave, free time that he used to study the geography and people of Goa, a Portuguese colony south of Bombay; the southwest Indian coast; and the valley of the Indus River in what is now Pakistan.

Drawn by foreign cultures, Burton evidently never thought of joining them—of "going native." His roots remained in England, to which he returned in 1848. Living with his family, which had moved to Boulogne, he began to write—and to plan a great exploit. In 1852, he proposed one to the Royal Geographic Society of London: "For the purpose of removing," he wrote, "the huge white blot which in our maps still notes the Eastern and Central regions of Arabia," he would explore that secret, hostile land.

His choice of exploits challenged an ancient prohibition. The Islamic holy cities of Medina and Mecca were closed to nonbelievers. Although the restrictions had eased somewhat in recent years—Burton would not be the first European into the region—his intrusion into the holiest of temples carried the penalty of death or circumcision. Ig-

noring the risks, and disguising himself as an Arab pilgrim on the hajj, Burton penetrated to the core of Mecca, making detailed measurements and observations of the holy city and its shrines. He debated Islamic theology, flirted with veiled young women, and departed wearing the green turban coveted by all Muslims and permitted solely to the hajjis—those who had completed the pilgrimage to Mecca. Only at the end did his Arab hosts realize they had shown one of their holy cities to an infidel. Then, just thirteen months later, and again disguised as an Arab, Richard Burton had set out for the forbidden city of Harar.

These clandestine sorties into other cultures were only the beginning of his explorations, however. A few months after his visit to Harar, Burton turned to the "unveiling of Isis"—the search for the source of the Nile River. He and a few companions narrowly escaped death at Berbera, in Somaliland; holding off attacking natives with his broadsword, Burton received a horrible wounding by a native spear that pierced both cheeks and his palate. A year later, Burton was serving in the Crimean War. Then he returned to Africa on an exhausting trek that brought the discovery of huge Lake Tanganyika and, by a companion—

John Hanning Speke—Lake Victoria, eventually confirmed as the Nile's true source.

Months after Burton's return to England in 1859, he set off to North America, where, among other things, he stayed in Utah with another tribe that interested him: the Mormons. Two years later he was in Africa again, trekking the deserts and jungles of the continent's west, then in South America to take up a diplomatic post—and explore the jungle highlands—in Brazil.

In 1861, between Utah and Africa, Burton took time to marry his fiancée of several years, Isabel Arundell. With typical disregard for public opinion, the thirty-nine-year-old iconoclast chose a wife from a devout British Catholic family, not one from the ranks of the Anglican upper classes. But there was already much between the pair. Isabel had adored Burton from their first encounter in Boulogne ten years earlier and was overjoyed finally to take her place at his side.

During all his travels, Burton sustained an astonishing output as an author. Besides writing his official reports, he wrote books on each of his expeditions; nearly fifty were published, and dozens more existed in manuscript. More remarkable for a man of such incessant action, he

possessed the deep-seated curiosity and mental acuity of a scholar. Bolstered by his fluency in twenty-five languages and fifteen dialects, he could not only disguise himself as an Arab, he could assume the accent and appearance of many kinds of Arabs. His prolific writings opened the Eastern world to Western readers. Out of Burton's Indian experiences, Europe learned of the great Hindu book of love, the *Kama Sutra*. From the Arabs, Burton brought his sixteen-volume translation of the *Arabian Nights*, formerly read only selectively in expurgated form. Much of what he revealed he had discovered for himself.

Certainly, he was a rough-edged scholar. Though a professional soldier and explorer by vocation, Burton described himself as an "amateur barbarian." Many at home in England thought the description quite apt, not only for his exploits, but for his personal life as well. He criticized colonial bosses for what he deemed stupidity in their rule and spoke out loudly for women's sexual freedom. He made no attempt to hide his own fascination with exotic sexual practices—as one biographer noted, men's vices interested Burton far more than their virtues did. Still, one of Britain's enduring heroes, Burton was knighted in 1886.

For the last eighteen years of his life, Burton lived with Isabel in Trieste, where he was a minor British foreign service functionary. Upon his death in 1890, his remains were returned to his homeland and interred in a marble mausoleum sculpted into the shape of a British officer's tent. It, and the work he had already published, would be all that remained of Richard Burton.

Near the end of his life, in spite of his declining health, Richard Burton wrote or translated scores of books—indeed, he had planned to complete his English translation of *The Perfumed Garden,* a compendium of sixteenth-century Arabic erotica, on the day that he died. That volume, along with dozens of books in various stages of completion, died with him. Claiming to act on the orders of her husband's shade—but possibly wishing to keep private the more lurid entries in his richly detailed journals—Burton's widow destroyed virtually all within a few months of his death. Surprisingly, the same public that had largely ignored Burton's writings when he most needed popular support pilloried Isabel for the destruction of his works. In a final irony, Isabel passed into history not as the loyal and devoted wife she had been, but as the woman who burned Richard Burton's books. □

The Short Happy Life of Mary Kingsley

For the first thirty years of Mary Kingsley's existence, the world knew nothing of her, as she lived the quiet life of a dutiful daughter. Then, after twice plunging into the wilds of what was then darkest Africa, she returned with tales of adventure that shocked Britain's proper Victorians, excited them, and stirred their consciences. She wrote with charm and humor about cannibals and naked warriors, capsized canoes, ferocious leopards, and ravenous crocodiles. But more than that, she introduced her compatriots to the notion—radical at the time—that the cruel continent of Africa was also a place of great beauty, populated by people who, while different, were not inferior.

Kingsley was born in 1862, the daughter of a London doctor, George Kingsley, and his wife, the former Mary Bailey, who had been a Cockney maidservant. George Kingsley's brother Charles was a celebrated writer; George himself was simply restless, and four weeks after the birth of his daughter, he left for the South Seas on the first of many trips to the far reaches of the earth. He seldom returned home, making his presence felt by letters and the publication of an occasional, forgettable book.

Mary's mother, virtually abandoned by her husband and uneasy among her neighbors, followed the Victorian expedient of taking to her bed. Learning early to care for both her mother and her fragile younger brother, Mary also learned how to shift for herself. Unable to attend school, she taught herself to read and write and promptly absorbed the works in her father's library. For the first twenty years of her life, those volumes were her school and her university—especially her favorites, the books on Africa. In 1882, the family moved to Cambridge, where the university's fine library fed the young woman's questing spirit. A researcher at heart, she spent her years there writing up her father's anthropological findings and reading the best science of her time, by such men as Charles Darwin and Thomas Huxley. By the end of her twenties, while still without formal training, she had become a keen biologist and anthropologist; and, although her family could not have known it, she was prepared for adventure.

In February 1892, her father died; her mother followed him only two months later. Suddenly, at the age of thirty, Mary Kingsley was free of her domestic responsibilities. By June she had broken free of England as well, taking passage on a ship to the Canary Islands. Though a habitually lonely woman, owing to her isolating years as her family's keeper, Mary Kingsley was no shrinking violet. The Canaries were a rest-and-recreation center for Europeans who made their livelihood in Africa, and Kingsley soon introduced herself to the rough characters who traded there. From them she learned the reality of the continent, for the traders knew the native tribes and their customs, the coastal geography, and the practical economics of doing business in a savage land.

Because they were not soldiers, politicians, or missionaries, they had no agenda beyond the straightforward urge to make a profit. To the traders, Africans were customers—and equals, not subjects. For their part, the Africans usually responded in kind, welcoming traders where they would have shunned missionaries or colonial overlords. The knowledge and per-

Mary Kingsley's determined features *(below)* appeared in *The Bookman* following her second expedition to Africa, where she netted *Ctenopoma kingsleyae (above)*, one of the three African fish species named for her.

spective gained from the traders guided Kingsley's own travels in West Africa and shaped the way she thought about the continent for the rest of her life.

Kingsley embarked on her first journey in 1893, traveling as one of many traders plying Africa's rivers, understood and welcomed by most natives. But, dressed in her unvarying, Victorian-proper garb of white blouse, long woolen skirt, and boots, she also traveled as a secret scientist—she had learned from the traders that Africans would be suspicious of her technical curiosity. Starting in Luanda, Angola, she made her way through the French and Belgian Congo and returned to England with many specimens of fish and detailed notes about the people and places she had visited. Grateful scholars at the British Museum accepted her fish samples and named three new species after her. As successful as this trip had been, however, to Kingsley it was only a scouting foray for the expedition she had in mind.

That journey took place in 1894 and 1895 and carried Kingsley into the country of the Fang, a cannibalistic tribe far up the Rembwe River in present-day Gabon. Kingsley's trader persona afforded protection against human predation; her cool intelligence deflected other dangers, such as crocodiles and unruly river rapids.

When she returned, Kingsley published two books. The first, an 1897 travelogue, *Travels in West Africa,* was an immediate hit, not only for the insights she offered into an exotic land, but for her breezy style, bravado, and humor in recounting her adventures. "On one occasion," she wrote of an encounter with a crocodile, "a mighty Silurian, as

the *Daily Telegraph* would call him, chose to get his front paws over the stern of my canoe, and endeavored to improve our acquaintance. I had to retire to the bows, to keep the balance right (It is no use saying because I was frightened, for this miserably understates the case.) and fetch him a clip on the snout with a paddle." Kingsley was uncertain as to the creature's size, however. "I should think that crocodile was eight feet long; but don't go and say I measured him, or that this is my outside measurement for crocodiles. I have measured them when they have been killed by other people, fifteen, eighteen and twenty-one feet odd. This was only a pushing young creature who had not learnt manners."

Her second book, *West African Studies,* published in 1899, took a more serious turn, attempting to sway public opinion and press for justice for Britain's African subjects. It was no less popular or compelling than the first book, but her opinions earned her a number of enemies, whom she took on in a series of public appearances. Kingsley planned a third trip to West Africa but delayed it in order to continue her lectures.

In 1899, also, Great Britain launched its war with the Boers of South Africa, and Kingsley's restless nature drew her there, to help nurse the sick and wounded. She arrived in Simonstown in March of 1900. Soon stricken by enteric fever contracted from her patients, Mary Kingsley died on June 3, 1900. The remarkable woman who had entered the world at thirty was dead at age thirty-seven. According to her wishes, she was buried at sea, in the deep waters off the continent she had briefly illuminated. □

Desert Dreams

One of the world's harshest deserts stretches more than 1,500 miles across central Asia, from the Pamir Mountains eastward across China and southern Mongolia. The Takla Makan in western China and the Gobi in Mongolia are lands of extremes. Their terrain soars thousands of feet above sea level, and plunges hundreds of feet below. Summer temperatures regularly exceed 100 degrees Fahrenheit; in winter the mercury drops well below zero. Where the stunted vegetation fails, the surface is covered with gravel or sand. The one certainty is the wind: A dry, unceasing blast scours the land, sucks moisture from animals, plants, and soil, and fills the air with ever-present grit. Howling across one of the sandiest deserts on earth, this eternal wind, with audible effort, propels great pyramidal dunes across the withered landscape. The traders and herders who have traveled the desert for generations call it an evil place, the devil's own, where sand dunes sing and mysterious voices moan throughout the night.

During the 1870s, Lieutenant Colonel Nikolay Mikhaylovich Przhevalsky, an explorer from the Smolensk region, plunged into this scarcely inhabited wasteland and made it his own. The thirty-one-year-old geographer had surveyed portions of Siberia in 1867, and his account of the journey had earned him some repute. In 1870, the Imperial Geographical Society of St. Petersburg, under the aegis of the War Department, sent Przhevalsky eastward once again, this time to survey the rugged lands of south- ◊

Orange lines on a century-old Russian map trace the route of Nikolay Mikhaylovich Przhevalsky's first expedition across Mongolia and China, from the Russian town of Kyakhta *(1)* to Beijing *(2)* to A-la-Shan *(3)* and back to Russia.

knowledge. Although other westerners had crossed it, no one had delineated the area in any detail.

On his first expedition, Przhevalsky, accompanied by Lieutenant Michail Alexandrovich Pyltseff, a handful of guards and bearers, a pair of cossacks, and a caravan of horses and camels trudged the length and breadth of the Asian desert with navi-

ern Mongolia.

At the time, the entire region was called Gobi—a Mongolian term that means "waterless place"—and its size and even the location of its few oasis towns was more a matter of desperate hope and conjecture than certain

gational instruments, surveyor's tools, and notebooks, mapping and measuring. Przhevalsky began in the Russian town of Kyakhta, near the Mongolian border, and headed south and east for more than 800 miles to Beijing. He then reversed his course, turning west and south along the meandering course of the Hwang Ho—the Yellow River—for more than 700 miles to A-la-Shan, then returned to Beijing. A second foray took him once more along the Hwang Ho to A-la-Shan, and some 500 miles beyond, nearly to the northern border of Tibet.

Among Nikolay Przhevalsky's Mongolian finds was a pony, since named for its Russian discoverer, reputed to be the world's only horse descended exclusively from wild stock.

Returning to A-la-Shan, he headed north, clambering across the vast wrinkles of Asian mountain ranges and again traversing the Mongolian desert to his starting point in Russia. The expedition took three years and covered 7,000 miles.

Przhevalsky's attraction to the desert was spiritual and intellectual, not physical. A son of the moist birch forests of European Russia, he found the Mongolian plain to be hostile and trying. "The barrenness and monotony of the Gobi," he wrote, "produce on the traveler a sense of weariness and depression. For weeks together the same objects are constantly before his eyes: cheerless plains covered in winter with the yellowish withered grass of the preceeding years, from time to time broken by dark rocky ridges."

Yet he endured, drawn by the challenge of learning and filling his notebooks with detailed observations of flora and fauna and precise measurements of the terrain. Among the animals he described was a small, previously unclassified native of Mongolia: the wild pony now called Przhevalsky's horse.

Although he recorded everything he encountered, Przhevalsky viewed the wild terrain through the prism of his aloof gentility, learning little of the region's languages and dismissing most of the customs as uncivilized. But his gentlemanly reserve crumbled on his second exploration of the region from 1876 through 1877. Beginning at Alma-Ata, the capital of Kazakhstan, Przhevalsky made his way eastward over the Tien Shan mountain range before descending toward the blasting heat of the Takla Makan.

The descent took Przhevalsky and his companions through a land of charcoal-hued gravel, a moonscape that, he later wrote, filled them with foreboding. "There are no signs of waterholes, no signs of vegetation," he reported. Slipping and sliding over the shale and gravel, they stumbled toward the desert. When one of his bearers gave a water bag to a passing nomad, Przhevalsky flew into a rage—an uncharacteristic tantrum for the ordinarily phlegmatic Russian. One night, after two days of marching through the baking heat and wind, he lay in his yurt—the circular, domed tent of the desert nomads—listening to the voices of the dunes. The curious sighing of the wind-driven sand, he recalled, became a voice telling him, "Go back. This is the devil's country. We do not want you here."

The following day he encountered what seemed to be a caravan of twelve camels followed by a string of mule-drawn carts; no shimmering, ghostly image, the procession was so real that Przhevalsky could distinguish between Chinese and Turkic teamsters. And then the caravan—in fact, an elaborate mirage—vanished, leaving the explorer blinking and bemused.

Przhevalsky and his party endured another week of travel before they reached their first destination: Turfan, an oasis more than 400 feet below sea level at the very edge of the desert. There they were revived by the wondrously fertile fields of the oasis, where fruit grew plentifully and the residents survived the baking midday heat by retiring to the cool cellars of their houses.

Beyond this verdant island, Przhevalsky found salt marshes and black-sand mountains swept by wind that stripped the leaves from the few trees. The explorer often encountered whirling *kwei*—dust devils—that peppered the party with grit as the twisters swirled past. They reached Lop Nor, a lake visited by thirteenth-century traveler Marco Polo, but not surveyed before Przhevalsky's expedition. As winter gripped the band, cold days began to shade into sub-zero nights. Black and yellow sands became a land scattered with shiny, multicolored pebbles. At Lop Nor, the ardent surveyor announced that they would trek to Kiayukwan, the extreme western portal in China's Great Wall, and an ancient gateway to the Takla Makan. Entering the town through a passage known as the Gate of Sighs, Przhevalsky paused to watch two kwei spin across the plain. "Very full of dreams," he mused, his eyes on the desert.

His own desert dreams had only begun to unfold. In 1879, he journeyed into the forbidding mountain fastness of eastern Tibet and traced the sources of the Hwang Ho. On a later expedition from 1883 to 1885, he discovered the watershed between that river and its great southern sister, the Yangtze. When he died in 1888, aged forty-nine, his accomplishments trailed him like a wake—a line of closely mapped terrain more than 10,000 miles long. □

Modern adventurer Ned Gillette is scrupulous about the facts of an expedition when he is raising funds to finance it. But he does admit to one lapse: Promoting a trans-Sahara trek, Gillette used a dashing video of himself aboard a camel—without mentioning that, pressed for time, he had posed for the shot in a Moroccan theme park.

Northern Light

The greetings that passed between the two men were commonplace, if the circumstances were not: One waved his hat; the other did the same. Drawing closer, they shook hands firmly. "How do you do? I'm immensely glad to see you," said one. "Thank you," replied the other. "I also." One man was attired in the checked suit and rubber boots of an English gentleman on an outing—which, in a sense, he was. He was freshly shaven and smelled of soap. The other, as he later described himself, was "clad in dirty rags, black with oil and soot, with long uncombed hair and shaggy beard, black with smoke." The men walked together, chatting amiably. Finally, the Englishman stopped in his tracks and confronted the other: "Aren't you Nansen?"

The date was June 23, 1896. The Englishman was Frederick Jackson, who was then exploring Franz Josef Land, a fractured archipelago at the edge of the Arctic Ocean north of Russia. The bearded, dirty traveler he encountered was indeed Nansen: Fridtjof Nansen, a thirty-five-year-old Norwegian who had not been seen or heard from since the sum-

mer of 1893. When Frederick Jackson chanced upon him, Nansen and a companion, Hjalmar Johansen, were on their way home after pushing to within 224 miles of the North Pole—the farthest north any human being had yet traveled.

Their journey had begun exactly three years earlier, when Nansen, Johansen, and eleven others sailed from Oslo, Norway, in their 128-foot ship *Fram*—"Forward" in Norwegian—with the intention of becoming frozen in the polar pack ice and drifting with it across the North Pole. No human being had ever reached the pole, and no explorers had taken the time to make scientific observations in the polar regions. *Fram* was the ideal platform for both activities. She was specially built to take the punishment of the pack ice; her hull was more than two feet thick at the water line and shaped so that encroaching ice did not crush the vessel, but forced it to ride up out of the water. In addition, the expedition carried five years' worth of provisions; the men expected to remain icebound for most of that time.

Nansen was the ideal leader, intelligent, physically capable, and possessed of a shrewd tactical sense. In 1888, he and five other men had traversed Greenland in two

months, a 400-mile journey that earlier expeditions had tried and ultimately abandoned. His predecessors had started at the government outpost of Godthaab on the island's west coast; their goal was the desolate, steep eastern coast. Nansen successfully attacked Greenland from the opposite direction, beginning in the isolated east, reasoning that Godthaab—no matter how primitive—was a more attrac-

Norwegian arctic explorers Fridtjof Nansen *(above, foreground)* and Hjalmar Johansen paddle kayaks in the summer of 1896 near Franz Josef Land. Earlier in the expedition, a reflective Nansen *(left)* sits by the icebound *Fram*, whose rigging flies drying animal pelts.

Fridtjof Nansen *(back row, fourth from left)* gathers with his hardy twelve-man crew on the deck of *Fram* shortly before their voyage into the polar ice.

tive and encouraging destination.

Fram performed as she had been designed to do, rising onto the ice as it closed in. The crew busied itself admiring the northern lights, charting their progress, making frequent weather observations, measuring the ice, and taking soundings of the Arctic Ocean, which turned out to be far deeper than they expected. Most important, Nansen proved correct in his theory that the ice drifted with ocean currents. But gradually, as they measured their position with the sun and the stars, they saw that the currents would not bear them poleward after all. As early as September, they realized that, after fifteen months of northward trending, they had begun moving south, away from their goal.

Thanks to Nansen's thoroughness and intelligence, the long and difficult expedition had been notably devoid of hardship. Despite the cold and close quarters, the explorers had passed two years in relative comfort, compared with most arctic expeditions, protected from the elements by the carefully designed ship—and from one another by Nansen's sensitive selection of crew members. Now, as the goal slipped further away, Nansen exhibited the boldness of his leadership. Assembling his party in the spring of 1895, he announced he and one other man would leave the ship on its southward drift and make a dash for the pole on foot. He selected Hjalmar Johansen, a reserve naval officer who had been so eager to join the expedition he had signed on as a stoker in the engine room. They would take minimal provisions.

For three weeks the men slogged over the ice, sometimes scrambling and hauling their sleds over twenty-foot-high pressure ridges thrown up by colliding floes, sometimes slipping into snowmelt pools that soaked their clothing, which then froze solid. Eventually, their navigational sightings told them that their desperate march was making almost no progress: The ice on which they traveled was drifting away from the North Pole almost as rapidly as they were walking toward it. Just 224 miles from their goal, Nansen and Johansen admitted defeat—and terrible isolation. They could not return to *Fram;* the ship, too, was drifting away, and they had no way of finding it. The pair seized the only option available to them and turned toward Franz Josef Land, 400 miles to the south.

Their hardships were unceasing, made worse by the melting of the pack ice as they moved southward under the sun of the brief arctic summer. Reaching the edge of the pack at the end of July, they could just make out the islands of Franz Josef Land in the distance. They launched two kayaks they had carried for the purpose and paddled to the shore. There they were forced to stop, for the polar winter was al-

ready approaching. They hurriedly killed walrus, using the hides for tents and the meat for food, and polar bears for food and warm rugs. They dug in for the long arctic winter, at times nearly hibernating, for they spent as much as twenty hours a day sleeping in their shelter as the blasting northern winds shrieked around them.

In May, as the arctic spring began, they set off toward the south and encountered the British expedition about a month later. The Englishman's supply ship bore them south to the Norwegian mainland. Within a week of their return, Nansen and Johansen learned that the *Fram* had recently broken out of the pack ice near Spitzbergen with all hands safe. It marked a happy ending to Fridtjof Nansen's final arctic venture. By now a national hero, the Norwegian turned during the next thirty years to another kind of expedition. In 1922, Nansen received the Nobel Prize, not for pioneering arctic exploration, but for his humanitarian efforts on behalf of prisoners of war and refugees following the First World War. □

Pony Tale

Before World War II, few true roads linked the countries of South America. The principal interchange between North and South America was carried on by sea and, in a rudimentary way, by early air transports. But the lack of established land routes failed to deter a Swiss-born, British-educated Argentine teacher named Aimé Felix Tschiffely, who in 1926 set out from Buenos Aires for Washington, D.C. The 10,000-mile journey would have taken less than three weeks by ship. For Tschiffely,

who opted to travel by horseback, the trip lasted two and a half years.

Whim played no part in Tschiffely's decision to use literal horsepower for his long trek. Like most venturers, he had a purpose beyond the journey itself: to draw attention to the plight of the wild horses of South America. His mounts, Mancha and Gato (in Spanish, "Spot" and "Cat"), were descended from the horses brought to the New World by Don Pedro Mendoza, the founder of Buenos Aires, in 1535. When Indians sacked the early Spanish settlement, the horses scattered, becoming, over successive generations, the wild ponies of the Argentine pampas. By the 1920s, however, predation and competition for their natural habitat had pushed these

creatures to the brink of extinction. By dramatizing the wild horses' strengths, Tschiffely hoped to convince the Argentine government that they were worth saving. What could be hardier, after all, than a horse capable of walking nearly halfway around the globe?

Tschiffely cantered across the pampas, surmounted the frigid, foggy Andes mountain range at 18,000 feet, plodded along Peruvian beaches, and skirted mudholes in Ecuador. He and his horses swam as much as walked through the Colombian rain forests. In the Panamanian jungle, Tschiffely ate iguanas, rhea eggs, and armadillos, while pestiferous mosquitoes and ticks fed on him and his steeds. Mexico brought bandits and revolu-

As gaucho-garbed Aimé Tschiffely looks on, New York mayor Jimmy Walker holds his visitor's pampas pony during 1928 ceremonies celebrating the Argentine's 10,000-mile ride to New York.

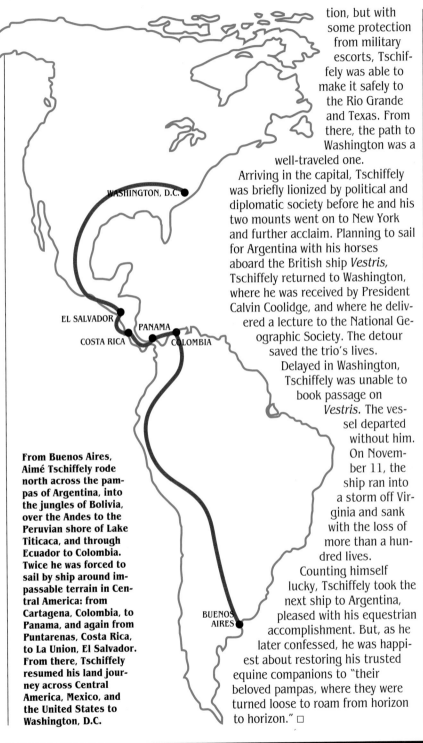

tion, but with some protection from military escorts, Tschiffely was able to make it safely to the Rio Grande and Texas. From there, the path to Washington was a well-traveled one.

Arriving in the capital, Tschiffely was briefly lionized by political and diplomatic society before he and his two mounts went on to New York and further acclaim. Planning to sail for Argentina with his horses aboard the British ship *Vestris*, Tschiffely returned to Washington, where he was received by President Calvin Coolidge, and where he delivered a lecture to the National Geographic Society. The detour saved the trio's lives.

Delayed in Washington, Tschiffely was unable to book passage on *Vestris*. The vessel departed without him. On November 11, the ship ran into a storm off Virginia and sank with the loss of more than a hundred lives.

Counting himself lucky, Tschiffely took the next ship to Argentina, pleased with his equestrian accomplishment. But, as he later confessed, he was happiest about restoring his trusted equine companions to "their beloved pampas, where they were turned loose to roam from horizon to horizon." □

From Buenos Aires, Aimé Tschiffely rode north across the pampas of Argentina, into the jungles of Bolivia, over the Andes to the Peruvian shore of Lake Titicaca, and through Ecuador to Colombia. Twice he was forced to sail by ship around impassable terrain in Central America: from Cartagena, Colombia, to Panama, and again from Puntarenas, Costa Rica, to La Union, El Salvador. From there, Tschiffely resumed his land journey across Central America, Mexico, and the United States to Washington, D.C.

Great Dame

Dame Freya Stark is the unchallenged doyenne of all those indomitable female travelers who have sallied forth from Britain to explore some of the world's least hospitable regions. But Dame Freya, more than most, journeyed as a kind of Victorian Empire in miniature, convinced of the rightness of British reign, and careful neither to break nor adopt the customs of strange lands. Whatever the conditions and however wild her companions, as she might have put it, she made it a rule never to make the coffee or her own camp bed, for appearances were important. Even when facing the possibility of death during a siege of the British embassy in Baghdad in 1941, she managed to smuggle in cosmetics for the womenfolk. "A woman asked if I didn't think it time for us to give up using our lipsticks," she wrote; "but I mean to be killed, if it comes to that, with my face in proper order."

The daughter of artist parents who divided their time between Dartmoor in England and the town of Asolo in northern Italy, ◊

Dame Freya Stark poses in Arab dress for the dangerous journey described in her 1928 book, *Beyond the Euphrates*.

Dame Freya was born to a life of adventure. As a baby, she was carried by guides on treks across the Italian Alps into Austria. A disfiguring accident in her teens, when her hair got caught in machinery and one of her ears was torn, led her to dress to conceal the mark; broad, floppy hats became a Freya trademark. Although she married briefly, she seems never to have had the slightest interest in quiet conformity: Life, Dame Freya apparently believed, was intended for learning and adventure.

Her earliest trips took her to some of the wildest parts of the Middle East, where she visited remote corners of Turkey, Iran, Syria, Afghanistan, and Arabia. She usually traveled on her own, by horse, donkey, or camel, picking up guides as they were needed. Although she often crossed bandit country, she relied on her friendliness and her skills as a linguist to see her through. Fluent from childhood in French, Italian, and German, she prepared herself for her adventures by adding Arabic, Persian, and Turkish to her repertoire. In addition, she always took care never to offend any local custom or belief.

Nevertheless, there were times when she was at risk. In Iran in the 1920s, during the troubles accompanying the establishment of the Pahlavi dynasty, she even forswore her hats so that passing gunmen could see her long hair hanging free and not mistake her for a male enemy. On another trip she found that her guides were trying to smuggle opium hidden in her possessions. Refusing to be intimidated, she threw the packet in a river. The guides raged but did not molest her. In all her travels, that was something no one dared.

Dame Freya has described her journeys in more than thirty books, which have won her fame and honors; in 1942, she became the first woman to win the coveted gold Founder's Medal of the Royal Geographic Society, for her explorations in Arabia. Yet the testimonial Dame Freya treasures most was given to her by desert Arabs. "This is a certificate to Miss Freya Stark, English, traveler," the document reads, "that she is conversant with laws and guided by religion, and of an honorable house, and is the first woman to travel from England to Hadhramaut alone—and is mistress of endurance and fortitude in travel and the suffering of terrors and danger."

Dame Freya continued her travels well beyond the age when most explorers are content to settle down with their memories. At the age of eighty-four, resplendent in a large-brimmed pink sun hat, she floated down the Euphrates River on a raft in the company of a television crew. Three years later, she undertook a three-week pony trek in the Himalayas until forced to turn back by blizzards. "Of course my doctor did his best to prevent me," she said later, "but I don't think at eighty-seven one ought to be afraid of dying." She lives today, not quite a century old, in an apartment in Asolo, where she began the life that became her epic journey. □

Frail Vessels

Norwegian zoologist Thor Heyerdahl is one of the world's best-known adventurers, but an adventurer with a difference: His daring exploits are, in fact, searching anthropological experiments—of which he himself has usually been the subject. Since the 1940s, Heyerdahl has crossed oceans in primitive craft and undertaken ambitious experiments in living to test the abilities of preindustrial technology and the resourcefulness of ancient societies, which Heyerdahl claims were far more accomplished than is generally believed. He suspects that, using primitive but effective technologies, antique civilizations were able to forge far-flung global networks. His exploits have sparked awe in millions of admirers around the world; but Heyerdahl's unconventional approach has failed to win favor where he needs it most of all—among fellow scientists.

Heyerdahl began what was to become a lifelong enterprise in 1937, at the age of twenty-two, when he and his wife, Liv, sailed from Norway to the South Pacific island of Tahiti, thence to Fatu-Hiva, a tiny atoll in the Marquesas group a thousand miles away. The couple established themselves in a bamboo hut beneath the island's looming mountain rain forest, intending to stay for a year. At first their tiny clearing seemed like paradise. They plucked tropical fruit from trees and bathed in clear mountain pools. When the rainy season came, however, their tiny hand-built hut was flooded, and they both became ill. Still, they persevered through the year before returning to Norway.

The Pacific interlude led Heyerdahl to wonder about the true origins of the island people. One night, as he and his wife sat on the beach at Fatu-Hiva, she remarked on the fact that weather came to the island from the east—not from the west, as it does at higher latitudes. An old chief had told Heyerdahl that his ancestors had also come from the east, and Liv's comment set the scientist thinking. After pondering the question, and after considerable study back in Norway, Heyerdahl thought he had the answer: The islanders had come from Peru. His next project was designed to prove it.

In 1947, Heyerdahl launched the raft *Kon-Tiki (below)*, a forty-five-foot vessel built of balsa logs lashed with rope, equipped with a square sail and a mango-wood tiller, and topped by a banana-leaf hut. By sailing from Peru to Polynesia with the prevailing winds and currents, Heyerdahl hoped to demonstrate that early South American seafarers could have colonized the South Pacific atolls ◊

aboard such craft, bringing with them their art and sun-worshiping rituals—a hypothesis very much at odds with conventional anthropological wisdom.

On the seventh of August, 101 days after leaving the port city of Callao, Heyerdahl and five companions completed their 4,000-mile journey. It would be for others to argue whether Polynesia had in fact been colonized by early Americans, but Heyerdahl and his companions established the fact that the feat would have been within their grasp. Experts notwithstanding, Heyerdahl's book about the journey became a bestseller.

Over the next few years, Heyerdahl increasingly turned toward another Pacific mystery: Easter Island and the enormous stone heads that stand above its shores, staring out over the sea. The Norwegian directed an extensive archaeological dig on the island and advanced explanations for how the heads had been carved, transported from quarries, and erected. Seeking to link the culture that produced the heads—now long disappeared—to other cultures, Heyerdahl proposed a link between Easter Island, South America's pre-Inca cultures, and the ancient Egyptians. Once again, others would argue the theory's

merits, while Heyerdahl attempted to demonstrate that the basic requirement for a cultural interchange—the transportation of people across the Atlantic Ocean—was possible. His vehicle was a boat built of papyrus reeds in North Africa. Two were built. The first, *Ra I,* became waterlogged and sank before reaching the West Indies. But the second boat, *Ra II,* made it from Morocco to Barbados.

Heyerdahl went on to study the ancient Sumerians, again by building and sailing an ancient kind of vessel: the reed sailboat *Tigris,* which he piloted in the Red Sea, the Persian Gulf, and the Indian Ocean. He wanted to learn if such craft could have plied the sea lanes between Africa and India. In 1992, at the age of seventy-eight, the intrepid Norseman was still busily trying to solve the puzzles of peoples' origins. His latest effort centered on the ancient Peruvian settlement of Tucume, which he believes was once a trading hub on the Pacific coast. The remains of Tucume are marked by 1,000-year-old adobe pyramids—structures he finds tantalizingly similar to the pyramids of Egypt. □

Treasure of the Himalayas

At two o'clock in the afternoon of June 3, 1950, three years before Sir Edmund Hillary and Tenzing Norgay scaled Mount Everest, before helicopters and high technology became routine on mountaineering expeditions, two Frenchmen—Maurice Herzog and Louis Lachenal—stood in blinding sunlight, numbing cold, and howling wind on the summit of Annapurna in the Himalaya Mountains, 26,493 feet above sea level. Thousands of feet below them, clouds blocked their view of the tortured valleys and steep green fields of Nepal. If this was not the roof of the world—nearby Everest, the planet's tallest peak, rises 29,028 feet—it was one of a handful of towering columns supporting that symbolic roof.

Herzog and Lachenal—members of the first French Himalayan expedition to be mounted after World War II—had achieved their goal of becoming the first men in history to scale a mountain higher than 8,000 meters (26,271 feet). Their climb was a stupendous accomplishment, in that or any other era. Herzog, the leader of this French Himalayan expedition, was an amateur climber, as were eight other members of the team. Lachenal, Gaston Rébuffat, and Lionel Terray were professionals who made their living as mountaineering guides in the rugged Chamonix Valley region of France. Although all members of the expedition had extensive experience on Europe's Alpine peaks, only one of them—photographer Marcel Ichac—had ever climbed in the much more difficult environment imposed by the Himalayas.

In 1986, nearly forty years after he first advanced his migration theories of how the South Pacific was settled, Thor Heyerdahl (left) was still pondering the enigmatic statues of Easter Island.

The climbers endured the usual hardships attending Himalayan expeditions: The route had to be scouted through the poorly mapped Nepalese mountains; ice, snow, avalanches, crevasses, and cold hampered the climbers' progress. For most of them, the thin air at high altitude meant constant fatigue, headaches, and reduced mental acuity. Above 20,000 feet, where air is only about half as dense as it is at sea level, even the simplest tasks required intense concentration and effort. And, like every other expedition to the Himalayas, the French were engaged in a race to complete their work in the brief window of opportunity between the retreat of winter and the onset of the storms and snows of the summer monsoon. Delay could bring failure—and death.

Herzog and Lachenal reached Annapurna's summit after spending a sleepless night huddled in a tent that teetered on a steep, icy slope at the 24,600-foot level. Lack of oxygen and fatigue made them too weak to eat or even heat water for tea. Cold numbed their hands and feet. But euphoria gripped the pair as they stood at the peak. "I was stirred to the depths of my being," Herzog wrote later. "Never had I felt happiness like this—so intense and yet so pure." Herzog unfurled the French tricolor, and both men took the obligatory photographs.

Lachenal broke the summit's spell. "We must go down at once," he yelled above the screaming wind. "Come on." Both men's feet felt like blocks of wood. Already clouds were sweeping across what had been a clear, blue-black sky. Herzog trailed

his companion as they descended. On the way down to their precariously perched campsite, Herzog paused to open his pack. With that brief, seemingly unimportant act, the Frenchman transformed their triumphant descent into a nightmarish, five-week-long retreat from the mountain.

Later, Herzog could not remember why he stopped. Soon his original intent became irrelevant, for the events that followed changed his life: "My gloves!" he remembered crying out. "Before I had time to bend over, I saw them slide and roll. They went further and further straight down the slope," he wrote. "The movement of those gloves was engraved in my sight as something ineluctable, irremediable, against which I was powerless."

Like most prudent hikers and ▷

Bound for Annapurna *(inset),* France's 1950 Himalayan expedition members wave goodbye to Paris from the door of their airplane. From left: Louis Lachenal, Maurice Herzog, Gaston Rébuffat, Lionel Terray, and Marcel Ichac.

mountaineers, Herzog carried an extra pair of socks in his pack for use in just such situations. But he forgot them in his panic and oxygen-starved confusion and, leaving his hands unprotected, plunged downhill toward the safety of the tent. The temperature, though unrecorded, was certainly far below zero, and the wind grew stronger.

Back at the campsite, Herzog and Lachenal found two more members of their expedition, Lionel Terray and Gaston Rébuffat. Herzog's euphoria returned, and he bubbled over with enthusiasm at the day's accomplishment. Terray, too, was overcome with joy. But abruptly, Terray's smile faded. "Maurice—your hands!" Herzog's fingers were violet and white, frozen as hard as ten small sticks. Lachenal's feet seemed to be in little better condition. Terray and Rébuffat spent the entire night massaging their comrades' extremities and flogging them with the end of a rope, hoping to restore circulation.

Their troubles had barely begun. All four nearly died during the next day's descent in a snowstorm. They became lost in the jumble of ice at the edge of the Annapurna glacier and spent the night bivouacked at the bottom of a crevasse. A small avalanche covered them with snow, and they nearly lost their boots. The following day was worse: Not only were Herzog and Lachenal severely frostbitten, but Rébuffat and Terray were snow-blind, having removed their goggles the day before. Herzog was convinced he would die.

Staggering and sliding, they continued downward. Another avalanche engulfed the party, which now included two Sherpas, the Himalayan tribesmen who tra-

ditionally guide and assist mountain climbers. At last the group reached the expedition's Camp II, where the party's doctor, Jacques Oudot, waited to treat them. Louis Lachenal still showed his old bravado. As he approached the camp on painful, frozen feet, he called out, "Want to see how a Chamonix guide comes down from the Himalaya?" By then, strips of blackened skin hung from Herzog's hands.

The immediate dangers were behind them. Now began an even more grueling ordeal. Herzog and Lachenal had to be carried quickly out of the mountains. The monsoon rains had begun, and the pair needed prompt medical attention in a well-equipped hospital. The descent became the rout of a small, battered army. By day, Herzog and Lachenal were carried by porters on makeshift seats and stretchers. At rest stops and at night, Oudot administered

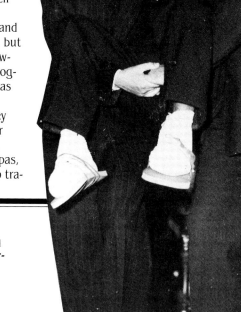

painful injections of antibiotics and anesthetic drugs to combat the effects of frostbite. Then the injections stopped, and trail-side amputations began. One by one, Lachenal lost his toes; Herzog lost his toes and fingers. Their dressings stank in the growing heat and dampness. Flies swarmed over them. Both men burned with extreme fever, and Herzog lost more than forty pounds. But somehow they survived.

They returned home to France as heroes and changed men. "Annapurna," wrote Herzog, "was a treasure on which we should live the rest of our days. With this realization we turn the page: a new life begins. There are other Annapurnas in the lives of men." Although Herzog would never climb another mountain, he plunged into his new life, devoting his considerable energies to a career as a corporate executive. He eventually became France's secretary of state for youth and sports.

No one knows if the spiritual treasure that served Herzog so well would have been sufficient for Lachenal. On November 26, 1955, some five and a half years after his ordeal on Annapurna, Lachenal was skiing with another Alpinist, Jean-Pierre Payot, on the Col du Rognon, near Chamonix. As they passed over a snow bridge, the fragile structure gave way, casting Lachenal into a steep crevasse. When rescuers finally reached him they found that the fall had broken his neck—Louis Lachenal had been killed by a mountain after all. □

Maimed by the mountain he defeated, Annapurna expedition leader Maurice Herzog is carried into Paris's Elysée Palace by Marcel Ichac and Lionel Terray.

Born Sailor

Tristan Jones was born on the South Atlantic Ocean aboard his Welsh father's ship and named for the nearest bit of land: the lone rocky islet of Tristan da Cunha, located about halfway between South Africa and Argentina. That was 1924. For the next fourteen years, young Tristan Jones lived ashore, in Wales, then returned to the sea—this time for good.

As a youngster, Jones shipped aboard small sailing vessels carrying cargo in the English Channel and North Sea, then, like nearly every other British sailor, served in the Royal Navy during World War II. But after his discharge in 1952, Jones returned to small sailing craft, which, in the ensuing four decades, he has sailed an estimated 450,000 miles—almost a round trip to the moon. He has crisscrossed the Atlantic Ocean twenty times—nine trips solo—and circumnavigated the globe three times. He has rounded every major cape, challenging the Southern Ocean between the major continents and Antarctica. He once spent more than a year frozen in the pack ice above the Arctic Circle, in deliberate imitation of the 1896 polar expedition of Fridtjof Nansen *(pages 18-19)*.

Jones made a point of sailing the world's lowest body of navigable water—Israel's Dead Sea, 1,296 feet below sea level—and the highest, Lake Titicaca, perched two miles high on the border of Peru and Bolivia. In both places, he battled political interference and physical obstacles. Both waters are landlocked, and Jones, having little money, improvised arrangements to move his vessels. When Peruvian officials blocked his return from the Bolivian end of Titicaca, for example, he hauled, trucked, dragged, drifted, and sailed his twenty-foot boat 700 miles eastward down the eastern slope of the Andes, across the Mato Grosso—the huge area of swamps, streams, and rain forests in central South America familiarly called the Green Hell—and down the Paraguay and Paraná rivers to Buenos Aires.

Where others have seen obstacles, Jones has always detected opportunity—even when the barrier is one to dampen the largest of spirits. In 1982, Jones's left leg was amputated above the knee as a result of an injury sustained while he was in the navy. Undeterred by the setback, Jones was once more at sea within a year, skippering the thirty-six-foot trimaran *Outward Leg*, which had been specially fitted to accommodate his new shortage—he despises the term *handicap*, a "hateful word" that evokes "visions of cap-in-hand!" Beginning in San Diego, California, Jones voyaged eastward with a new purpose, to "show what other people in my physical state can do."

Outward Leg stopped in Mexico, Central America, and North and ◊

South America. Tristan Jones and his craft crossed the Atlantic and struck off across Europe along the Rhine and Danube. With a young German by the name of Thomas Ettenhuber serving as mate, Jones pierced the Iron Curtain, still in place in 1985, and sailed into the Black Sea and then back into the Mediterranean. They traversed the Suez Canal, voyaged down the long, pirate-infested Red Sea, set a 4,000-mile course across the Indian Ocean, and finally dropped anchor in Phuket, on the west coast of Thailand, in the summer of 1986.

In thirty-four countries on five continents, Jones preached his gospel that infirmity need not destroy a person; he organized the nonprofit Atlantis Society to "reach poverty-stricken and crippled kids and provide them where possible

with the basic means to earn a living." Noting that few among those he was trying to reassure had the wherewithal to test themselves in a costly seagoing trimaran, Jones set about designing a more accessible project. He set seven criteria for the project: It had to be done in a boat, be relatively inexpensive, and lie within the capabilities of disabled youngsters; it had to be within a day or two of medical help, be politically possible, and convey some kind of benefit to society; and it would have to do something no one had done before.

Turning over various possibilities in his restless mind, Jones soon settled on what the new adventure would be. Fitting out a Thai fishing boat—christened *Henry Wagner* after a friend—and rounding up a crew of three dis-

abled Thai youngsters, Jones and Ettenhuber set out to cross Thailand's narrow Isthmus of Kra by way of its rivers—an eighty-mile sail and portage that no one had accomplished before. "Between us," Jones wrote, "we have one arm, two legs, and half a head missing"—this last referring to the fact that the myopic Ettenhuber had smashed his glasses early in the trip.

The small, determined party set out in June 1987, dodging pirates and storms along the way. Jones endured sickness brought on by an infection in his foot. Time and again they pushed, levered, lifted, and dragged *Henry Wagner* across fallen trees, dams, and shallows. Frequently able-bodied villagers jeered the efforts of the one-legged European and his crippled crew. But the voyagers prevailed; each time they

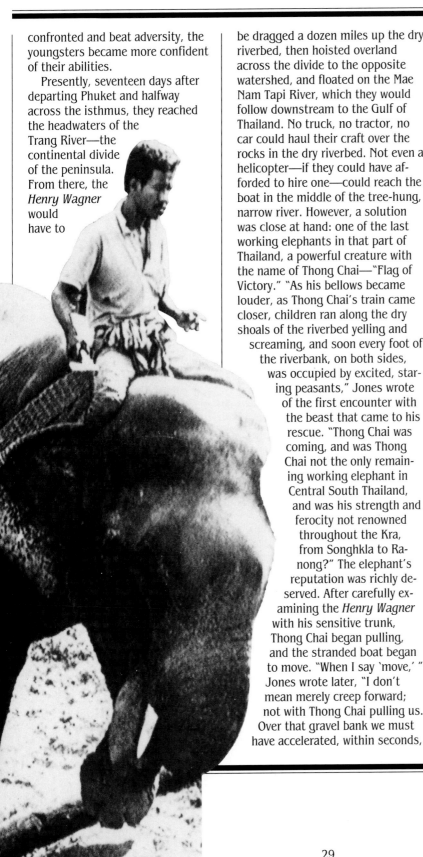

An elephant named Thong Chai, or "Flag of Victory," hauls Tristan Jones's boat *Henry Wagner* up the parched bank of the Trang River during a 1987 portage across Thailand's Kra Peninsula.

confronted and beat adversity, the youngsters became more confident of their abilities.

Presently, seventeen days after departing Phuket and halfway across the isthmus, they reached the headwaters of the Trang River—the continental divide of the peninsula. From there, the *Henry Wagner* would have to be dragged a dozen miles up the dry riverbed, then hoisted overland across the divide to the opposite watershed, and floated on the Mae Nam Tapi River, which they would follow downstream to the Gulf of Thailand. No truck, no tractor, no car could haul their craft over the rocks in the dry riverbed. Not even a helicopter—if they could have afforded to hire one—could reach the boat in the middle of the tree-hung, narrow river. However, a solution was close at hand: one of the last working elephants in that part of Thailand, a powerful creature with the name of Thong Chai—"Flag of Victory." "As his bellows became louder, as Thong Chai's train came closer, children ran along the dry shoals of the riverbed yelling and screaming, and soon every foot of the riverbank, on both sides, was occupied by excited, staring peasants," Jones wrote of the first encounter with the beast that came to his rescue. "Thong Chai was coming, and was Thong Chai not the only remaining working elephant in Central South Thailand, and was his strength and ferocity not renowned throughout the Kra, from Songhkla to Ranong?" The elephant's reputation was richly deserved. After carefully examining the *Henry Wagner* with his sensitive trunk, Thong Chai began pulling, and the stranded boat began to move. "When I say 'move,' " Jones wrote later, "I don't mean merely creep forward; not with Thong Chai pulling us. Over that gravel bank we must have accelerated, within seconds, to four or five knots." Dragging the vessel along the riverbed, the elephant worked for fifteen minutes at a time, then took a break to graze and rest. Two days later they arrived at a point where the boat could be taken from the river, placed on a truck, and driven to the next body of water. After nearly two more weeks of crossing more dams, evading more fallen trees, and coping with more injuries, Jones and his crew arrived at their destination on the Gulf of Thailand.

They had completed their journey and, more important, made their point. Television crews had covered the last stages of their struggle, demonstrating to the world what Tristan Jones had known all along: Injury and infirmity need not destroy the human spirit.

None of Jones's exploits has ever made him wealthy. Many times in his life, he found himself broke and alone in unfamiliar cities. At one point during the Kra journey, he sent Ettenhuber back to Phuket in the hope that his publisher had sent a payment. In the meantime, Jones calculated, the five dollars remaining in his pocket would last until Ettenhuber's return. "Such," the world traveler concluded, "is the reality of 'adventure.' "

A grimmer sort of reality crowded in after *Henry Wagner*'s Kra Peninsula voyage. In 1988, Ettenhuber died of a hidden, congenital heart ailment at the age of twenty-four. Jones, who settled in Thailand, ended the Kra journey with a badly infected foot that never healed; in 1991, that leg was amputated. But true to form, the indomitable sailor was soon back in Phuket, eagerly planning what he would do next in order to demonstrate the irrelevance of adversity. □

Wind Riders

Late one February night in 1977, insomniac Maxie Anderson flipped restlessly through the pages of a magazine in the study of his Albuquerque, New Mexico, home. He stopped at an article about Edwin Yost, an American balloonist, who had come closer than anyone else to completing the first manned balloon flight across the Atlantic. Yost's trip ended when a storm forced him into the Atlantic Ocean 700 miles off the coast of Portugal. Fortunately, a passing ship plucked him to safety. Anderson, at forty-two, had become bored by the mining businesses that had made him a millionaire and, for excitement, had taken up ballooning in the early 1970s. A transatlantic balloon flight seemed to be just the test he had been looking for.

Before long, the mining mogul was explaining his vision to his longtime friend and ballooning partner, Ben Abruzzo, a wealthy real-estate developer and avid sportsman who thrived on taking risks. Abruzzo leaped at the opportunity to succeed where Edwin Yost had failed. But, wisely, they promptly hired Yost to design and build their balloon. They would dedicate their flight to the memory of Charles Lindbergh, who had flown solo across the Atlantic in an airplane in 1927, just fifty years

earlier. In the spirit of honoring Lindbergh, who had become known as the United States' "Lone Eagle," their balloon would be called *Double Eagle*. Also like Lindbergh, Anderson and Abruzzo planned to drift beyond the European coast, all the way to Paris.

The duo had much to learn. Their own experience was in hot-air ballooning, in which air made buoyant by constant heating keeps the balloon aloft. Such lighter-than-air craft can be used only for short hops, however, because of the weight of the fuel required to fire their heaters. *Double Eagle*'s balloon would have to be an enormous bag filled with helium. Yost gave them some lessons, and after assembling a ground crew that included a meteorologist and a physicist, the two felt ready for anything. Abruzzo, quick thinking and quick to act, would be in charge of regulating the ballast, controlling the balloon's rise and fall—effectively, the pilot. The more deliberate and methodical Anderson would handle the radio and navigation.

Double Eagle took off from a field near Marshfield, Massachusetts, on September 9, 1977. The journey went

smoothly at first, with the balloon sliding along the northeastern coast of America at an altitude of 2,000 feet. This, however, was considerably below their planned cruising altitude of between 10,000 and 15,000 feet, higher than most heavy weather but not so high as to require the men to use supplemental oxygen. Fifteen hours into the flight, when they encountered a storm over Canada's Gulf of St. Lawrence, *Double Eagle*'s crewmen received their first taste of dangerous discomfort.

Living in New Mexico, the pair had given little thought to rain. Now water sluiced down *Double Eagle*'s smooth sides and into the open gondola. Anderson donned a waterproof poncho that his wife had thoughtfully packed for him. That and a sheepskin hat kept him snug. Abruzzo had naively chosen to wear the same goose-down jacket and trousers that kept him warm and dry on the ski slopes. Within minutes, his puffy outfit was a

10,000

6,500

The flight progressed as planned until August 13, when a layer of clouds screened the sun, cooling and reducing the buoyancy of the balloon's helium enough to drop the craft 3,500 feet.

LAUNCH

Double Eagle II's successful flight began on August 11, 1978, with a night launch that was timed to permit the balloon to ascend rapidly into a stratum of favorable winds.

PRESQUE ISLE, MAINE

soggy mess with no insulating value. For the remainder of the voyage Abruzzo suffered in his soaked clothing, too cold to eat or even sleep, while Anderson slept serenely and awakened refreshed. Indeed, despite the difficulties, Anderson seemed to be enjoying himself, while Abruzzo endured his own misery in silence.

For most of September 10 and 11, *Double Eagle* bounced like a yo-yo as it struggled across the Atlantic Ocean, thrust toward the sea one minute by a violent storm and rising the next as the weather cleared. Rain-soaked ra-

dios kept them from communicating with their ground crew. Then, on September 12, one of the receivers crackled to life as *Double Eagle* drifted through a clear sky over the Denmark Strait at 12,000 feet, the highest altitude of the voyage. After losing radio contact with Abruzzo and Anderson during a storm the previous day, a worried ground crew had turned to the U.S. Navy for help. A navy plane was now offering to send a rescue helicopter from Iceland. One could reach *Double Eagle* in about

three hours. Anderson ached to complete the trip: Paris was now out of the question, but they could land in Norway in ten hours. Recognizing the extreme physical toll the journey had exacted from his friend, however, he reluctantly—and somewhat resentfully—asked for the helicopter. Sixty-five hours after taking to the skies, Abruzzo and Anderson ditched their balloon off the coast of Iceland and scrambled into the warmth and safety of a navy chopper. They had traveled 2,440 miles. Only Edwin Yost had traveled farther or longer.

At first, Abruzzo wanted nothing to do with a second attempt. His left foot had been severely frostbitten, and doctors warned him that he could lose it if it were reinjured. But Anderson, quietly persistent, persuaded him to try again, and by August 1978, *Double Eagle II* was ready for takeoff from Presque Isle, Maine. Abruzzo and Anderson had ◊

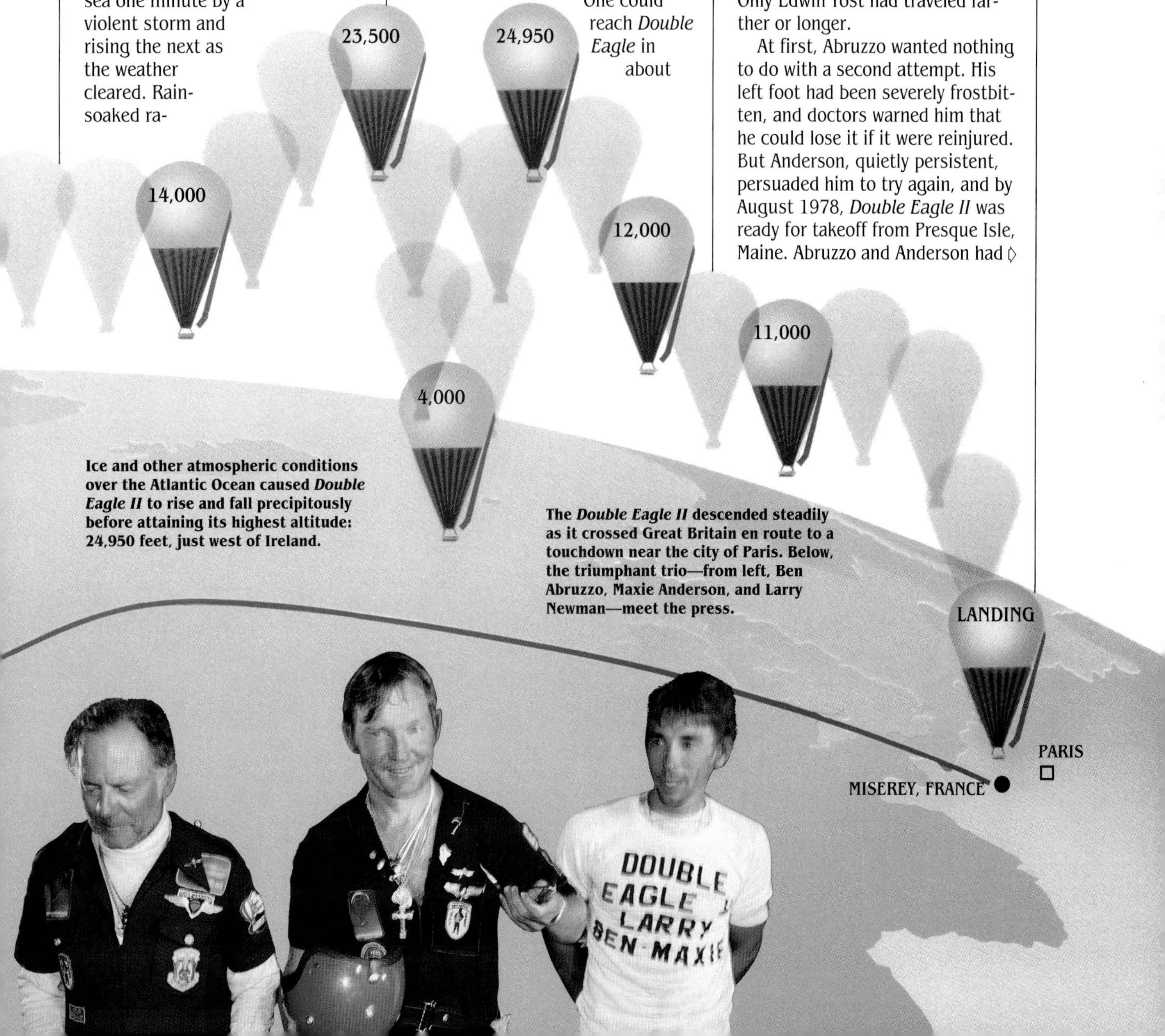

23,500

24,950

14,000

12,000

4,000

11,000

Ice and other atmospheric conditions over the Atlantic Ocean caused *Double Eagle II* to rise and fall precipitously before attaining its highest altitude: 24,950 feet, just west of Ireland.

The *Double Eagle II* descended steadily as it crossed Great Britain en route to a touchdown near the city of Paris. Below, the triumphant trio—from left, Ben Abruzzo, Maxie Anderson, and Larry Newman—meet the press.

LANDING

PARIS

MISEREY, FRANCE

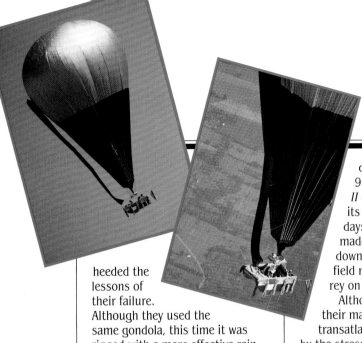

As *Double Eagle II,* its open gondola decorated with Irish and American flags *(left),* touched down in France near Miserey *(below),* motorists who had gathered to watch the landing swarmed to help deflate the giant balloon.

heeded the lessons of their failure. Although they used the same gondola, this time it was rigged with a more effective rain shield, shelter, and propane heater. The men brought plenty of warm, waterproof clothing, sleeping bags, and parkas. Abruzzo even wore battery-heated socks to give his left foot some extra protection.

The duo also added a third crewman. A close friend of Abruzzo's, thirty-year-old Larry Newman, was an excellent pilot and a successful hang-glider manufacturer. Although Newman had scant balloon experience, Abruzzo thought a third man sharing the chores and watches would reduce fatigue for everyone. Newman was also handy with radios, a talent that had been desperately needed on the first trip. Anderson felt that a third man was one man too many, but he respected Abruzzo too much to deny his re-

quest. On August 11 at 9:00 p.m., *Double Eagle II* departed for Paris with its three-man crew. Six days later, the balloon made history, touching down at 7:49 p.m. in a barley field near the village of Miserey on Paris's outskirts.

Although they had made their mark on aviation, the transatlantic team was strained by the stresses of success. Ben Abruzzo and Larry Newman loved the attention the press lavished upon them; it made Maxie Anderson uncomfortable. He began to resent his friends' popularity, sensing that the formerly reluctant Abruzzo was stealing the lion's share of the acclaim. The two had a falling out. Abruzzo and Newman went on to become the first balloonists to cross the Pacific Ocean in 1981. Anderson and a new partner died in 1983 in a ballooning accident in Bavaria. Two years later,

Abruzzo died in an airplane crash in New Mexico.

But Newman was not through with ballooning on the grand scale. In January 1992, he and two fellow crewmen—Donald Moses, a Hawaii-based airline pilot, and Major General Vladimir A. Dzhanibekov, commander of the Russian astronaut training program—were standing by near Akron, Ohio, waiting for suitable conditions to launch a giant new balloon dubbed *Earthwinds* on a nonstop drift around the world. The unsettled midwestern winter proved their undoing, however, aborting their attempted liftoffs with sudden storms and gusty winds. Finally, near the end of February, the balloonists decided to postpone the attempt. But the false starts had taken their toll. The huge balloon, already stressed beyond its designed abilities, had to be scrapped, and the hundreds of volunteers drawn by Newman's dream scattered back to their everyday lives, to await a new venue and less treacherous currents for *Earthwinds.* □

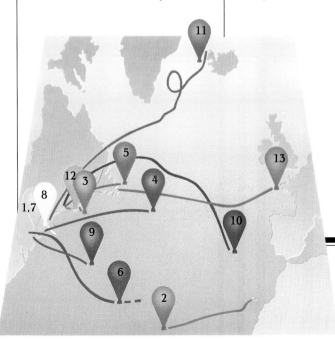

Thirteen failed attempts preceded *Double Eagle II*'s transatlantic success. The first, in 1873, flew only forty-five miles. A century later, Edwin Yost *(10)* ditched in the ocean near the Azores in 1976; the first *Double Eagle (11)* went down off Iceland in 1977; and Donald Cameron and Christopher Davey *(13)* landed in the sea short of France in 1978.

The Deep

Yorkshiremen Geoff Yeadon and Oliver Statham, better known as Bear for his great strength, began their careers in speleology—the exploration of caves—in grammar school. By the time they met in 1970—appropriately, in a cave in Norway—both were accomplished underground explorers. They soon forged a bond that made them formidable pioneers in a dangerous subspecialty of their subterranean pursuit: cave diving.

Traditionally, cave exploration had been limited largely to areas in which people could walk or crawl. Unless underground streams and pools were small enough to be traversed on a single gulp of air, they remained impenetrable. In the early 1970s, however, cavers adopted the wet suits, air tanks, and other apparatus of the scuba diver. No longer impeded by water, those explorers with the courage and skill to press downward began to open vast flooded subterranean labyrinths that human beings had never seen before.

Yeadon and Statham were among the cavers who took to diving, Yeadon after some instruction and Statham after perfunctory training in the use of their newly acquired equipment. In 1973, the pair loaded up fins, masks, suits, and tanks and headed for Boreham Cave, a cavern in the upper Wharfedale section of the Yorkshire Dales, now known to be riddled with hundreds of miles of flooded—and often interconnected—limestone chambers.

Boreham Cave, intended as more a practice site than a serious exploration, quickly introduced the divers to the special terrors of descending in the narrow spaces of a cavern, in darkness except for their lamps. About 100 feet into the first section of the cave, the exhaust valve on Statham's breathing apparatus failed, blocking his air. Because neither man had yet mastered the art and discipline of buddy breathing—sharing the use of the same air tank—Statham was forced to kick frantically for the cave opening, barely reaching the surface before his lungs gave out. When the pair returned to the site a few weeks later, Statham stayed on the surface, paying out a safety line attached to Yeadon, who this time penetrated more than 500 feet along a snaking route. At points, the passage was so narrow he barely wedged through; at others, it expanded into chambers where he could surface for a breath of subterranean air. On the way back, Yeadon swam blind through a haze of fine silt that had been stirred up by his fins. Even with the lifeline to follow, he almost became lost.

Perhaps rattled by his narrow escape from Boreham Cave, but also to pursue his pottery business, Statham gave up cave diving for a while. But the attraction of these dark dives was compelling. In ◊

Silhouetted against the beam of his single light, British diver Geoff Yeadon hovers in the inky blackness of Boreham Cave.

1975, he rejoined his partner to explore Keld Head, a pool in the Yorkshire Dales that they were certain must connect to a cave called Kingsdale, about a mile distant. More important, they believed, that connection was part of a larger flooded network now known to extend for hundreds of miles through the permeable limestone substrate of the Yorkshire Dales. For centuries, this system had sat unexplored, although geographers had inferred from surface pools and stream patterns that there must be extensive networks of interlocking caves. Now the pair set out to map what the geologists had guessed at.

Working on weekends, they made multiple dives, Statham from the Keld Head side, Yeadon from the Kingsdale end, each time pushing back the watery barrier of unexplored cavern a few more yards. Frequently, the turbid waters pushed back. Once, after navigating a maze of confusing junctions and dead ends, Yeadon's mouthpiece became disconnected from the air-supply regulator. Before realizing what had happened, he inhaled a mouthful of water. Alone and far beneath the surface, Yeadon somehow staved off panic and groped for a reserve regulator line running off his second tank. The ticking seconds seemed like hours.

Finally, Yeadon felt the regulator, brought it to his mouthpiece, connected and purged it of water . . . and breathed. He lay on the sandy bottom for several minutes, gathering his wits.

Despite this close call, Yeadon was more determined than ever to establish the Keld Head-Kingsdale link. Word of their exploration had spread to the Continent, and Statham, perhaps wanting to internationalize their efforts, invited a third partner to join them: Jochen Hasenmayer, a highly experienced German cave diver and holder of an underground distance record. Hasenmayer had been diving into holes since 1957, when, at fifteen, he had explored the Falkenstein Hölle between Stuttgart and Ulm. Over the ensuing decades, always operating alone, Hasenmayer had explored some of Europe's most demanding subterranean passages. Since the Keld Head-Kingsdale link—if there was one—exceeded his Swiss record, he was glad to be on the team. He displayed his abilities on his first dive, swimming right to the end of the lifeline laid down by Yeadon and Statham. On a murky February 5, 1978, the trio clambered into Keld Head, determined to find a way to the other side.

Hasenmayer led off, again swimming to the end of the line. Sensing that a passage had been overlooked, he reeled in part of the line, then added another 300-foot reel to it and pressed farther into the cave, past a constriction into what he later described as a "spacious tunnel." But, more than 3,000 feet into his dive, swimming in water with barely 5 feet of visibility, he found himself in a side channel. Statham, who had followed thirty minutes behind Hasenmayer and carried a smaller air supply, was by then dangerously low on air and retreated before reaching the German diver. Encountering Yeadon, who was heading in, Bear scribbled a note on his partner's slate: "No Jochen, Trouble?" Yeadon wrote back, "I will go and look and then turn back."

Yeadon trailed Hasenmayer's lifeline until he came to a tiny hole.

Oliver Statham (*in mask*) and Geoff Yeadon probed the buried waters of Keld Head until they discovered a route through the maze of flooded caverns in January of 1979.

The German had evidently found a route to the other side of the gap, but Yeadon did not feel safe trying. In the darkness he could see nothing stirring ahead but nevertheless waited. He calculated that Hasenmayer's air would be almost exhausted. Then, as he was on the verge of giving up, Yeadon said after the dive, he felt the line jiggle and gave it a couple of tugs. Then he shoved his hand through the tiny opening and into a short, tight tunnel. Hasenmayer, thrown off balance by the tugs, was pulled into the constriction. In his account, he said that he quickly made his way along the line and grabbed Yeadon's hand

to make sure there was no further tugging. But it had served a useful purpose. "I knew the right direction in principle," Hasenmayer wrote, "but Yeadon had taught it to me in an unforgettable way."

Not knowing this, and certain that Hasenmayer must be nearly out of air, Yeadon thought that the German might be signaling him to leave, to save himself. He thought he had shaken hands with a dead man, he told reporters afterward. But moments later, Yeadon saw the unmistakable glow of Hasenmayer's lamp. Guided by Yeadon's emphatic yanks on the line, the German, still with plenty of air, calmly emerged

from the constriction, gathered up the line reel, and, with his partner, headed back to Keld Head. To Hasenmayer's annoyance, the incident was treated in the press as a near-fatal event, echoed by the name given the narrow passage: Dead Man's Handshake.

The German generously stepped aside when it came time for the final dive to link Keld Head and Kingsdale. That triumph went to Yeadon and Statham alone. On January 16, 1979, they entered at Kingsdale and emerged at Keld Head. Although it had taken almost four years to identify the mile-long route, their final trip consumed just two and a half hours and set a world record for a continuous underwater dive between two caves.

Yeadon continued his cave diving, but his triumphs were tinged with sadness that Statham could not be there to share them. No one knows what killed Bear. Perhaps it was the stress of the dives into darkness or the strains of being famous. But, sadly, nine months after their victory deep below the Yorkshire Dales, Statham committed suicide.

Hasenmayer and Yeadon have not dived together since Keld Head, but the German has kept up his daring underground explorations. In 1989, diving in the open water of Wolfgangsee, a deep Austrian lake, a faulty depth gauge led Hasenmayer to surface too quickly. He suffered a disabling case of the bends, caused when nitrogen bubbles are not purged from the bloodstream during a diver's ascent. Hurried to a decompression chamber ashore, Hansenmayer was again brought up too quickly. Partially paralyzed by the curious pair of accidents, the determined explorer has recently begun to dive again. □

Exhausted but triumphant, Geoff Yeadon *(yellow helmet)* and Oliver Statham emerge from the Keld Head spring at the end of their successful mile-long underground swim.

Southern Comfort

A seventy-knot wind howled through the rigging of *Ice Bird*, David Lewis's thirty-two-foot yacht, and forty-foot seas smashed onto the decks. Inside, the cabin was littered with the contents of shelves and lockers, spilled by the storm-tossed heaving of the boat. And Lewis—cold, wet, frightened, and exhausted—braced himself in a bunk to keep from being hurled about. Lifting and falling, *Ice Bird* pitched through the night in a hysterical rhythm, until one wave fractured the cadence of the storm and lifted the seven-ton steel boat, twisting and smashing it and its helpless occupant. Lewis, squeezing his eyes tight against the impact, was tossed from his bunk like a rag doll. When he opened his lids, water was pouring through *Ice Bird*'s shattered hatch, the interior was awash, and the boat's thirty-six-foot aluminum mast had been snapped in half. The broken spar, still tethered to the boat by the shrouds that had once supported it, banged dangerously against the hull. *Ice Bird* and David Lewis had been rolled completely over. Then a second mammoth wave smashed into the capsized craft and righted it.

The date was November 29, 1972, and Lewis and his boat were in the extreme southern Pacific Ocean, about 1,000 miles north of the Antarctic continent, and some 2,500 miles short of Lewis's intended destination, the British Antarctic survey's Faraday Station in the desolate Argentine Islands. Sailing near sixty degrees south latitude, Lewis had been undone by the unceasing high winds for which the area is known as the Screaming Sixties. The fifty-five-year-old New Zealand physician had for years let his medical practice take a backseat to his love affair with the sea. He had circumnavigated the world with his family, crossed the North Atlantic alone several times, and crisscrossed the Pacific without map or compass to teach himself the ancient techniques of Polynesian navigators. The voyage to Antarctica was to have been another test in self-sufficiency at sea.

Six weeks and 3,600 miles before *Ice Bird* was rolled over, Lewis had left Sydney, Australia, intending to become the first lone sailor to reach Antarctica. After calling at Faraday, Lewis planned to return to Sydney by circling the southernmost continent, propelled by the intense prevailing westerly winds.

Vast distances are diminished on a map of the Antarctic. During his voyage on *Ice Bird*, David Lewis sailed from Sydney, Australia *(1)* to New Zealand's Stewart Island *(2)* before heading across 4,500 miles of wild open ocean. Less than halfway there and 1,000 miles from any land, storms capsized and dismasted *Ice Bird (3)*, then a second time *(4)*, forcing Lewis to alter his course. Three months after leaving Sydney, he landed at Palmer Station on Antarctica *(5)*. After refitting his damaged vessel, Lewis continued his attempt to circumnavigate the southern continent, but a third dismasting *(6)* compelled him to seek refuge in Cape Town, South Africa *(7)*. Lewis's son, Barry, later sailed *Ice Bird* the remaining 6,000 miles back to Sydney—like his father, alone.

Now, as he struggled to bail out his boat, secure the broken hatch, and clear the dangerous broken mast before it smashed through the hull, Lewis was concerned with survival, not setting records. The radios had been shorted out by seawater, and the waves had washed away his life raft. The temperature was below freezing; snow swept over him and his boat. When he lowered his shredded sail, Lewis cut his hand deeply but felt no pain and saw no blood; though a doctor, he did not immediately realize the terrible meaning of that bloodless injury: Frostbite had added itself to the many risks of this journey. Lewis's hands survived, however, thanks to massive doses of the antibiotic tetracycline.

That storm raged for a week, only to be replaced by another howling gale. Once more, *Ice Bird* was rolled over, like a toy in the surf, then righted itself in the dark watery valleys between the racing waves. Part of the makeshift mast crumpled in the storm, as Lewis frantically bailed out the stricken craft. By Christmas, he had nearly run through his supply of drinking water and had to ration it.

But here a curious change came over him. "Whenever I was not otherwise occupied I turned to escapist novels, so that I could forget for a while the surrounding squalor and misery," he wrote. "I longed to be able to pray, to cry out for help, but strangely I was not lonely. My drama was being played out on the vast stage of the ocean, with death lurking in the wings, but I was never lonely." Gradually, the dazed doctor began to take a keen interest in his surroundings. He was constantly reminded that he sailed the richest waters on earth: Whales and dolphins were his constant companions and large ocean birds inspected him as they skimmed past. There was a menacing beauty present as well. Icebergs—at once luminously graceful and dangerous—dotted his path. When the skies cleared to reveal the polar summer dawn and sunset, they merged into a single flaming event—the perpetual light of the austral summer. Once more, Lewis began to smell the exciting aroma of the sea—as he put it, he was coming to life again. Examining his situation more closely, he decided to alter his course to head for Palmer Station, an American research outpost that was more accessible than Faraday.

On January 29, 1973, just two months and 2,500 miles after *Ice Bird* was dismasted, David Lewis gingerly guided his shattered craft through floating ice into a landing at Palmer Station.

It was nearly a year before Lewis returned to his voyage. *Ice Bird* needed extensive repairs, and Lewis had unfinished business—books and magazine articles to complete—in New Zealand and the United States. His boat was fully repaired at the research post, and on December 12, 1973, after a month of feverish final preparations, Lewis was able to resume his circuitous return to Australia.

It was not to be. Although experience had enabled Lewis to improve *Ice Bird*'s preparations for the Antarctic Ocean's fierce weather, the two capsizes of the previous summer had left him terrified of the region's gale-force winds. "I lived through each one in an agony of fear," he said later. His fear was justified. More than seven weeks after his departure from Palmer and 800 miles south of Africa, a hurricane packing eighty-knot winds once more rolled *Ice Bird,* shattered her mast, and put a finish to Lewis's plans for an Antarctic circumnavigation. Using the remaining stub of a mast and an oar, the voyager set his tattered sails northward toward Cape Town, South Africa, arriving there after an arduous, month-long sail, on March 20.

Shaken by the ordeal, David Lewis swore he would never go to sea again. Time, however, eases hard memories. Sailing *Solo,* the trim successor to *Ice Bird,* Lewis made three more voyages to Antarctica and has spent more than a dozen years since at the head of the Ocean Research Foundation, collecting data on sea life and oceanic movements near the North and South poles. In the end, it seems, the ocean always has its way. □

Shortly after leaving Australia for Antarctica, physician-sailor David Lewis cruises past Sydney Heads in his thirty-two-foot steel-hulled vessel, *Ice Bird.*

Trekster

In the mountains of Turkey, near Mount Ararat, Steven Newman was arrested, kicked, and questioned by jackbooted secret policemen. Housed for the night in a cold stone hut guarded by a soldier, Newman escaped through a window and found refuge in the basement of a hotel. He slipped out of town several days later. Months further into his journey, on a lonely road south of Bangkok, Newman fought off two machete-swinging Thai bandits with an umbrella, then made good his escape by diving into a passing truck. A mob of panhandlers and hustlers nearly picked him apart in Morocco. Elsewhere, he was attacked by wild boars and ants and nearly crushed by a runaway team of horses. On the other hand, according to Newman at least, such dark moments were merely dips in an exhilarating round-the-world roller-coaster ride—on foot.

Newman's four-year, 21,000-mile trek was the first recorded circumnavigation of the planet by a lone walker. Despite some desperate moments, he has preferred to accentuate the positive—to remember not the Turkish police who jailed him, but the school janitor who hid him for three days, bringing him food and questioning him interminably about the lot of janitors in the United States. The same seesawing balance held true elsewhere. In Australia, for example, a chance meeting led Newman to a remote opal mine, where a miner gave him one of the rare stones. A few days later, he lost the gem when a murderously drunk construction worker ransacked his pack and tried to shoot him. Then, four days after that, short of water and miles from nowhere, Newman encountered two rough miners who drove him back to the site of the attack—and miraculously recovered the lost opal on the barren desert.

Newman, then a twenty-eight-year-old journalist, left his home in Bethel, Ohio, on April 1, 1983. He had no corporate sponsors, no publicity agent, very little money—but a large ambition "to see what the common people of the world were like." Accordingly, his game plan demanded that he pay for no lodging—Newman slept in parks, highway culverts, under bridges, and in the homes of people who befriended him. And he would shun celebrity and hobnob with the hoi polloi. Such journalism as he did was rationed out to a relatively small audience: readers of the *Columbus Dispatch* and *Capper's* magazine, and some third graders in Bozeman, Montana; near the conclusion of his journey, Newman detoured 500 miles to visit his young correspondents.

From Bethel, Newman's route took him eastward to Boston, where he boarded a plane to London. Bus and boat carried him to Dublin, Ireland. He walked from there to Belfast, hopped a ferry to Scotland, and hiked from Scotland to the southern tip of England. Crossing the English Channel, he walked from the French city of Cherbourg southward into Spain, then to Tangier on the far side of the Mediterranean, and back into Europe by way of Sicily and Italy. Turning toward the east, Newman crossed Yugoslavia and Greece into Turkey.

War and politics kept Newman out of Iran and Afghanistan, but he did manage to walk from Peshawar, near the famous Khyber Pass, to Lahore in Pakistan, then to Calcutta, India. A boat carried him to the city of Bangkok, Thailand, but his feet bore him down the Malay Peninsula to Singapore and across the entire breadth of Australia. Arriving back in North America, he trudged from Vancouver, British Columbia, to Ohio—contriving to reach his hometown, Bethel, exactly four years after his departure, on April 1, 1987.

Newman returned to a hero's welcome but demured: "The people all over the world were the true

High above California's Yosemite Valley, photographer Galen Rowell is snapped en route to a higher vantage point by his intended subject, climber Ron Kauk.

heroes of the worldwalk," he wrote in his account of the journey. "It was the acts of love from the people I had met—and the people who had cheered me on—that had enriched my life beyond description." Still, the trek had been enriching in other ways as well. For his investment of four years and $4,000, by the end of 1990 Newman had earned more than $500,000 talking and writing about what he had done. □

Carrying his home on his back (below), hiker Steven Newman eschewed paid accommodations throughout his four-year walk around the world, preferring to rest his head on his boots for a night of sleep in fields such as the one at left in Greenville, Illinois, near the end of his Ohio-bound trek.

Intrepid Imager

In the most striking of Galen Rowell's photographs, one is moved first by the drama of the subject—a rock climber, for example, halfway up a sheer face on ropes and pitons, seen from a point just above. Then one asks: To take this photograph, where was the photographer? In a Rowell picture, the answer is that the photographer is always just ahead of the subject, sharing—often leading—the dangerous ascent. The fit, hawk-eyed adventurer photographs climbers from points they have not yet reached, mountaineers from the slope no one has climbed. Each image captures the adventure of someone else and the natural world as few have seen it; but, more often than not, each frame also suggests a photographer at risk. One of the world's premiere wilderness photographers and expedition leaders, Rowell has traveled from California's Yosemite National Park to Tibet, and everywhere in between, to capture the unforgettable images that are his trademark.

Rowell grew up with a passion for the outdoors. As a teenager in the 1950s, he favored seventy-mile hikes, mineralogy, and mountaineering. He also dabbled in photography, though without professional plans. "I took pictures," he says now, "to communicate about the outdoors." Meanwhile, he had entered and left the University of California at Berkeley and started a car-repair shop to support himself. On weekends he went to the mountains. Gradually, as his pictures began to sell, photography moved closer to the center of his life. Final-

ly, in December 1972, Rowell took the plunge. Although friends told him there was no way he could combine a career with the outdoor life he loved, the thirty-two-year-old mechanic sold his repair shop and gave himself a year to become a successful photographer.

At first, his income barely covered the cost of supplies and equipment. But a 1973 assignment from *National Geographic*—as second photographer for a sheer climb up Yosemite's Half Dome—turned things around. Having demonstrated a keen eye, daring spirit, physical toughness, and climbing prowess, he became a frequent contributor to the Society, providing the photographs that few other nature photographers would try.

In the nearly two decades since then, Rowell has published books and articles that combine personal narratives of his adventures with riveting photographs. Although he has photographed more than 1,000 mountain-climbing trips on four continents and has participated in forty major expeditions, Galen Rowell refuses to rest on his laurels. "All the adventures have not been done," he says. "You just have to be a little imaginative." □

Love Boats

Bundled against the winter cold, Valerie *(left)* and Verlen Kruger paddle across Lake Huron in December 1986 on their way to South America.

Soon after they were married in 1986, Verlen and Valerie Kruger embarked on a honeymoon cruise. But rather than relaxing with room service and dinner at the captain's table, the newlyweds paddled two canoes 21,246 miles from Inuvik in Canada's Northwest Territories to South America's Tierra del Fuego and Cape Horn. The Krugers made one concession to convention, however: Although each of their canoes carried all the requirements for its occupant's survival alone, the couple shared a single tent.

Before they met, both Verlen and Valerie were experienced paddlers. In the 80,000 some miles of long-distance canoe trips he had taken, Verlen, at sixty-three, had paddled 28,000 miles around North America with a partner. Valerie, at thirty-five, was a champion canoe racer. So it seemed perfectly natural when they tied the knot to make canoeing part of the celebration.

Their thirty-three-month honeymoon was certainly more eventful than most postnuptial sojourns. The Krugers were attacked by a bear, charged by a moose, and literally frozen into their boats during a blizzard on Lake Superior. The two of them island-hopped across shark-infested fetches of the Caribbean, evaded swarming Africanized bees, and endured the buffeting of 100-mile-per-hour winds in the South Atlantic.

Their indomitable good cheer helped them survive these and other travails, as did the generous hospitality they encountered everywhere along their route. In South America, Valerie noted that they sometimes packed more material possessions into their seventeen-foot, 300-pound canoes than entire families did in their rustic homes. Yet people pressed small gifts of food on the foreign travelers wherever they went.

As part of their own desire to give something back, the Krugers carried out scientific tests, measuring acid rain and water quality for university and corporate sponsors. Valerie also kept extensive journals and, even as their odyssey unfolded, produced a newsletter describing what they had seen. Once back in the United States, the intrepid canoeists took to the lecture circuit to share what they had learned about nature and other cultures, aided by a selection from the 35,000 transparencies they had taken along the way. It was not just the thrills they relished, but the simple truths they learned about themselves and their place on what must seem to them now a *very* large planet. □

Verlen Kruger paddles past Lago Argentino's glacial ice near the finish of a hemisphere-spanning trip.

OUTRAGEOUS EXPLOITS

Adventure may be savored in small bites as well as in large, in escapades that make up in novelty what they lack in scope and grandeur. These miniature adventures take distinctive forms—a secret leap from some forbidden height, driving on the sea, cycling the roof of the planet, moving only in reverse. Some are defiant intrusions, elaborate competitions, or acts notable for their duration, distance, and endurance. Sometimes they involve great danger, sometimes less than meets the eye, the hazard muted by technique or technology—going over Niagara Falls in a barrel, the quintessential stunt, is both more and less perilous than it seems.

These brief exploits are usually tasted just once, for a moment, and put away; to repeat them may ask more than the adventurer wants to spend. But other excitements demand to be sampled again and again, their thrill endlessly accessible both to the performer and to the crowd that dependably gathers to watch. Perhaps the appeal flows from a general human longing to experience one thing—and it must be different for everyone—whose brief, sweet taste can last the remainder of a quiet lifetime.

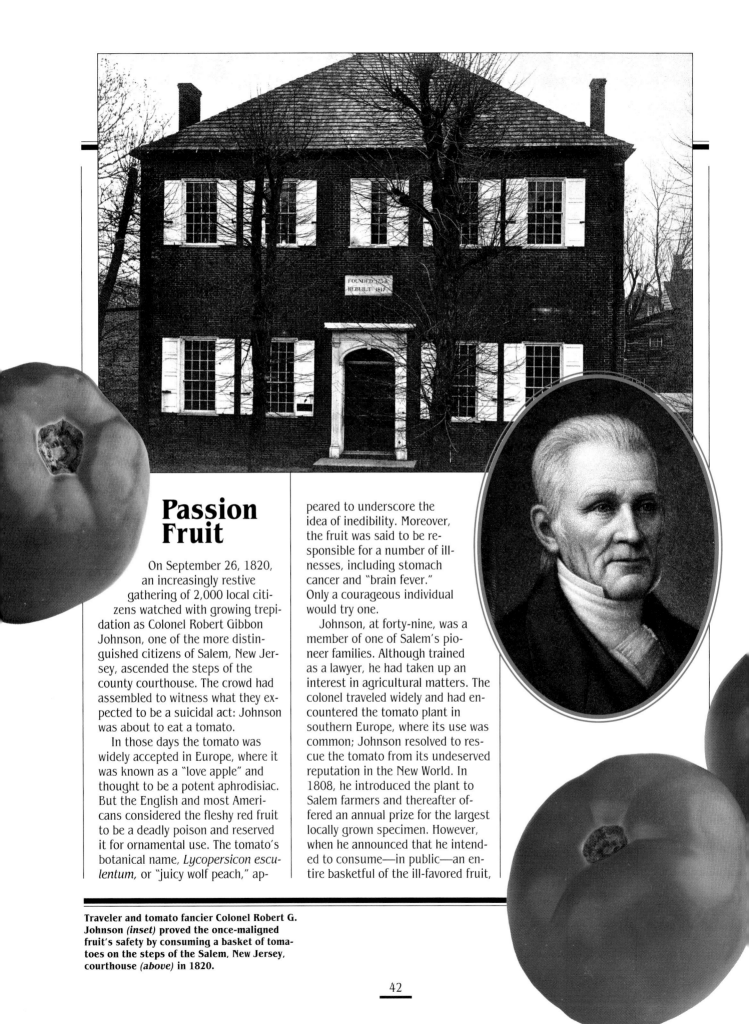

Passion Fruit

On September 26, 1820, an increasingly restive gathering of 2,000 local citizens watched with growing trepidation as Colonel Robert Gibbon Johnson, one of the more distinguished citizens of Salem, New Jersey, ascended the steps of the county courthouse. The crowd had assembled to witness what they expected to be a suicidal act: Johnson was about to eat a tomato.

In those days the tomato was widely accepted in Europe, where it was known as a "love apple" and thought to be a potent aphrodisiac. But the English and most Americans considered the fleshy red fruit to be a deadly poison and reserved it for ornamental use. The tomato's botanical name, *Lycopersicon esculentum,* or "juicy wolf peach," ap-

peared to underscore the idea of inedibility. Moreover, the fruit was said to be responsible for a number of illnesses, including stomach cancer and "brain fever." Only a courageous individual would try one.

Johnson, at forty-nine, was a member of one of Salem's pioneer families. Although trained as a lawyer, he had taken up an interest in agricultural matters. The colonel traveled widely and had encountered the tomato plant in southern Europe, where its use was common; Johnson resolved to rescue the tomato from its undeserved reputation in the New World. In 1808, he introduced the plant to Salem farmers and thereafter offered an annual prize for the largest locally grown specimen. However, when he announced that he intended to consume—in public—an entire basketful of the ill-favored fruit,

Traveler and tomato fancier Colonel Robert G. Johnson *(inset)* proved the once-maligned fruit's safety by consuming a basket of tomatoes on the steps of the Salem, New Jersey, courthouse *(above)* in 1820.

42

his fellow citizens were convinced that he had gone too far. Perhaps, some townsfolk speculated, the tomatoes he professed to have eaten privately had affected his sanity. Even Johnson's physician predicted that his client would "foam and froth at the mouth and double over with appendicitis. All that oxalic acid!" the doctor exclaimed. "One dose and you're dead."

When Johnson reached the top of the courthouse steps, a local band serenaded him with a dirgelike melody. Undeterred, the audacious colonel held up one of his tomatoes and delivered his pitch. "The time will come," he intoned to the crowd, "when this luscious, golden apple, rich in nutritive value, a delight to the eye, a joy to the palate, whether fried, baked, or eaten raw, will form the foundation of a great garden industry." Then, "To show you that it is not poisonous, that it will not strike you dead, I am going to eat one right now!"

Members of the disbelieving audience screamed as Johnson took one bite, then another. Men and women swooned at each loud and juicy chomp. The courageous colonel ate the entire basketful—and still stood strong and healthy on the courthouse steps.

Colonel Johnson's stunt was reported in newspapers across the nation, and the publicity helped turn the cultivation of the tomato into a major American business, just as its proponent had predicted that it would. In fact, to this day tomatoes are a principal crop—and food—of Salem County farmers. □

Riding High

Of all the daredevils who have challenged Niagara Falls, perhaps the bravest was an unremarkable little man named Henry M. Colcord. Colcord was business manager for Charles Blondin, the flamboyant French tightrope walker who became the first aerialist to cross the Niagara River near its famous falls, on June 30, 1859. Colcord had helped Blondin engineer the stringing of a 1,100-foot manilla cable, about two miles below the falls, and ably promoted the feat.

Blondin's performance itself was worth every bit of the twenty-five cent admission fee charged on the American side of the falls. In pink tights and dazzling yellow tunic, the Frenchman strode to the middle of the rope, lay down, got up, balanced on one leg, sat on the rope, and performed other "gymnastic evolutions," according to a contemporary newspaper account. He carried a bottle of wine with him and, midway across and 150 feet above the river, lowered the libation on a string to the captain of the *Maid of the Mist*, the sightseeing steamboat that had taken up a position below Blondin. The aerialist's exploit was hailed the next morning in newspapers across the country. Also noted was an offer Blondin had made in his limited English as he stepped onto the rope: "Gentlemen, anyone what please to cross, I carry him on my back." There had been no takers.

What was no doubt a facetious offer gained momentum in the days that followed. Blondin—having gone to some effort to set up his rope-walking apparatus across the gorge—intended to stage still more crossings. But he and his manager faced a challenge equal to that of the Niagara itself: how to improve an already stunning act. Clearly, carrying a passenger would qualify. There was, however, one persistent problem. They could find no one brave, foolish, or greedy enough— Blondin reportedly was ready to pay handsomely—to take the ride. The stunt was stalled until somehow the Frenchman talked Colcord into joining him on the tightrope. Colcord had been quite content advertising Blondin's exploits rather than participating in them, and it is not known what threats or inducements drew the manager into the act. But once he agreed, the wheels of publicity began to roll.

Blondin's reputation for delivering on his promises soon had throngs of spectators converging on Niagara Falls. Wooden grandstands a half-mile long were built on each side of the river. Excursion trains arrived from the cities of Buffalo, Rochester, Chicago, Detroit, and Milwaukee. Overbooked hotels had patrons sleeping in the lobbies and concessionaires were deluged with business. The roads to the river were clogged with carriages and pedestrians. Trains stood on the bridges. All in all, a record crowd of 100,000 gathered along the gorge on August 17, 1859, to witness Blondin's crossing.

Shortly before 5:00 p.m., Blondin took to his rope on the American side of the falls. First he performed solo, thrilling the spectators with a half-hour of somersaults, headstands, and other gymnastics. He leaped and jumped; he swung from the rope by his feet and hands; he lay down on it; he performed a kind of double-tightrope act by balancing his thirty-foot-long, forty-pound steadying pole across the rope, then lying on his pole. When Charles ▷

Blondin finally stepped onto the Canadian shore, the crowd was in a frenzy of cheering, clapping, and whistle blowing.

After Blondin rested for a brief period, the main event began. Colcord, who matched Blondin's own 140-pound weight, mounted his boss's shoulders. His businesslike shirtsleeves and straw hat contrasted with Blondin's gaudy costume. After admonishing his companion to "keep looking up," Blondin stepped onto the rope.

As they made their way toward the center of the river, they descended into the gorge; the 1,100-foot-long two-inch rope under Blondin's feet sagged some fifty feet from its anchor points on either shore. A complex webbing of

guy ropes—some 26,000 feet in all—steadied the main span. But still, the wind that constantly eddies through the Niagara River gorge nudged the rope one way and another. Several times Blondin stopped to rest and Colcord dismounted. Once Colcord was asked to relax his grip, which was threatening to cut off Blondin's breath. When they were little more than halfway across, at a gap in the guy ropes, the main rope began swaying violently. At that, Blondin ran for the safety of the next

stabilizing rope. They rested again. Finally, Colcord remounted, and the two men made their way up the incline to the welcome safety of the American shore. The aerialist was reported to be "very much fatigued" by his ordeal. Colcord—whose mental toil no doubt matched Blondin's physical exertions—was described simply as looking pale.

For a time, Colcord shared his employer's international fame, but he never repeated his feat. According to one explanation, the president of the New York Central Railroad had offered Colcord two $1,000 checks, one for crossing with Blondin and one if he promised never to do it again. Colcord reportedly accepted both without hesitation. □

Weighed down by manager Henry Colcord and a forty-pound steadying pole, aerialist Charles Blondin (above) tightropes his way across the Niagara River gorge two miles below the famous falls.

Boatmen prepare to seal Anna Edson Taylor inside her barrel *(below)* as it bobs in the Niagara River a few minutes before the current swept the schoolteacher over the 160-foot Horseshoe cataract, shown in background.

Over a Barrel

On October 24, 1901, Anna Edson Taylor, a straight-laced, stout, forty-three-year-old widow and schoolteacher from Bay City, Michigan, became the first daredevil to plunge over Niagara Falls in a barrel. Hers was a truly remarkable venture. Only a handful of people—and no other women—have followed her brave lead, and no wonder. Water roaring over the two cataracts—167 feet high on the American end and 158 feet at the Canadian end—shakes the ground and fills the air with spray and the awful sound of a mighty torrent. At the base of the falls lies a treacherous combination of rocks, whirlpools, and rapids. Boulders frame the foot of the falls. In the center, where the cataracts land with their full force, a powerful undertow tends to submerge anything—and anyone—surviving the water and the rocks. Going over Niagara Falls in a barrel was once a paradigm of risk, offering fame and fortune to that handful who survived. In fact, as Taylor's story shows, only the falls are real—the rest is an illusion.

As Taylor prepared to launch her vessel, the undertaking seemed more likely to result in suicide than success. The schoolteacher had no previous credentials as an adventurer; she devised the scheme simply to make money. The oak barrel she brought to Niagara from Bay City was an unlikely conveyance. Weighing 160 pounds, four feet in diameter at its widest, and four and a half feet long, the barrel contained a 100-pound anvil as ballast to keep it upright in the water. A crude pump supplied its occupant with air and a system of leather straps and cushions were intended to protect her from injury. Seven iron hoops were all that held the bulging wooden cylinder together.

Shortly after four in the afternoon of the appointed day, a crowd numbering in the thousands, attracted by newspaper accounts of the impending lunacy, watched as a rowboat towed Taylor's barrel into the fast-flowing river about one and a half miles above Horseshoe Fall on the Canadian side of the river. The crew cut the towline, and Taylor drifted inexorably toward the rim, faced with all the usual dangers, plus one other: If Taylor's tub was destroyed and she somehow survived, she would still be doomed; ◊

Bruised and groggy from her bout with Niagara Falls, Annie Taylor accepts the helping hands of onlookers guiding her across the rocks to terra firma.

the woman could not swim. Minutes after the release, the barrel plunged over the edge.

It took three seconds for Taylor and her keg to reach bottom. They disappeared below the waves for another ten seconds. Then, to the relief and surprise of all, they bobbed to the surface intact and floated into what is known as the Maid of the Mist eddy—a current named for the steamboat that carries tourists to the base of the falls. When the barrel was hauled to shore intact, Taylor climbed out relatively unharmed. She was bruised and bleeding from a cut behind her right ear, and she babbled incoherently for a few moments. But she had survived.

Later she described her wild ride as a terrible nightmare. "Of course," she added, "I don't regret it. It will help me financially." But if her characterization of the plummet was on the mark, her expectations were not. She was a failure on the lecture circuit. Dubbing herself Queen of the Mist, Taylor delivered her story to audiences in a raspy monotone, unaided by a smile, humor, or en-

thusiasm. Because she had not bothered to save the vehicle of her fame—the improbably sound keg— she had nothing with which to distract her listeners from a dull presentation. And Taylor's timing was poor. Other events soon captured the world's attention: That fall and winter newspapers heralded Guglielmo Marconi's transatlantic wireless transmission and the Wright brothers' historic first flight. Annie Taylor quickly became old news.

Broke, the widow returned to Niagara Falls and scraped out a meager living signing autographs while sitting beside a phony facsimile of her barrel. Eventually, the bitter and penniless widow was taken to the Niagara county infirmary where she died on April 29, 1921, at the age of sixty-three. She was buried at Niagara Falls, New York, in a section of Oakwood Cemetery called Stranger's Rest. Annie Taylor was not entirely forgotten, however. The community paid to erect a small tombstone bearing the epitaph "First To Go Over The Horseshoe Fall In A Barrel And Live." □

Windbag

The English Channel's capricious weather, rough seas, and powerful currents have long qualified it as a worthwhile challenge for swimmers, boaters, and a host of less conventional travelers—among them the unsinkable Paul Boyton of Atlantic City, New Jersey, and the United States Atlantic Life-saving Service. In May of 1875, the twenty-seven-year-old Boyton slipped into the waters at Cap Gris-Nez, France, and began paddling toward England. Slightly less than twenty-four hours later, Boyton, appearing none the worse for wear, walked ashore at Dover. His conveyance: an inflatable India-rubber suit.

The apparatus was definitely something new in the water. Weighing just thirty-five pounds and covering everything but a small part of the wearer's face, the garment provided enough buoyancy to float up

to 300 pounds. Although it necessarily lacked such twentieth-century refinements as Velcro closures and automatically deployed flashing lights, Boyton's suit was similar to the survival suits worn by modern sailors and aircrews. By inflating or deflating certain chambers, Boyton could float horizontally or vertically. Included with the suit was a waterproof satchel to hold flares, food, drinking water, and, in Boyton's case, cigars. He was also known to carry a bugle and a small sail.

The English Channel feat—later reproduced there and elsewhere—was in fact one of a series of publicity stunts to promote the suit's virtues and enrich Boyton and its inventor, American rubber manufacturer C. S. Merriman. Paul Boyton's single-minded quest for publicity and his almost insane courage severely tested the contraption; his demonstrations often careened dangerously out of control.

Boyton's first major stunt involved jumping from a ship fifteen miles off the west coast of England. Gale-force winds and heavy seas arose unexpectedly; the daredevil fought the ocean for several hours, armed only with a small double paddle, before staggering ashore in Ireland. But his life as a rubber-suit test pilot was inherently perilous. Boyton was attacked by sharks while floating through the Strait of Messina between Sicily and Italy, nearly skewered on a chain of iron spikes in France's Rhone River, and attacked by North African soldiers who thought that the oddly attired stranger must be the devil. American Indians attacked the adventurer when he floated down the Missouri River, and he had countless close calls with rocks, rapids, waterfalls, whirlpools, strong tides, fever, and exposure.

Through it all, neither Boyton's remarkable suit nor his indefatiga-

ble enthusiasm failed him. He became one of the world's most successful publicity seekers. He was feted as a hero everywhere he went, regularly earned large lecture fees, and once performed before the queen of England. For a time Boyton operated a lucrative aquatic and Wild West show.

Paul Boyton finally hung up his buoyant costume in 1892. Ironically, the rubber raiment that made Boyton famous evidently did nothing for his sponsor: There is no record of a single sale of Merriman's floating suit. □

Curious steamer passengers hail Paul Boyton as he floats across the English Channel in a buoyant rubberized suit, propelled by a miniature sail and a kayak paddle.

Hand Stamped

In the winter of 1914, the parents of little May Pierstorff of Grangeville, Idaho, wanted their four-year-old daughter to visit her grandmother in Lewiston, some sixty-five miles away. Transportation was not a problem; the Camas Prairie Railroad connected the two towns. But a youngster traveling alone was required to buy a full-fare ticket, an impossible burden for the impoverished Pierstorffs. Nevertheless, May made the trip; her parents sent the tyke to her granny—by mail.

Postal regulations, which clearly forbade the shipping of live animals, nearly derailed the ploy. But good-hearted Grangeville postmaster Lloyd A. Wisener dug through his rule book and discovered one exception: Baby chickens could be sent via parcel post—in fact, poultry growers throughout the country relied on the service.

Following regulations to the letter, Wisener identified May as a "forty-eight-pound baby chick"—two pounds under the fifty-pound parcel-post limit. The Pierstorffs paid fifty-three cents' postage and glued the stamps to a tag on the youngster's coat. May had to forgo carrying luggage; as freight, it would have cost extra.

May spent the trip in the baggage car under the watchful eye of the train baggage man. In Lewiston, a kindly clerk delivered her to her grandmother. There is no record of when, or how, the child returned to Grangeville. □

Driven

For the publishers of the popular French newspaper *Le Matin,* the idea of an automobile race from Paris to China was strictly a commercial proposition, albeit a novel one, that would publicize the paper and the growing French automobile industry. On the front page of the January 31, 1907, edition, the paper issued a call for willing participants in an automobile race. "Is there any one who would agree to drive an automobile this summer from Paris to Peking?" the paper asked. With that was launched the first and perhaps the most grueling intercontinental race in automotive history, covering 10,000 miles of camel track and ox road across deserts, mountain ranges, rivers, swamps, and through farmland and forests. Most of the route lay across the vast empire of Russia, where civil unrest had begun to stir. Bandits and vicious weather plagued the rest of the course.

This would be an event of heroic proportions, said *Le Matin,* whose courageous entrants and their mettlesome autos would "have a dozen nations as spectators." The winner, it was promised, would find himself famous in "the four corners of the earth." So, too, would the sponsoring newspaper, its publisher believed, for this was the golden age of the motorcar, when glamour, not utility, was prized and the public eagerly lapped at each manufacturer's attempt to field faster and flashier automobiles than the competition's. Celebrity for all involved would be the greatest prize, but it would come at a hefty price. The entry fee was fixed at 2,000 francs (refundable at the start), and competitors had to be prepared to foot expenses of another 100,000 francs.

Perhaps to give the grand finish greater visibility, the organizers soon reversed the direction of the automobile race, placing the start in remote Beijing (Peking) and the finish line in Paris. The official reason given was avoidance of Beijing's rainy season.

Ten entrants initially came forward, but within weeks the field narrowed to half that number. Georges Cormier, an automobile dealer and endurance racer, entered a French-built, ten horsepower de Dion-Bouton *voiturette.* Victor Collignon, another experienced driver, also planned to race a de Dion-Bouton. Auguste Pons, later the father of opera star Lily Pons, piloted a Contal tricar, the only three-wheeled vehicle entered in the race.

The most flamboyant entrant was Charles Godard, an ebullient confidence man who persuaded Dutch auto manufacturer Jacobus Spijker to donate an automobile—his brand was the Spyker—and a 10,000-franc bonus for Godard should he win. Theirs was an enterprise built on prevarication, duplicity, faith, and bravado. Godard, who was responsible for the race expenses, was broke. He raised money to ship his car to Beijing by selling the spare parts and tires provided by Spijker. The manufacturer, for his part, was nearly bankrupt; he made his promises to Godard knowing that victory would result in sales and the cash to deliver. Failure would cost nothing.

The fifth and most formidable motorman—owing both to his bank account and his experience—was a former Italian diplomat and explorer named Prince Scipione Borghese. An aristocrat of considerable means, Borghese ordered a custom-made forty-horsepower Itala automobile for the race. To assure proper publicity, *Le Matin* signed on a handful of journalists and attached one to each driver. After all but Borghese signed a contract promising mutual assistance, the racers and their machines were shipped ◊

The sponsoring French newspaper Le Matin announced the start of its Beijing (Peking)-Paris race with a front-page depiction of the men, their cars, and the grueling 10,000-mile route across two continents.

On the steppes of Central Asia, contestant Victor Collignon had horsemen tow his car *(above)* as he headed for Moscow, where racers parked beneath a sign describing their route *(right).*

to Beijing via the port of Shanghai.

They arrived in China in May, and on June 10, 1907, the five contestants set out from Beijing to the strains of the *Sambre-et-Meuse,* played by a French navy band.

Auguste Pons was the first to taste disaster; he was captured by Kurguze horsemen in the Gobi Desert just ten days after the start. Pons was rescued several weeks later, but the delay ended his participation in the race. The favorite, Prince Borghese, narrowly missed forfeiting his chances while driving along the Trans-Siberian Railroad, when his Itala fell through a bridge and into a river. Borghese and the car were rescued by twenty muzhiks with a long rope.

Similar hazards—including no fewer than 117 flood-wrecked bridges—hindered the other contestants. Local laborers were hired to haul supplies and, as often as not, the cars themselves. The competitors had agreed to travel as far as Germany in a convoy, but, before three weeks were out, hundreds of miles separated the first motorcar from the last. Nevertheless, one by one the obstacles fell: the Gobi Desert, the rough lands south of Siberia's Lake Baikal; the endless

plains and swamps of Siberia; the Ural Mountains.

And it was true, as the newspaper had promised, that the racers were the toast of every nation they visited. In Urga, Mongolia, they met the Grand Lama, "living God and incarnation of Buddha." They were toasted by Moscow's social elite. High society in St. Petersburg, Warsaw, and Berlin cheered them on.

By the time Borghese reached Moscow on July 27, it was clear that, barring tragedy, he would fin-

Taking a respite from the rigors of the Beijing-Paris race, the de Dion team of Georges Cormier and Victor Collignon *(right)* camp in the Mongolian desert. Victory went to Prince Scipione Borghese, who entered Paris *(below)* three weeks ahead of the pack.

ish as the winner. The others languished nearly two weeks behind. On August 11, having outplanned, outspent, and out-driven his rivals, the Italian drove triumphantly into Paris. The race was over. But the intrigue had just begun.

With Borghese's victory in an Italian car, the race organizers decided to have the remaining vehicles enter Paris together, sharing second place. Such a finish would extract maximum publicity for *Le Matin* and for the French manufacturer of two

of the cars, de Dion. That agreed, there remained only the matter of disposing of Godard and his Dutch-built Spyker, for the managing director of *Le Matin* had decided that the Spyker's second-place finish would be an intolerable embarrassment to the French automobile industry, already compromised by Borghese's victory. Perhaps he was correct; the Dutch car must have been exceptionally resilient to survive the grueling miles with little else supporting it except Godard's

wit and driving ability—the driver had sold most of his spares long before the race began.

The solution to such an embarrassment was to have Godard arrested in Germany on trumped-up charges of fraud. (He was later freed.) But the ploy failed. Jacobus Spijker, anticipating just such a blow, had arranged for a replacement driver and, on August 31, the Spyker was one of the three second-place cars that entered the city of Paris together. □

Sea Rider

While a stream of visitors gawked at the might of the British navy assembled in the harbor of Chatham, a few miles away an English motorcycle racer by the name of H. S. Perrey prepared to make seagoing history by crossing the English Channel from the cliffs of Dover to the French port of Calais and back again—on his motorcycle. Perrey had motored down to Dover from the Midlands on August 12, 1929, riding his two-cylinder Aerial cycle. After reaching Dover, the cyclist installed his machine on a sixteen-foot twin-hulled craft. The rear wheel of the motorcycle was connected to a drive that turned the boat's propeller; the bike's front wheel was hitched to the craft's rudder. Perrey seated a passenger—one Harry Thacker—behind him on the bike, and at 7:35 a.m., the pair sputtered out upon unusually calm Channel waters, accompanied by a motor launch.

The cycle sailors stopped twice for refreshments aboard the escort launch, then paused in Calais harbor for a leisurely forty-minute shipboard lunch before their non-stop return trip. They bumped the beach at Dover at 3:00 p.m. Perrey later boasted that his round trip to France had cost him less than ten shillings, and had taken—including lunch in Calais—just seven hours and twenty-five minutes. □

Motorcycle-mounted H. S. Perrey, with passenger Harry Thacker, guided his double-hulled craft on a round trip from Dover to Calais in seven and a half hours.

Old Glory

The eccentric excesses of the Roaring Twenties may have been epitomized in the unusual career of Alvin "Shipwreck" Kelly, who gained fleeting fame and glory by spending more than 5,000 hours of his life perched atop the flagpoles of American cities.

In 1924, the thirty-nine-year-old Kelly was hired by a Hollywood press agent to promote a new film by sitting for ten hours at the top of the flagpole above the Los Angeles theater where the movie was showing. Kelly fulfilled his duties and then some: He remained on top for thirteen days and thirteen hours and in the process started a new national craze. He also launched a lucrative personal career.

Kelly needed a vocational readjustment at the time. He had been a boxer, going by the name Sailor Kelly. But fight fans, who knew a loser when they saw one, had thought "Shipwreck" more appropriate. The name stuck but did nothing to dent the general admiration of his flagpole-sitting abilities. Soon after his Hollywood debut, Kelly rose on the popularity scale; by 1928, when he spent 145 days aloft, he was earning $100 a day.

To ease the rigors of his life at the top, Kelly devised an ingenious seat: an eight-inch rubber disk with holes drilled around its circumference. The rubber provided marginal comfort, and by jamming his thumbs into the holes Kelley could take five-minute naps. Any loss of balance while napping would strain his thumbs, causing excruciating pain that would awaken him. Stirrups allowed Kelly to stand and stretch his legs from time to time.

Not only did Kelly spend long hours aloft, but he also sought out occasions to climb to ever-greater heights. On November 17, 1928, for example, he shinnied to the top of an iron pole only 10 feet long—attached to the wing of a biplane flying 500 feet over Long Island's Curtiss Field. In the summer of 1930, Shipwreck Kelly reached the apex of his career ◊

Dressed in sailor's cap and pea jacket and reading a newspaper, a jaunty Shipwreck Kelly perches atop a sixty-foot flagpole near College Park, Maryland.

when he thrilled some 20,000 cheering fans on Atlantic City's famous Steel Pier by spending 1,177 hours—more than forty-nine days—on top of the pier's 125-foot flagpole.

But Kelly's popularity, like the stock market, had begun a disastrous slide. At the end of 1930, he braved zero-degree temperatures, snow, sleet, and freezing rain for thirteen days, thirteen hours, and thirteen minutes—coincidentally, almost the same duration as the stunt that had catapulted him to fame in 1924—atop New York's Paramount Hotel. This time his take was only thirteen dollars.

Kelly's second career was virtually on the rocks. He tried to revive it in

1939. In order to promote National Donut Week, promoters paid Kelly to eat thirteen doughnuts, on Friday, October 13, while standing on his head on a plank extending from a fifty-six story New York skyscraper. It was Kelly's final appearance of any consequence.

In 1952, broke and on welfare, Shipwreck Kelly fell dead between two parked cars in New York City. Clutched tightly in one arm was a scrapbook filled with yellowing newspaper accounts of his lost, high-flying glory. □

High above Manhattan's Times Square, Shipwreck Kelly waves from a sixty-five-foot flagpole that graces a fifteen-story hotel. Intended to last eight days and settle a $250 wager, the stunt was quickly aborted when police hauled Kelly down after a mere four hours.

Headlights facing rearward, the Back-Up Boys leave Los Angeles for New York City, halfway through their retrograde transcontinental round trip.

Route 66

One summer day in 1930, two men from Missouri, Charles Creighton and James Hargis, backed their Model A Ford roadster out of New York's Battery Park and onto the streets of lower Manhattan. They backed up Broadway and kept right on backing until they reached Los Angeles. No sooner had they arrived than the two Back-Up Boys, as the press dubbed them, promptly reversed course—but not gears—and backed all the way to New York again, arriving forty-two days after their July 26 departure, having covered 7,180 miles at an average speed of 10 to 12 miles per hour. Theirs remains a unique automotive achievement.

To ensure that their claims would not be disputed, Creighton and Hargis removed all of the car's forward gears before embarking. Having thus guaranteed their direction of movement, they mounted the headlights on the rear of the car. To torture their long-suffering automobile even more, Creighton and Hargis never once shut off the motor. The Ford spent each night tucked away in a Texaco station with its engine running to help test and promote a new Texaco motor oil.

Hargis, a twenty-six-year-old interior decorator, first got the idea for the stunt when his car broke down during a fishing trip, forcing him to drive home in reverse. He and Creighton, a twenty-one-year-old automobile mechanic, braved heavy rains, temperatures up to a scorching 121 degrees Fahrenheit, high altitudes, and long stretches of wind-blown desert.

Despite its novelty, it was an uneventful journey. The most serious difficulty arose early in the trip when a New York City taxicab—perhaps confused by the reversal of custom—rammed the roadster, lightly denting the fender and running board. Without bothering to repair the damage, Creighton and Hargis backed away. □

Daring Dick

Some sixteen years after the Panama Canal opened, the 700-ton entry gates of its Gatun Locks parted to admit the smallest transit in their history: Richard Halliburton, an American adventurer and travel writer who became the first swimmer ever to pass through the Panama Canal and its three sets of locks. The twenty-eight-year-old, 150-pound journalist was accorded all the services of the largest freighter and, like all vessels, paid a fee that was based on his weight: thirty-six cents, as duly calculated by a canal official.

On his way from Atlantic to Pacific through the canal, Halliburton overcame a number of hazards, both real and imagined. When he sought permission for the swim, General Meriwether L. Walker, governor of the American Canal Zone, tried to dissuade him, warning of typhoid, barracuda, sharks, and alligators, some reputed to be thirty feet long. But the governor neglected to mention the greatest peril, one that almost aborted the stunt: sunburn. The searing equatorial

rays plagued Halliburton from the very first day.

Having received permission and paid his canal toll, Halliburton launched his adventure on October 26, 1928, by diving into the Atlantic Ocean from the waterside veranda of the Strangers Club at Colon. He set out across the harbor with a lazy sidestroke. Beside him was a rowboat carrying a reporter and a photographer, and an army sharpshooter to fend off hungry predators. They would escort him throughout most of the swim.

Despite warnings about alligators, it was six days before one of the creatures slithered from the banks and knifed through the water, escaping notice until it was close enough to lunge at the swimmer. Halliburton scrambled into the rowboat to elude the powerful jaws; the sharpshooter fired once, the water churned, and the great beast disappeared from sight.

The following day, however, a more dismaying adversary threatened the swim; the sunburn that began as an annoyance had become

a serious medical threat. Doctors warned Halliburton that it would be dangerous to continue the swim before his skin had healed. He accepted their first aid and ignored their advice. Instead, he fashioned a jacket that would protect his shoulders and arms from the rays without hampering his stroke and continued on his way.

Swimming during daylight hours and resting at night, Halliburton completed his journey in ten days. In each lock he treaded water or swam in circles for as much as fifteen minutes as water filled or drained from the chamber to raise or lower him. Three locks brought Halliburton up to the level of the canal's central feature, twenty-four-mile-long Gatun Lake; three more locks lowered him to sea level on the Pacific side of the isthmus. For safety reasons, the sunburned swimmer had each lock all to himself, with the exception of his escort boat. Between locks, Halliburton paddled steadily, sometimes in a sidestroke, sometimes in a lazy crawl. His actual swimming time was fifty hours.

The Panama Canal swim was

just one of many headline-grabbing exploits that earned Halliburton the nickname Daring Dick during a seventeen-year career of travel and adventure. Throughout the 1920s and 1930s, Halliburton gained modest fame as a madcap journalist who would do anything, anywhere, in pursuit of a good yarn. He earned a handsome living writing best-selling travel books that incorporated his adventures. Sometimes, Halliburton's schemes invoked official censure; in 1925, for example, he briefly went missing and let the world presume he was dead.

That oversight may have contributed to Richard Halliburton's real demise in 1939. His popularity waning and book sales at a low ebb, Halliburton, now thirty-nine, made a bid to regain the limelight by attempting to sail a Chinese junk, the *Sea Dragon*, 9,000 miles from Hong Kong to San Francisco. On March 24, during a typhoon, a passing ocean liner picked up what may have been a distress call from Halliburton's junk. No one knows whether a rescue attempt would have succeeded: The navy delayed beginning a search for six weeks, apparently suspecting that Halliburton was again playing possum somewhere on the sea. This time, however, Daring Dick was on the level; he was never seen again. □

Richard Halliburton **(left)** swims behind a rowboat through the Panama Canal, which is visible in this false-color Landsat image **(above)** as a sinuous line running northwestward; an arrow marks the Pacific mouth of the canal.

Edifice Complex

New Yorkers are known for their blasé acceptance of strange sights and bizarre activities, but on the morning of May 26, 1977, George "Human Fly" Willig got their attention and held it for three and a half hours as he scaled the 110-story South Tower of Manhattan's World Trade Center, a climb of 1,350 feet.

At first, spectators thought that Willig was staging a unique suicide attempt. However, when police officers arrived they found the climber, by now well on his way to the top, to be perfectly content and rational. He was, in fact, quite well prepared for his climb.

A twenty-seven-year-old Queens toymaker and an experienced rock and ice climber, Willig had been planning the ascent of the World Trade Center for a year. In that time he had carefully measured the metal tracks built into the flanks of the structure that guide the window-washing scaffolding. After hours of work, he fabricated two sets of clamps—based on climbing tools called "ascendeurs"—that fit into the tracks and allowed him to walk up the side of the building. Each clamp incorporated a handle and a rope sling. Willig's foot rested in the sling; when he applied his weight, the ascendeur locked in place and supported him; when he shifted his weight to his other foot, the device unlocked so that he could slide it up the track by its handle. "It was like climbing a rope ladder," Willig said later.

In his red nylon backpack, the intrepid climber carried a spare set of clamps, a boltlike device that he could lock in place in case of ◊

After scaling the walls of New York's 110-story World Trade Center *(left)*, human fly George Willig cheerfully pays a $1.10 fine to New York mayor Abraham Beame *(below)*—a penny per floor.

emergency, a jug of water, a nylon jacket, sunglasses, and some wrenches. A blue nylon line was slung over one shoulder. It was tested to hold 3,500 pounds, considerably more than Willig's sinewy 155-pound body.

With his brother Steve and friend Jery Hewitt standing by, Willig began his climb at 6:30 a.m., as the morning sun glinted from the tower's glass walls. George's girlfriend, Randy Zeidberg, arrived a few minutes later. Security guards and police officers soon converged on the departure point, arresting Willig's well-wishers and screaming for him to descend. "There's only one way

to go," he called down to them, "and that's up." There were no arguments after that. Soon crowds of morning commuters packed the sidewalks. Television crews sent news of the climb nationwide. News helicopters circled the building.

When Willig reached the tower's sixtieth floor, he saw a party of police officers descending toward him on a window-washing scaffold. Thinking they were trying to rescue him against his will, the human fly used his rope to swing to an adjacent set of tracks, out of the "rescuers'" reach. Reassured that the police were only there to help if he needed them, Willig swung back to

his original route and continued his ascent—this time trading jokes and small talk with his escorts.

Finally, at 10:00 a.m., George Willig conquered the tower and crawled to safety. The police officers, most of whom by now had been won over by Willig's matter-of-fact skill, asked for autographs, then amiably arrested him for criminal trespass, reckless endangerment, and disorderly conduct. New York police commissioner Michael J. Codd—himself amused by Willig's audacity—nevertheless threatened to sue the climber for $250,000 to reimburse the city for traffic control and other expenses—and to deter future urban adventurers.

But to the huge crowd below and his even larger television audience, Willig was a hero. Perhaps recognizing that, New York mayor Abraham Beame settled Willig's official difficulties the next day with a fine of $1.10—one penny for each story the human fly had climbed. □

Cyclorama

The Himalayan village of Lukla is one of the principal jumping-off spots for expeditions to the world's highest mountain, Everest, and its neighbors. Generations of Lukla's Sherpa residents have served as the climbers' guides and porters.

When Fritz Öttinger, Hans Koller, and Hermann Schuschke stepped from the cabin of a small plane one spring morning in 1987, their seasoned hosts thought they were no different from all the other mountain climbers who came there. Like the others, the trio brought an abundance of hiking and mountaineering gear—stoves, tents, sleeping bags, insulated jackets, and the like. But these men were different. Among the packs and parkas were two eighteen-speed aluminum bicycles, on which Öttinger and Koller planned to cycle to the top of 18,200-foot Kala Pattar, whose peak commands a panoramic view of majestic Everest. Schuschke would walk behind them and photograph their exploits.

Öttinger, a thirty-three-year-old auto electrician, and Koller, a forty-year-old toolmaker, had prepared for their climb by pedaling for a year through the mountains of their native Bavaria. Schuschke was a marathon runner. Despite their preparations, some uncertainty persisted in the three men's minds. They had told only their closest friends and relatives what they were up to; most people at home thought that the trio had taken a vacation at the beach. "We didn't want to be laughed at if our plans didn't work out," said Schuschke.

The fear was misplaced; the trip proved a rousing—but not an easy—success. On March 31, only a few hours after their airplane deposited them in Lukla, the trio and three newly hired Sherpa porters started on their way. Just outside the village, the track became steeper with every revolution of their wheels. The trail traced hundreds of switchbacks. Frequently debris and boulders blocked the way; then, the two dismounted and carried their twenty-four-pound bicycles. Behind them trudged Schuschke and the three Sherpas carrying stoves, clothing, tents, and spare parts for the bicycles.

At the entrance to Everest National Park, they encountered an almost insurmountable obstacle: Gatekeepers refused to admit the vehicles. There was a misunderstanding that required an afternoon to overcome; bicycles were permitted, it turned out, but motorbikes were not. From there, the trip was a roller-coaster ride through the shadows of Everest and its neighbors. Grinding ascents were followed by wild, plunging descents. ◊

Rough terrain frequently forced Fritz Öttinger *(on right)* and Hans Koller to carry their bikes while ascending Kala Pattar, near Mount Everest.

They passed through stunning rhododendron forests and teetered on swinging cable bridges over churning glacial streams. At times the path was so difficult that photographer Schuschke and the Sherpa porters walked past the riders.

Distances in the Himalayas are measured vertically, not horizontally. The bikers and their train traveled more horizontal miles than they bothered to count. By April 4, their vertical progress had taken them to an elevation of 13,000 feet; an icy storm swept through, coating the path with bumpy, frozen mud. The next morning, struggling to breathe even as he traversed level ground, Öttinger wrote in his diary, "I'm gasping like a carp. My temples are pounding. A collapse here would be fatal. It would take days for a helicopter to get here." The cyclists shouldered their bikes and trudged on to the Khumbu Glacier, a 300-foot-thick monster of ice and debris only a few hours from the summit of Kala Pattar. In Lobuche, a five-hut village perched above 16,000 feet, they rested and composed themselves for the next day's final assault.

At 6:00 a.m. they set out, alternately riding and carrying their bicycles. At Gorak Shep, 500 feet below the top of Kala Pattar, they dismounted for the last time and carried their vehicles—which by now seemed to weigh more than their riders—until they reached the summit at 10:00 a.m. After a two-hour sojourn, gulping tea and drinking in the view of Everest, they retreated.

It had taken them seven days to travel to Kala Pattar's peak from Lukla; their return consumed just three. The spare bicycle parts that the Sherpas carried were never used; not even a tire had failed. □

Gadfly

When a nineteen-year-old computer operator and freshly minted private pilot named Mathias Rust rented a single-engine, 160-horsepower Cessna 172 Skyhawk from a local flying club in May of 1987, he told friends and family that he was headed off on a 1,300-mile journey from Hamburg, Germany, to Reykjavik, Iceland. The long flight, Rust explained, was intended as a shortcut to the flying hours he needed to qualify for a commercial license. No one thought it unusual that Rust removed three of the plane's four seats and fitted the space with extra fuel tanks to stretch the Skyhawk's normal three-and-one-half-hour range and provide a safety margin for the long overwater portions of his trip.

Rust departed from Hamburg on May 13, flying first to the German island of Sylt in the North Sea. He stopped in the Shetlands off northern Scotland, then completed his journey with a long crossing of the North Atlantic to Reykjavik. On his return trip, Rust made his way to Helsinki, Finland. The young pilot was in no hurry. By the time he departed from Helsinki, more than two weeks had passed since his roundabout flight had begun.

Lifting off from Vantaas International Airport at 12:21 on the afternoon of Thursday, May 28, Rust pointed his Skyhawk west toward Stockholm, Sweden, his stated destination. But just twenty minutes after Helsinki's radar operators first picked up the Cessna's blip on their screens, its track turned left—southeast, toward the Soviet Union where, ironically, the date was designated as "Border Guard's Day."

The center of attention after landing his Cessna 172 Skyhawk in Red Square, German airplane pilot Mathias Rust *(above, in red flying suit)* four months later stood trial in a Soviet courtroom *(right)* for illegal entry and "hooliganism."

Soon Rust's aircraft disappeared from the Finnish radar screens.

What happened during the next six hours may never be fully known, for Rust's left turn took him on a daring—some would say foolhardy—400-mile excursion across some of the most heavily guarded air space in the world, concluding with a landing in Moscow's Red Square. Soviet—now Russian—military experts have discussed Rust's escapade only reluctantly and without much detail. Nor has Rust himself spoken in detail about his intrusion. But the young pilot's penetration into the heart of Moscow shook the Soviet empire and ultimately cost several military leaders their jobs.

It is known that soon after Rust turned toward Moscow, his aircraft was spotted by a Soviet radar operator as it slipped along the Finnish coast, low over the Baltic Sea, moments before Rust reached the Russian mainland. Between there and Moscow were said to lie 10,000 radar units, 14,000 missile launchers, 2,200 jet interceptors, and countless antiaircraft emplacements. The registration numbers painted on the plane's fuselage clearly identified it as West German. A small West German flag was painted on the airplane's tail.

Yet hardly a finger was raised to halt Rust as he cruised at around 330 feet, at a little more than 100 miles per hour. At least three Soviet air-force jets intercepted Rust, buzzing his small craft and circling it menacingly for a time. Apparently no other aircraft were deployed—not even helicopters, which could have forced Rust to the ground.

The intruder kept on. Shortly before 7:30 p.m. Moscow time, tourists in Red Square were startled to see a small blue-and-white aircraft approach low from the west, circle the square three times, buzz the Lenin Mausoleum, then settle to the cobblestones behind the onion domes of St. Basil's Cathedral, just yards from the Kremlin wall. One British tourist captured the entire event on videotape.

The crowd was agog. Tourists,

Muscovites, and police thronged the plane as Rust, dressed in a crimson flying suit, stepped from the cabin. Police gaped as he nonchalantly signed autographs, adding the phrase "Hamburg-Moscow" to each. Before long, however, the gears of Soviet officialdom were grinding at full speed. Rust was bundled off to prison, where he spent slightly more than a year before being sent home. Within the military, heads rolled, at least figuratively. The largest were those of Defense Minister Sergei Sokolov and Aviation Marshall Alexander Koldunov.

West Germans fell in love with Rust's daring. One opinion poll showed 79 percent of his compatriots were "tickled" by his exploit, and within weeks Germans were sporting T-shirts bearing the words "International Airport, Red Square, Opening May 28, 1987."

Rust denied participation in any elaborate spy scheme or complex plot. He told reporters that he had made the daring flight as part of a campaign for better East-West relations and because "I just wanted to talk with Russians." There might have been yet another reason. Rust's flight took place on the Christian holy day marking the ascension of Jesus Christ into heaven—and an old German pilots' toast promises that "On Ascension Day, we land in Red Square."

Rust's popularity waned in the years after his return to Germany in August of 1988, and his stability must have declined as well. In April of 1991 he was convicted of stabbing a nurse—for refusing to give him a kiss. □

Beearded Man

In 1969, retired engineer Don Cooke began wearing a beard that sometimes stretched an impressive seventeen and one-half inches from his ears to his waist and weighed as much as six pounds. It was a honey of a beard—comprising as many as 21,000 live Italian bees. Cooke grew the writhing wreath by putting a queen bee into a gauze cage and tying it to his chin; once the queen's thousands of subjects landed on his face, Cooke's evidently unflappable stylist shaped the bees with gentle swipes of a file card. Cooke donned his bee beard more than 150 times during the 1970s for the entertainment of spectators at farm shows and to prove that bees are not dangerous to those who know how to handle them. But Cooke's wife, Marge, was the real hero of these demonstrations. Although allergic to bee venom, Mrs. Cooke would unhesitatingly plant a big kiss on her spouse's bee-fringed lips. □

One of ten cameras mounted on Gregg Riffi and his helicopter captured the start of his 2,400-foot bungee jump over the Loire Valley, 2,600 feet below.

Yo-Yos

Gregg Riffi is a twenty-six-year-old poly-athlete who holds several French national swimming records and golfs with a seven handicap. He has skied the highest slopes of Mont Blanc and has set a world record for "barefooting"—water-skiing without skis—at more than 130 miles per hour. He is a licensed airplane and helicopter pilot. But all these credentials were irrelevant near noon on Wednesday, September 18, 1991, as Riffi sat in the open door of a helicopter piloted by Michel Beaujard. Some 2,600 feet above the green fields of the Loire Valley, photographer Tim McKenna thrust a camera into Riffi's hands. Beaujard brought the craft to a hover above Grangent Lake. Then Riffi pressed the button that started his camera and fell out of the helicopter door into the void—sans parachute.

The falling Frenchman quickly accelerated to 120 miles per hour as he plummeted earthward. Then, at first imperceptibly, the diver's descent began to slow. Some 200 feet above the lake's surface—2,400 feet below the hovering helicopter—Riffi's fall suddenly ended, and he was flung wildly upward for hundreds of feet. He fell once more and once more rebounded. Even as Beaujard gingerly steered the helicopter toward land, Riffi continued to bounce like a yo-yo, still snapping pictures of himself as photographer McKenna recorded the events from above.

The occasion was worth preserving: Riffi had just concluded the world's longest bungee jump. Snubbing his free fall from the helicopter was an 800-pound elastic cord about three inches in diameter ◊

secured by a harness to the jumper's waist. At rest the cord was 750 feet long; Riffi's momentum stretched his elastic tether to 2,400 feet before it stopped his descent.

Safely landed a few minutes after his bungee plunge, Riffi had a sudden urge to try it again—an urge that has prompted Riffi to complete more than 5,000 bungee jumps and has made him one of the world's leading practitioners of the sport. Curiously, his enthusiasm is not unique. Though not for everyone, bungee jumping has gained a large international following. Since 1979, when members of Britain's aptly named Dangerous Sports Club donned top hats, tails, and elastic cords to plunge from Bristol's Clifton Suspension Bridge, bungee jumping has become the pastime of preference for the thrill deprived of Europe, America, Australia, and New Zealand.

Jumpers claim that the experience produces a "natural high," in pursuit of which some men and women will leap from almost any elevated site. Bridges are common and convenient, although their use for jumping is illegal in the United States. But commercial operators offer virtually all comers the opportunity to dive from towers, cranes, hot-air balloons, and helicopters.

Today's upscale, high-tech bungee jumpers are far removed from the pastime's origins on Pentecost Island in the South Pacific's New Hebrides. Each spring for thousands of years, Pentecost islanders have been leaping from rude wooden towers more than ninety feet tall.

The divers are tethered not by an elastic cable, however, but by woven vines tied to their ankles. On Pentecost, land diving, as it is called, is a ritual of manhood and prayer for a successful yam harvest. It is decidedly dangerous, and divers have been known to be injured or killed when their vines failed or proved to be too long to arrest their fall before they hit the ground.

For the most part, modern bungee jumpers are able to obtain the thrill without the risks incurred in the primitive ritual. Rather than vines, the ties that bind them to safety are supersize versions of the elastic bungees that have been used for years as shock absorbers in airplanes and tie-down cords on trucks, trailers, and motorcycles. They consist of hundreds of elastic strands encased in a woven nylon sheathing. One end of the cord is fastened to a jumper's ankles or a body harness such as that used by mountain climbers. After the required length is calculated by taking into account the height and the jumper's weight, the other end is fixed to the jumping platform. Under ideal conditions, the cord is just long enough to snub a jumper's fall a few feet from the ground.

A study published in 1991 revealed that only six minor injuries—and no fatalities—had resulted from more than 14,000 bungee jumps arranged by one California vendor of thrilling sports. Why do jumpers keep bouncing back for more? The name of one such operator—Adrenaline Adventures—may say it all. □

Hanging On

On June 25, 1989, after two years of preparation, twenty-four-year-old dental student Zoltan Ovari packed a toothbrush and a change of clothes and embarked on a flight from Donaueschingen, Germany, to Adelaide, Australia. This might have been an unremarkable event, except that Ovari's mode of transportation was not much more than an oversize tricycle fitted with wings and a tiny engine—a propeller-driven hang glider.

The aircraft weighed 330 pounds and carried less than nineteen gallons of fuel, giving it a cruising range of about 450 miles at a speed of 50 to 60 miles per hour. Its Volkswagen engine prompted one newspaper to dub the craft the Flying VW. But it was no sturdy beetle—Ovari's hang glider lacked even a rudimentary cabin to shield the pilot from the fierce elements he would encounter along the way.

Despite his Spartan equipment, Ovari was well prepared for the journey. He had canoed alone for weeks in Alaska, hiked 600 miles across Norway and Sweden, and motorcycled through Mexico and Nicaragua. In the scant space available aboard his aircraft, he packed maps, visas, landing permits, a hand-held aviation radio, a compass, an altimeter, a parachute capable of safely lowering the entire machine in the event of an emergency, and a transponder that made his tiny craft visible on air-traffic-control radar screens. Ovari skillfully piloted the offbeat flier over eighteen nations and some of the most hostile terrain in the world. His original flight plan called for an eighty-day jaunt. Instead, the journey became a fourteen-month odyssey, plagued

In a sixty-year career that encompassed sidecar races, cross-country record setting, and leisurely touring, Dot Robinson, the "First Lady" of motorcycling, logged more than 1.5 million miles astride a string of shocking pink motorcycles.

Photographed over Thailand, Zoltan Ovari flew low and slow for 13,000 miles in a frail motorized hang glider, following the route mapped below.

WEST GERMANY

TURKEY

SAUDI ARABIA   PAKISTAN   NEPAL

MYANMAR

INDONESIA

AUSTRALIA

by bad weather, crash landings, and officious bureaucrats.

Ovari was buffeted by wild turbulence over the Taurus Mountains in Turkey and blistered by 120-degree-Fahrenheit temperatures over the desert of Saudi Arabia. There, a minor miscalculation in navigation—easily accomplished, since his instruments were a portable compass and a wristwatch—would have meant going down in an uninhabited wasteland. In India, he endured a drenching by torrential monsoons. Rain or searing sun, Ovari pressed doggedly onward.

Determination was not enough to overcome the bureaucrats who forced Ovari to accept sixty-six-octane gasoline in Myanmar, formerly Burma. So feeble was the fuel that it caused his sixty-horsepower engine to falter, then quit as he flew over the jungle between Chittagong and Rangoon. The hang glider was severely damaged in the ensuing crash, but Ovari escaped serious injury. The plane's twisted remains were shipped to Bangkok, where Ovari waited three months for repair parts. Finally, he was in the air again—but not for long. The earlier crash had caused hidden damage to the engine's crankshaft; it snapped over Sumatra, forcing another crash landing of the craft, this one on a lonely palm plantation. Once more, there was a three-month delay before the necessary parts arrived and the aircraft's engine could be reassembled by the village blacksmith.

But now Ovari was nearing his goal. Only one major obstacle remained: a 450-mile stretch of the Timor Sea between Dili on Timor and Melville Island, Australia. Although the hop was within the nominal range of his aircraft, adverse winds could easily double his flight time—and put him in the water. Ovari chose a relatively cautious course: He jettisoned his parachute in order to save weight, added five gallons of fuel, and made the trip in two hops, using the tiny Indonesian island of Saumlakki as an intermediate stop. During the flight, Ovari's mind was filled with worries. Was the engine running a little roughly? Was the wind blowing him off course? Was his compass pointing true? The anxieties proved to be no more than that. No difficulties arose, and the flier's navigation was perfect. Ovari's prudence had been justified, however—he landed in Saumlakki with a scant half-gallon of fuel in his aircraft's tanks.

From there he flew to Melville Island in a mere five hours. Another short hop carried him to Darwin, and five days after that, on August 31, 1990, Zoltan Ovari landed in Adelaide. He had spent 299 hours, 50 seconds in the air, and flown some 13,000 miles—the longest flight ever made in a motorized hang glider. But the new record-holder had little time to celebrate; Ovari was due to report to the University of Budapest on September 2 to resume his studies. He hurried back, but not the way he had come. While his little aircraft headed home by ship, Ovari traveled on a commercial Boeing 747. □

Mountain Son

It surprised no one in his home town of Talkeetna, Alaska, when twelve-year-old Taras Genet became the youngest climber ever to scale 20,320-foot Mount McKinley, North America's tallest peak. Mountaineering was in Taras's blood.

Taras is the son of famed Alaska mountaineering guide Ray "Pirate" Genet and Kathy Sullivan. Sullivan scaled the Western Hemisphere's highest peak, Argentina's Aconcagua, with Taras in her womb. Years earlier, in 1967, Ray Genet was a member of the first team to scale McKinley during the winter. Later, he started the first guide service on the mountain and in 1979 he led the previous youngest climber, fourteen-year-old Mark Edwards, to the summit. A few months later, Ray Genet died while descending Mount Everest in the Himalayas. The year-old Taras and his mother were in the expedition's base camp at the time of the accident.

The boy grew up in Talkeetna dreaming of climbing McKinley. That was inevitable; he could see the mountain from his front door, and he absorbed the lore of its trails and weather from his mother and their mountaineering friends. And there was an expectation that Taras would follow in his father's footsteps. "Throughout his life," Sullivan said of her son, "people asked, 'Are you going to climb the mountain because of your father?' " Taras's own motives were mixed. "I've dreamed about climbing McKinley forever," he told reporters after his climb, "partly because of my dad and because I just wanted to climb it."

He got his chance to fulfill the dream on June 6, 1991, with a seven-member expedition that was one of scores that ascend McKinley every summer. Although the mountain is a popular ascent and hundreds scale its peak every year, the climb is hazardous. In 1990 alone, three climbers died on McKinley. Even during the summer, sub-zero temperatures grip the mountain and violent storms sweep across its slopes on winds reaching more than 150 miles per hour.

The mountain's capricious weather did not disappoint Taras and his party. Early in the climb, it was so hot that they traveled at night, when the snow froze and afforded more secure footing. But at times the temperature plummeted to fifteen degrees below zero Fahrenheit. Then, five feet of snow fell and halted progress for four days. For some climbers, the wait might have been excruciatingly boring, but not for Taras; he filled his time reading a book about the Matterhorn and staging food fights with his tentmate. "We threw anything," he grinned, "beans, baby powder, water. The tent was a mess." Taras never complained of the hardships, and his fellow climbers never gave a thought to his age—except, perhaps, when they caught him playing with the teddy bear he had brought along.

On June 21, the group surmounted the peak's 400-foot, thirty-five-degree headwall and walked the final few feet to the summit. Taras looked out and waved triumphantly to his mother, who was circling above them in a small plane she had rented for the occasion. □

Twelve-year-old mountaineer Taras Genet scales an ice wall en route to the summit of Alaska's Mount McKinley.

This fleeting, fuzzy image of the elusive "John Vincent" was caught by a tourist's video camera as the outlaw parachutist leaped from the 1,300-foot-high observation deck of New York's World Trade Center.

Skyscraper

On May 8, 1991, a young man joined sightseers in the elevator that carried them to the observation deck of New York's 110-story World Trade Center. Then, disengaging himself from the others, the man eluded security guards, somehow climbed an electrified fence intended to prevent people from jumping, tossed a small yellow cloth into the wind to test its direction, and—blowing a kiss to startled tourists and shouting something that sounded like "Geronimo"—quickly followed the cloth into the void.

The man harbored no death wish, however. The shocked witnesses soon saw a colorful blue-and-white parachute bloom above the jumper like a soft wing. With practiced skill, the mysterious leaper steered himself to a perfect landing on a small patch of green grass 1,368 feet below and hit the ground running. Within seconds, and long before startled police could react, he had folded his equipment, scampered to a waiting red car, and escaped into Manhattan's rush-hour traffic.

A local television station, alerted by a telephone call, captured the parachute descent on videotape. But, like the police, the television journalists found the jumper to be mysteriously elusive. Reporters had been told that the leaper was a twenty-three-year-old Texas deep-sea diver named John Vincent. But, having made good his escape, Vincent—if that was indeed his real name—has since eluded all attempts to locate him and learn the rest of his story. □

Mexican Dive

It is never long before a visitor to Mexico's famous seaside resort of Acapulco gravitates to a place called La Quebrada, where, four or five times a day, bronzed men clad in spandex swimsuits climb the rocks overlooking the Pacific Ocean, pose briefly at the edge for the benefit of awed spectators, then execute a graceful swan dive 135 feet into a rock-fringed, twelve-foot-deep pool of surging seawater. Acapulco's cliff divers are among the world's best-known tourist attractions.

Less well known is the Club de Clavadistas, the "Club of High Divers," which may be one of the world's most exclusive labor unions, numbering fewer than forty men. The club, founded in 1949, negotiates with hotels and other institutions to stage special events. Members who are not diving during a show help solicit the tips from tourists that are the divers' major source of income. The Clavadistas earn between $650 and $700 per month, significantly more than the average Mexican worker. ◊

Raul Garcia poses after one of hundreds of high dives from Acapulco's cliffs.

Body rigid and arms out-
stretched, a member of Acapulco's famed Club de Clavadistas
soars from the cliffs of
La Quebrada.

But then, Acapulco's cliff divers are not typical workers. They are distinguished not only by the obvious danger of their occupation but by the years of training each undergoes before being admitted to the Club de Clavadistas. Although informal, their apprenticeship is lengthy. It is also effective in developing the strength and rigid adherence to style that allows divers to complete as many as 1,000 plunges a year without serious injury.

Beginning at a young age—eight or nine is not unusual—aspiring Clavadistas attach themselves to the community of divers, running errands and generally ingratiating themselves with their heroes. To prove their mettle, the boys dive from ever-higher positions on the cliff, mimicking the Clavadistas' form and soliciting their advice. By the time they reach their mid-teens and are eligible for club member-

ship, the aspirants have proven themselves thousands of times by climbing the cliffs and completing successful dives.

The endless hours of climbing help the young cliff divers develop massive neck and shoulder muscles. These are necessary to prevent spinal injury by absorbing the shock of hitting the water. The fledglings have also perfected the Acapulco diving style that impresses audiences and—more important—saves the divers from the many hazards of their plunge.

One danger is the cliff itself, which tapers so that its base juts twenty-one feet out from the top. In order to hit the center of the fifteen-foot-wide pool, the cliff diver must make a horizontal leap of twenty-seven feet during his fall. The Clavadistas' characteristic swan-dive position helps them soar outward; its graceful appearance is a pleasing side effect.

The second menace is the water, which a diver strikes at more than forty miles per hour with a force that could cripple the unprepared. For protection the Clavadistas employ their hands and heads, using an unwavering formula. Before entering the water, the diver raises his head, joins his hands above his head, and tenses his muscles. One medical researcher compared the effect to that of the nose cone of a rocket. The position prepares the diver for a smooth entry: Locked fists break the force of the impact of hitting the water, rigid muscles absorb much of the shock, and upturned head straightens the spinal column and distributes the remaining forces evenly down its length.

By sticking to the formula, the Acapulco divers have pleased audiences for half a century—and avoided death and disabling injury. Raul Garcia, a founder of the Club de Clavadistas and now in his sixties and semiretired from diving, made more than 37,000 dives in his fifty years on the La Quebrada cliffs—and suffered only minor bone fractures and a dislocated shoulder. □

Call to Grapeness

Paul Tavilla of Arlington, Massachusetts, a produce dealer, earns his living selling grapes, along with such other staples as lettuce, tomatoes, cabbages, broccoli, and melons. But grapes, although they have not earned Tavilla a fortune, have been especially good to him: They have become his ticket to fame, allowing him to put his mouth where his money is by setting a cluster of records for catching—in his mouth—an assortment of grapes dropped from great heights and hurled long distances.

In setting his latest mark on May 27, 1991, at a field in East Boston, Tavilla grabbed a juicy projectile thrown by a friend, Bostonian James Deady, from a distance of 327 feet, 6 inches. The catch was added to other Tavilla exploits in grape catching noted in *The Guinness Book of Records.* It also returned him to his roots, for this was the way that Tavilla had first captured the category in 1977.

Tavilla's produce customers had long admired his oral skill at catching peanuts, grapes, and other snacks on the fly. As a result, Tavilla

was talked into appearing that July at a benefit baseball game in Dedham, where he snared a dark purple grape hurled 251 feet down the foul line by former semiprofessional player Mike Weir. The Dedham town clerk certified the feat, and Tavilla entered the record books.

Tavilla's efforts since then have borne considerable fruit. On July 7, 1985, he mouth fielded a large red seeded grape that was dropped 520 feet, 5 inches, from the Shawmut Bank building in Boston—a record. Less than a year later, Tavilla surpassed himself in Tokyo, where he caught a grape dropped from the 660-foot-high Sumitomo Insurance building. He sundered that record a little more than two years later by catching one of seventy grapes that were dropped on him by his son-in-law—a Boston-area dentist—from Boston's 788-foot John Hancock Life Insurance Tower. The purple projectile was traveling about 110 miles per hour when it smushed into Tavilla's mouth.

Such sweet glory is not without its price. Tavilla has sustained swollen lips and other minor injuries associated with ingesting high-velocity fruit. Because he must spend long minutes staring straight up into the sky searching for small, falling spheres, neck strain is another avocational hazard. But the risks are as nothing next to the satisfaction Tavilla receives from pleasing his audiences. "When you read in the papers about all these disasters happening," he says, "it's kind of nice to read about a human achievement." □

A handful of grapes at the ready, Paul Tavilla demonstrates grape form as he prepares to field a falling fruit.

Surf Bored

Surfers have been known to travel to the ends of the earth in search of the perfect wave. But Frenchman Laurent Bouquet has carried the quest to new heights. His sport is sky surfing, practiced by plunging from an airplane at an altitude of 12,000 feet and performing loops, rolls, and other aerobatics perched on a surfboard. About 9,000 feet later, he opens his parachute and floats quietly to earth.

The first sky surfer is said to have been Bruno Gouvy, a French skydiver and skier who first took the plunge with a board in 1988. Bouquet, then twenty-eight and a champion skydiver who had logged more than 2,200 jumps, soon followed. "I think I was mad," he said much later. "It was impossible to control the board. It took me wherever it wanted."

Today, Bouquet makes the board go where *he* wants. He built and tested a total of thirteen designs in the first two years before arriving at the right sky-surfing board, a streamlined length of plastic less than four feet long and one foot wide, weighing only two pounds. Straps secure his feet to the top, and an emergency cord allows him to jettison the board—which can quickly become a dangerous projectile—at the first sign of trouble.

After innumerable practice jumps, Bouquet found that, at the 120-miles-per-hour speed at which a sky surfer falls, the air can be as solid as an ocean wave. Soon, the Frenchman had taught himself to ride the invisible breakers that he had discovered in the atmosphere, pulling loops, carving turns, and tumbling forward and backward in his all-too-brief falls back to earth. □

High above Israel's Negev Desert, Laurent Bouquet, the Silver Surfer, poises at the aircraft door *(top)* before spreading his arms, soaring into space *(center)*, and executing intricate turns and flips on his return to earth.

UNTO OTHERS

Although human beings are quite capable of unspeakable cruelty, cowardice, selfishness, and greed, they also have a powerful instinct toward doing what is right for their fellows. Disregarding great personal risk and spirit-breaking adversity, men and women follow that reflex to help others without a moment's hesitation and with no thought of reward. Compelled by their vision of a kind of golden rule, they brave every imaginable hazard merely to do for others what they would expect to be done for them. Often, they do even more—many die that others may survive.

Nothing is beyond such selfless individuals. They have dared infernos and tempests on the sea, polar wastelands, ice-choked rivers, the terrifying cauldron of a shattered nuclear core, the cruelty of evil empires—the automatically brave are not easily deterred. Sometimes they are driven by devotion to their comrades and the responsibilities of leadership; but usually they are simply swept up by circumstance and follow their innate generous impulse. Thus, mild clerks, encountering an accident, stop to help or die trying. Frail girls plunge recklessly into harm's way. Gentle teachers place themselves between their little flocks and violent intrusions. The lesson of this diverse, courageous band is clear: Within us all, there lives a hero.

3

Rider to the Sea

Driven onto treacherous offshore shoals by a North Sea storm, the coal brig *Hermione*, southbound from Sunderland, ran aground off England's Lincolnshire coast on August 31, 1833. As the wind and waves pounded the doomed craft, the eight men aboard the *Hermione* saw a sight as astounding as it was welcome: Plunging toward the sinking ship through the surf and spindrift were two men, mounted on sturdy farm horses.

The riders, Richard Hoodless (*below*) and Joseph Dobson, each took two mariners onto their horses—one ahead of the rider and one behind—and carried them safely through the pounding surf to shore. But before they could return for the remaining four crewmen, the ship disintegrated in the hammering waves, and the sailors drowned.

Hoodless and Dobson modestly declined a reward that was offered by Lincolnshire's lord lieutenant, Earl Brownlow. But the pair could not escape official recognition of their heroism. The following spring, at Earl Brownlow's urging, the Royal Humane Society awarded Hoodless and Dobson its Silver Medal, citing Hoodless's "noble courage and humanity" and "the praiseworthy manner in which he risked his life on that occasion, by swimming his horse through a heavy sea to the wreck, when it was found impossible to launch the life-boat."

Hoodless richly deserved the recognition, for the *Hermione*'s crew was only the latest that he had pulled from the deadly shoals of that stretch of coast. Nor were they the last. Rescue was the plan and pattern of the square-jawed Briton's life. Hoodless spent most of his time farming a small plot of land reclaimed from the North Sea near Grainthorpe, in Lincolnshire. But atop his house he built a lookout post, mounted a telescope, and in stormy weather climbed to his aerie to scan the coast. When northeast gales blew, he seldom had to look long, for sandy shoals and shifting banks extended well out from shore, waiting to entrap ships, such as the *Hermione*, that failed to maintain a respectful distance.

When he saw a vessel in trouble, Hoodless raced to the rescue, usually astride his horse, which he had trained to plunge into heavy seas—an equine skill that he said was not very difficult to teach. "Hoodless declares," reported one contemporary journal, "he could manage the most unruly horse in the water; for that, as soon as the animal finds that he has lost his footing, and is obliged to swim, he becomes as obedient to the bridle as a boat is to its helm."

Docile or not, the aquatic mount made rescue possible in some otherwise hopeless situations. In one exceptional case, Hoodless brought a ship's captain, the captain's wife, and ten seamen to shore at one time by draping some over his horse's flanks and having others hang onto the stirrups. Still, the equestrian rescues required great care, especially where the wrecked ship had rolled on its side, with masts, sails, and lines just out of sight underwater. At least once Hoodless's steed was almost his undoing when its feet became tangled in a ship's submerged rigging. Hoodless escaped by slashing the entangling lines with a pocketknife.

Although lionized after the *Hermione* incident, the taciturn farmer shrugged off his accomplishments. It was enough, said Hoodless, to have saved the lives of fellow creatures. Uncomfortable with fame, he returned to his farm and the selfless work that so compelled him. His cherished anonymity had been lost, but not his gallant partner's: There appears to be no record of his swimming horse's name. □

Amazing Grace

At twenty-two years of age, Grace Horsley Darling still lived with her parents and brother in the Longstone lighthouse, off England's craggy northeast coast. Located in the Farne Islands near the Scottish border, the Longstone light warned ships in the North Sea away from the reefs and shoals of the rough Northumberland shore. Grace's father, William Darling, had succeeded his own father as keeper of the lighthouse; but it was she who became the heroic figure of the Longstone saga and one of the foremost heroines of the Victorian age.

Grace Darling's reputation was earned early on the cold morning of September 7, 1838, during the fiercest storm in decades. As the young woman watched the sea heaving in the pale dawn light, she spotted wreckage floating on the waves offshore. She immediately summoned her father. The lighthouse keeper scanned the foam-streaked waters and the scatter of low, stony islands with his spyglass, seeking signs of a shipwreck. Sure enough, he spotted nine souls clinging desperately to the ragged flank of the large, flat stone known as Big Harcar, about a quarter of a mile offshore and intermittently buried in the heavy seas. They were the only survivors of the paddle steamer *Forfarshire,* which had come to grief during the night on its run from Hull to Dundee.

Both Darlings knew that the castaways would undoubtedly be swept to their deaths in the sea if they were not rescued promptly. But the nearest lifeboat station was at Seahouses, on the coast about five miles to the south; its rescue boat would never reach the castaways in time. The only craft available for the task was the Darlings' own coble, a hefty rowboat twenty feet long and six feet in the beam—far too much boat for one man to handle in those seas. Grace's brother, named ▷

Inspired by the heroism of father and daughter, artist James Wilson Carmichael depicted William and Grace Darling rowing through the seas off Britain's Longstone lighthouse toward the ill-fated *Forfarshire.*

William after the father, was also at Seahouses on a visit. Without hesitating, the delicate young woman volunteered to take her brother's place at the coble's oars.

The pair stowed blankets in the boat to warm survivors; Grace removed her voluminous petticoats to make rowing easier, and she joined her father at the oars. Although Big Harcar was not far from the lighthouse, strong tidal currents, rocks, gale-force winds, and a heavy surf forced the Darlings to row nearly a mile before they could approach the storm-swept island. Time and again, the little coble came close to sharing the *Forfarshire's* fate.

Father and daughter rescued and took five people to safety; one was a woman hugging two children who had died during the night. While Grace and her mother took care of the first group of survivors, the lighthouse keeper and one of the steamer's rescued crewmen braved the storm waters once again to retrieve the remaining four. Later, a lifeboat arrived from Seahouses with the younger William Darling and a rescue crew, who had the grim task of gathering the steamer's dead from the sea. But Grace was the heroine of the day.

Word of Grace Darling's exploit soon spread across Britain, and she became an instant celebrity. Souvenir hunters throughout the kingdom cherished tiny scraps of the clothing that she had worn that fateful morning, and so many wrote to request locks of her hair that, one historian quipped, she faced the danger of baldness. Plays, novels, and fanciful illustrations commemorated her deed, and her idealized likeness adorned nearly every surface that could accommodate it. Grace and William Darling both received medals and pensions from the government.

The daring rescue also left a more enduring legacy. The Royal National Lifeboat Institution, a charitable organization that developed from England's Shipwreck Society, spread throughout the British Empire, offering aid and comfort to survivors of lost ships and support for lifeboat stations.

But Grace Darling's life, like her single adventure, was fleeting. She was not lured by fame, but chose to remain with her family at the Longstone lighthouse. Never robust, the courageous young woman died there of consumption only four years after rowing her way into the hearts of Victorian England. □

Riding a national wave of adulation, Grace Darling's friend Henry Perlee Parker portrayed the Victorian heroine in action.

Hinckley's Holocaust

To the residents of Hinckley, a busy lumber center in east central Minnesota, the forest fire that leaped from the woods into town on September 1, 1894, signaled the end of their world. Striking at the end of a hot, dry summer, the fire consumed more than 400 square miles of pine forest. Its smoke blackened the daytime sky. Heat from the blazing timber created its own tornado-like wind, a searing blast that hurled balls of flame miles through the air. These bombs of red-hot embers rained on the wooden buildings of Hinckley, setting fire to structures far removed from the advancing wall of flames. The town's main street turned into a gauntlet of fire. The village that owed its life to the forest was now destroyed by it.

In and around Hinckley, 418 persons died. That so many were killed was unre-markable. The miracle was that so many more survived the fire—saved by the courage of a handful of hardy railroad men.

As the wall of flames advanced on Hinckley from the south and buildings were ignited by flaming wind-borne debris, many of Hinckley's terrified inhabitants instinctively ran to the railroad tracks that bisected the town. The rights of way of two competing railroads cut wide swaths through the forest north and south of Hinckley and represented a possible safe route away from danger.

The only train in Hinckley waited at the depot of the Eastern Minnesota Railroad. There, prevented by the fire from proceeding southward to St. Paul, engineer ◊

Hundreds of citizens of Hinckley, Minnesota, owed their lives to engineers Edward Barry (top left) and William Best (left), who coupled their trains together and carried panicked citizens out of the blazing center of the town. On another track at the edge of Hinckley, engineer James Root (below) backed his crack express train through the fire to safety.

Edward Barry had coupled his freight train to the passenger express of engineer William Best and conductor Harry Powers, the senior railroad man on the scene. They decided that survival—if, indeed, survival was possible—lay to the north, toward Duluth, eighty miles away. As fire consumed the tracks at the south end of the yards, they hustled frightened refugees on board. Several times Barry tried to get under way but Best, whose passenger train was closest to the approaching flames, applied his air brakes, holding fast to allow more people to scramble aboard. The smoke-filled sky turned black; flames licked the train itself and ignited the clothes and hair of the panicked townsfolk. Finally, at 4:00 p.m., the Eastern Minnesota Railroad train pulled away with 350 people aboard.

Although two engines pulled its two sets of cars, the overloaded train labored mightily to outrun the fire. Eight miles north of town, Barry found that the timbers supporting the 850-foot span of the Kettle River bridge were already ablaze. The crew gingerly inched the locomotive and cars across the span; they had proceeded less than half a mile beyond the bridge when it collapsed. Even after the train had traversed the most dangerous fire zone, refugees appeared on the tracks and from time to time Barry and Best stopped along the way to let people board. By the time the train arrived in Duluth at 9:00 p.m., they had rescued a total of 500 people. Duluth's residents did not have to be persuaded that those on the train had suffered; although the nearest fires were more than fifty miles distant, flames lit the southern sky and the wind bore the acrid aroma of burning pine into the city.

Even as Barry, Best, and the trainload of fire victims inched out of the Eastern Minnesota station, one of the competing line's trains—the St. Paul and Duluth's crack express, the *No. 4 Limited,* hurried southward from Duluth, driven by engineer James Root. Soon the tracks became obscured with thick smoke and the fire's fumes burned Root's lungs. The *No. 4 Limited* never reached Hinckley. A mile north of the town, Root brought his train grinding to a stop when he encountered 150 men, women, and children who were fleeing from the advancing flames.

Root boarded the refugees, then began a retreat, backing the train toward Duluth. The fire was moving faster than Root's train, however. Wooden ties ignited and hot metal rails began to warp. The heat shattered the locomotive's windows, peppering Root with broken glass. Blood streamed from a gash in his neck, and he passed out. Fireman John McGowan revived Root with a quickly hurled pail of water, and the engineer, by now burned and blistered as well as cut, pressed the train onward.

The passengers were no better off than the crew. Ash-laden smoke choked the parlor cars. Fire charred the exterior, and wooden window frames began to blaze. The stunned riders—many of whom had boarded in Duluth, prepared for nothing more than a fast run to St. Paul—prayed, screamed, or lapsed silently

into shock. One man dived through a broken window, and conductor Thomas Sullivan had to restrain another from following.

Doubting that he could escape the onrushing flames, Root determined that he would stop five miles up the track, where the railroad crossed a shallow, muddy pool known as Skunk Lake. There he halted the burning train. Passengers and crew ran for the water, where they waited out the passage of the flames that swirled everywhere around them. Although they had to spend the entire night in the lake, they emerged alive.

When rescue workers entered Hinckley and its surrounding villages the next day they found hundreds of charred corpses. Entire families had been incinerated by the flames. For several years afterward, hikers and surveyors continued to stumble over the burned remains of those who had been caught in the woods during the fire.

James Root became a celebrated hero and even appeared on stage in a specially concocted play about the tragedy. Edward Barry, the other engineer, was awarded a gold medal, and eventually a town in the region was named for him. William Best, the man who had held the Eastern Minnesota train to the last minute possible, was largely ignored in these celebrations, except for a gift of sixteen dollars he received from a newspaper fund drive. He turned the money over to charity. □

Four-year-old Cecilia Cichan was the sole survivor of the crash of a Northwest Airlines jet that killed 154 people at Detroit in 1987. Rescuers think her mother, Paula, may have sacrificed herself by shielding the child with her own body. Cecilia's father, Michael, and brother David, six, also died in the crash.

Towering Midgetts

In the four centuries since Florentine navigator Giovanni da Verrazano first noted their treacherous presence, the far-reaching shoals and barrier islands that protect nearly 200 miles of North Carolina's coast have proved the undoing of nearly 700 ships. Thousands have died in the wrecks, but thousands more have been saved by the waterwise residents of Okracoke, Hatteras, and the other sandy offshore islands that compose the Outer Banks. During the nineteenth century, the United States Congress formalized the rescue activities of the islands' residents by establishing a chain of twenty-seven lifesaving stations. Erected at intervals of about seven miles along the Atlantic beach, each of these great, barnlike structures housed a crew of six to eight persons who kept watch and saved lives during the eight stormiest months of every year. In 1887, the Outer Banks lifesaving stations went on a year-round alert, and some are still in operation today as part of the U.S. Coast Guard. In all those years, the stations have produced their

share of heroes—among the best of them, several named Midgett.

In 1916, forty-one-year-old Captain John Allen Midgett, Jr., became keeper of Hatteras Island's Chicamacomico Station. The following year, a new menace joined the usual storms, tides, and shifting shoals that stalked shipping off the Banks: German submarines, sent forth to harass Allied shipping, brought World War I to the American East Coast. On August 16, 1918, one U-boat found a target in the British tanker *Mirlo*.

According to Midgett's official Coast Guard report, the *Mirlo* was within sight of Chicamacomico Station—about seven miles offshore— when she was torpedoed. Midgett and his lookout saw flames shooting upward and heard "heavy explosions." After "some difficulty getting away from the beach," Midgett skippered the station's power surf boat through heavy seas toward the burning wreck. Two miles from the leaking tanker, he met the *Mirlo*'s captain and sixteen sailors, pulling

for shore in a lifeboat. The captain said that the other two lifeboats were still near the fire, one of them capsized. Midgett advised the captain to get his boat closer to shore and wait but not to attempt a landing through the turbulent surf.

Then Midgett steered his craft into a roaring, floating hell that surrounded the ruptured oil tanker. Two fireballs, fueled by gas and oil bubbling to the surface, blazed about 100 yards apart. The sea around them was slicked with the burning cargo. In the acrid, greasy smoke that swirled between the fireballs, a capsized lifeboat could be seen. Six men clung to it. "With some difficulty," Midgett reported with characteristic understatement, "I ran our boat through the smoke, floating wreckage, and burning gas and oil and rescued the six ◊

One of a dynasty of rescuers, Captain John Allen Midgett, Jr., proudly wears the gold Lifesaving Medal for a formal portrait in his Coast Guard uniform.

men from the burning sea."

To the rescued seamen, Midgett and his men must have appeared like angels come to snatch them from the fires of hell. They were plastered with the goo from *Mirlo*'s bunkers and terrified that at any moment the surface of the sea would burst into flames. It had flared up several times, burning all of them; they saved themselves by ducking underwater. Sometimes, when they surfaced to gasp for air, they saw that shipmates had disappeared in the burning sea.

In this heaving field of fire, Midgett hauled the six survivors on board, then motored on in search of the third lifeboat. He found it nearby, laden with nineteen sailors. Midgett later reported that the boat was "overloaded and so much crowded that the men in it could not row: and it was drifting with the wind and sea." Taking the boat and its passengers in tow, the lifesavers headed toward shore and a rendezvous with the *Mirlo* captain's

boat. The three boats—Midgett's and the two remaining lifeboats—carried forty-two survivors of the torpedoed tanker. Getting them safely ashore required four round trips through hammering surf by the lifesaving station's surf boat and crew. Just ten *Mirlo* crew members were never found. The heroism of Midgett and his crew was kept secret until the end of the war. But finally each man involved was awarded the gold Lifesaving Medal of the United States and England's Victory Medal.

These were signal honors. But for Captain Midgett, who spent forty-one years in the Lifesaving Service, the deed that earned them had been a matter of simple duty. John Allen Midgett, Jr., came from a family of lifesavers. He had followed his father into the Lifesaving Service and had succeeded his uncle—Captain Little Bannister Midgett III—as keeper of Chicamacomico Station. If their calm heroism was not so well defined by actions, one might find it embodied in a story still told on the Outer Banks. In the tale, a grizzled old station keeper who many old-timers claim was John Allen Midgett, Sr., was about to launch a surf boat into a furious storm to aid a grounded ship. A visitor, concerned about the high winds and tumultuous sea, asked him, "Cap'n, you're not going out in a sea like this, are you?"

"Of course I am," Midgett reportedly answered.

"Well, you don't expect to come back, do you?"

"I don't know anything about coming back," the captain replied. "All I know is, the regulations say you have to go out. They don't say a word about coming back." □

Ice Man

Although he failed in two attempts to reach the South Pole, Sir Ernest Shackleton is considered one of the greatest polar explorers of all time. His first experience with the Antarctic came in 1901, when he joined an expedition mounted by Britain's famed arctic pioneer Robert Falcon Scott. The twenty-seven-year-old novice fell ill, however, and was sent home to England. Undaunted,

With the ship *Endurance* locked in the ice of the Weddell Sea, meteorologist L. D. A. Hussey exercises a dog team, preparing for a transantarctic journey led by Ernest Shackleton *(inset)*.

Shackleton joined a second expedition, this one aimed at reaching the South Pole. Sailing from New Zealand aboard the ship *Nimrod* on New Year's Day, 1908, he began an exploration that lasted through 1909. Shackleton led a team to the top of the 12,450-foot volcano Mount Erebus, pinpointed the southern pole of the earth's magnetic field, and—with Manchurian ponies bearing his equipment—marched to within 112 miles of the South Pole itself. Returning to England in 1909, Shackleton was knighted for his accomplishments. But he had not reached the pole.

On August 1, 1914, he left England aboard the aptly christened ship *Endurance* on another Scott-led expedition. This time he carried his country's hopes that the first men to cross the antarctic continent would be British. Instead, the expedition became a rout in which the stocky, sunburned, forty-year-old explorer established himself as an extraordinarily tireless and devoted leader—and living proof that, as he wrote later, "there is no limit to human endurance."

Shackleton had intended to land on the coast of the Weddell Sea on the eastern side of the Antarctic Peninsula, then march overland 2,350 miles via the pole to Mc- ◊

Murdo Sound on the shore of the Ross Sea. Despite the most careful preparations, however, polar explorers work at the whim of the weather. For nine months, the *Endurance* was trapped in pack ice in the Weddell Sea. Slowly but relentlessly, the drifting floes crushed the hull, casting the twenty-eight members of the expedition loose on the ice with three twenty-two-foot lifeboats and only a portion of their food and equipment. The *Endurance* sank on November 21, 1915—ironically, two months into the southern spring. Shackleton briefly considered their predicament and then calmly told his men, "Ship and stores have gone—so now we'll go home."

This was far easier said than done. At first, there was no open water for the boats to float on, and the vessels were too heavy to be dragged over the ice. The stranded party camped on the drifting ice, shooting scarce penguins and seals for meat and blubber. Finally, their ice raft was carried to warmer, open waters, and on April 9, 1916, the men were able to launch the boats. The lifeboats steered for Elephant Island, a steep, barren rock off the

northern tip of the Antarctic Peninsula. They reached the island after six perilous days and nights and made their crude camp ashore. On Elephant Island, they were safe from the sea but not from the antarctic winter. Without help they would die there.

Shackleton devised a plan as desperate as their circumstances. He would take five crewmen and one of the lifeboats—the *James Caird*—and make for the island of South Georgia, where there were a half-dozen Norwegian whaling stations. The journey required crossing 930 miles of the stormiest seas in the world in a small boat. Even a minor error in navigation could cause the party to sail past their destination into the oblivion of the Southern Ocean. "Clearly, it would be a big adventure," Shackleton wrote in one of history's magnificent understatements. The boat carried sails on two short masts. For ballast, the crew loaded a ton of stone from Elephant Island's beaches in the bottom of the boat. To provide some measure of protection for the crew, the expedition's carpenter fashioned a crude shelter for the *James Caird*, using wood from packing cases and canvas remaining from the *Endurance*'s salvaged stores. The men loaded one month's ra-

tions and set sail on April 24, 1916.

Fierce winds and heaving waves buffeted the tiny craft, and a seasick crew had to bail continuously to keep it afloat. "So small was our boat and so great were the seas that often our sail flapped idly in the calm between the crests of two waves," Shackleton recalled afterward. "Then we would climb the next slope and catch the full fury of the gale." Constantly cold and wet, the men stood four-hour watches and then made their way forward to sleep on the stones that were used to ballast the boat. Shackleton saw to it that there were two meals each day of dehydrated meat protein and a night ration of warm milk. The men slept and cooked under the makeshift—but lifesaving—canvas decking.

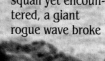

On the sixth day, Shackleton noticed that the *James Caird* "was becoming more like a log than a boat." Wind-driven spray had frozen over the craft, weighing it down to the point of sinking. Frantically the men jettisoned gear and hacked at the covering of ice; they barely succeeded in keeping afloat. On the eleventh night, during the worst squall yet encountered, a giant rogue wave broke

Four months after *Endurance* sank, Shackleton's crew dragged the lifeboat *James Caird* onto the icy beach at Elephant Island on April 15, 1916 *(left)*, fitted it with a crude canvas deck, then launched the vessel nine days later *(right)* on a desperate voyage to reach help on South Georgia, 930 miles away.

over the *James Caird,* tossing the craft "like a cork in breaking surf." Somehow the boat survived, and the men managed to bail it out.

Through it all Shackleton's adroit navigator, Frank Worsley, somehow held the boat on a proper course, carefully estimated its speed, and calculated its position from sextant sights taken in the rare, brief moments when the sky was clear. Shackleton had estimated that the voyage would take two weeks, and on the fourteenth day the rugged South Georgia coast came into view. But the crew of the *James Caird,* by now nearly out of drinking water, had to endure two more stormy days at sea, fighting to keep their boat off the rocks that guarded the shore. They pulled up on South Georgia on May 10.

Their arduous adventure was not over, however. To reach the whaling stations, Shackleton and his men would have to cross the island, scaling an unexplored mountain range in the process. The expedition leader set out with two men. They trekked for thirty-six hours without stopping, over mountains and across a glacier, hacking footholds in the ice, and more than once retracing their steps when they came upon a dead end. Shackleton wrote later that they began to hallucinate a ghostly fourth man trudging through the snow with them—although the explorer is known to have said dismissively, "*That* should please the old ladies of Holland Park." With or without this spectral companion, they finally spied a whaling station and stumbled down to its relative safety.

But Shackleton's ordeal continued. By now the Southern Ocean was in the grip of winter. After retrieving his men on the other side of South Georgia, Shackleton failed in three attempts to reach Elephant Island to rescue the twenty-two crewmen who waited there. At last, on his fourth attempt, after pleading with the Chilean navy for the use of their ship *Yelcho,* Shackleton reached Elephant on August 30, 1916. As he approached the icy shore, one of the men shouted out the words their leader wanted most to hear: "All safe! All well!"

The revered explorer made one final assault on the southern continent. His fourth expedition sailed from England in 1921 aboard the ship *Quest* but never reached Antarctica. Weakened by influenza, Shackleton was struck down by a heart attack on January 5, 1922, at Grytviken on South Georgia, where his third expedition had ended, and his final one began. □

Those remaining on Elephant Island wave and shout encouragement to Ernest Shackleton as he and five crewmen set off for South Georgia aboard the tiny *James Caird.* All survived to greet their leader when he returned by ship four months later.

Father Desert

California's Death Valley earned its forbidding name in the mid-nineteenth century, when pioneers seeking a shortcut to California paid for their impatience with their lives. The valley, a 150-mile-long basin that lies 282 feet below sea level, is the lowest point in the Western Hemisphere. The basin traps heat, the sun is merciless, and summer afternoon temperatures often rise above 130 degrees Fahrenheit. Surrounding mountains comb moisture from the air so that rain seldom falls within the valley. Although the desert is dotted with springs, many produce undrinkable alkaline water.

The nineteenth-century discoveries of gold, then borax and other minerals, lured droves of prospectors and miners to seek riches despite the harsh conditions. Many were lost without a trace, their bodies picked by vultures and covered by the shifting sands. Until the advent of road signs, restaurants, and telephones, Death Valley offered little comfort to the traveler, and untold numbers of people died trying to cross this punishing wilderness.

More would have perished had it not been for the selfless services of one man, Ralph Jacobus Fairbanks. From 1910 to 1930, he saved more than a score of men from death in the desert and recovered the remains of fifteen others who were not so fortunate. Fairbanks considered helping people his plain duty, and he never took any payment for his lifesaving work. He was known as the guardian angel of Death Valley—or, more simply, as "Dad" Fairbanks.

Drawn from Utah to Death Valley by the mining business late in the nineteenth century, Fairbanks made his home base in Shoshone, a tiny California trading post between the Nevada border and the eastern edge of Death Valley. He and his wife, Celestia Abigail, earned a living in the desert hauling freight and running a cafe and general store. But Fairbanks squeezed more than a living out of the unforgiving desert—he came to understand his new world. One of the first things he did after arriving in Death Valley had been to befriend the region's nomadic na-tive Paiute Indians. In turn, they helped "Long Man," as they called the tall, slender Fairbanks, learn the detailed texture of the terrain and taught him how to survive in the desert. He had soon begun using his abilities to save others.

Acting at the request of police or worried family members—or, more often, cued by the sight of circling vultures—Fairbanks would head into the desert in the hope of finding the hapless wanderer before the desert staked its fatal claim. Sometimes the rescue came too late; Fairbanks shipped the bodies home to relatives or, in the frequent instances when no identification was possible, buried the dead right where they lay.

But even when he found a wanderer still alive, his task was far from over. "A man dying in the desert from thirst is always loco," Fairbanks observed in 1930. "Every one of 'em goes off his buzz-wheel, tears off his shirt, and then starts to digging." One young man Fairbanks found was sifting sand through his fingers and laughing wildly. He was laughing, the victim explained, at the pollywogs that had to be strained out of this "water" before he could drink it.

On at least one occasion, according to legend, Fairbanks's savvy saved local people from their own familiarity with the desert—familiarity that fostered carelessness. Once, two sheriff's deputies guided by Fairbanks drove into the desert to search for a missing man. But their car broke down after penetrating twenty-five miles into the valley. The deputies—inexperienced desert men—immediately set out for home on foot, despite the blazing sun. They carried only small canteens, abandoning the large water jugs in the car because the vessels were too heavy. The scheme was a prescription for death. Fairbanks stopped the pair, ordered them to pass the afternoon in the shade, then led them home in the still-stifling darkness. Carrying the car's full ration of water, the accidental hikers were reduced to sipping it by the spoonful by the time they reached Shoshone.

Dad Fairbanks's forays into the hostile wilderness never harmed him, but he left it in the end. He died in 1943, eighty-six years old, about 200 miles southwest of his beloved Shoshone, in a Hollywood nursing home. □

Foreign Service

At the age of thirty-two, Giorgio Perlasca looked every bit the man in his prime. Tall, handsome, and elegantly dressed, Perlasca exuded self-assurance and authority. He personified what his Spanish diplomatic passport said he was—the representative of a neutral nation to the Nazi-leaning Hungary of 1944. Like many diplomats in difficult times, he lived on wit, charm, inventiveness, and a manner that could be as patrician and overbearing as circumstances required.

But Perlasca was both more and less than he appeared to be. To thousands of Hungarian Jews, he was a heroic benefactor, cleverly disguised. Perlasca was Italian, not Spanish, and no diplomat; he was an out-of-work meat buyer whose biggest customer had been the army of Germany's ally, Fascist Italy. Formerly a staunch Fascist himself, he had become disillusioned with the regime of Italian dictator Benito Mussolini.

Perlasca had come to Budapest in the summer of 1943, representing a company that supplied meat to the Italian army. When, coincidentally, Mussolini was overthrown and executed in Italy, Italy's alliance with Nazi Germany abruptly ended—and Perlasca was suddenly at risk. The pro-Axis Hungarian government began to round up and intern many Italians as enemy aliens. In April 1944, the net swept up the meat buyer as well.

Perlasca escaped from custody in October and quickly made his way to the Spanish legation, where he knew he had an ace in the hole. He was one of the Italian volunteers who had gone to Spain in 1936 to fight in the Spanish Civil War on the side of Nationalist leader Francisco Franco. In gratitude, the Franco regime had awarded him a document promising the protection of the Spanish government anywhere in the world. At the legation in Budapest, the assertive Perlasca asked for—and received—a Spanish diplomatic passport. It was a good choice. Because Germany was anxious to remain on good terms with the Fascist rulers in Madrid, the Nazis in Hungary would honor these new credentials. But Perlasca had already decided that they would be most useful to others.

While waiting for his documents, Perlasca had learned from the Spanish chargé d'affaires, Angel Sanz-Briz, that Spain and other neutral countries had joined in an effort to save Hungarian Jews from deportation to extermination camps in Germany. (Another participant in this effort was celebrated Swedish diplomat Raoul Wallenberg, who mysteriously disappeared after Soviet troops freed Budapest at the end of the war.) Flouting international law, Sanz-Briz was issuing letters of protection—documents that granted the rights and protections of Spanish citizenship—to all who sought them. Perlasca immediately volunteered to help and was given the task of finding housing, food, and medicine for the growing stream of refugees who had been placed under Spanish diplomatic protection. Before long, he was managing eleven apartment houses containing more than 5,000 Jews.

Perlasca was far more than a logistics officer, however. He and other diplomats regularly went to Budapest's railroad yards where, as Hungarian Nazis and German SS ◊

guards herded Jews into boxcars, the neutral visitors did their best to disrupt the operation. When they could, the diplomats removed individuals from the doomed crowd and took them under protection. One refugee saved by Perlasca recalled that the bogus delegate "was mesmerizing. He had such authority, he was so strong, that there was no way anyone could contradict him. They simply went away!"

On one occasion, an SS major, splendidly menacing in his gray uniform, attempted to remove two children whom the Italian had snatched from a death train and placed in the Spanish legation's car. Perlasca barked at the German officer, "No! This car has diplomatic immunity! Look at the license plates! Look at the flag of Spain!" The German drew his pistol, accusing Perlasca of interfering with his job. "You call this a job?" Perlasca bellowed back at the officer. Other diplomats crowded around and joined in the angry shouting match. The standoff was resolved by a lean SS colonel who barged into the group and brusquely told his subordinate, "Let them go. Their time will come." The newcomer was the notorious Adolf Eichmann, the ruthless SS officer in charge of emptying Hungary of its Jews.

While he could bluff such men as Adolf Eichmann, however, Perlasca could only watch the rising desperation everywhere around him in the city of Budapest. As Soviet troops advanced across southern

Hungary, the Germans ejected their puppet regime—which had never fully cooperated in the deportation of the Jews—and installed a more docile government. New goals were set: 50,000 Jews were to be shipped to Germany immediately; all others were to be put in labor camps. Soon, Eichmann demanded that 50,000 more Jews be sent to Germany. And speed was essential, because the Allied net was tightening around the Third Reich. As Soviet forces approached Budapest, the regime ordered the Spanish legation to move to Sopron, near the Austrian border. Knowing that transferring the legation would close Per-

lasca's base of operations, Sanz-Briz, the Spanish chargé, quietly slipped out of Hungary instead.

Working from the leaderless legation, Perlasca pushed his splendid diplomatic impersonation to new levels of audacity. When word of Sanz-Briz's departure reached the Nazis, they descended on Perlasca's apartments and began removing the frightened Jewish occupants. The Italian stopped them at the door of one house. "The legation is still in business," he boldly announced. "Sanz-Briz has gone to Switzerland for a diplomatic conference. The flag is still flying. I am in charge. I am the legal representative of

Spain." The government of Madrid, of course, had no idea of what was happening. Perlasca's ploy relied on the chaos of war—Budapest had by then entered one of warfare's epic sieges, with the Soviet army on every side. "Communications were impossible," he remembered many years later. "If somebody had managed to send a message, I would have been discovered."

Even without discovery, Perlasca's work became increasingly difficult, for the new Hungarian government refused to honor the letters of protection issued by Spain and other neutral countries. Perlasca's forceful personality became the last barrier between the Nazis and the remaining Jews. Through sheer bluster, Perlasca narrowly managed to sustain the fiction of his position for six weeks after Sanz-Briz left the capital. On January 16, 1945, Soviet forces entered Budapest.

Ironically, the liberation of the shattered Hungarian city meant the end of freedom for the self-styled Spanish diplomat: Giorgio Perlasca became a prisoner himself. Captured by Russian soldiers, he was put to work clearing corpses and rubble from the streets of Budapest, then shipped to Turkey—in a cattle car, the same kind of vehicle from which he had rescued so many Hungarian Jews. Perlasca eventually made his way back to his home in Padua, leaving a remarkable record in his wake. Between November 1944 and January 1945, he had helped save as many as 10,000 Hungarian Jews from deportation to Nazi Germany.

Perlasca's exploits went largely unnoted for nearly half a century—the only acknowledgment he received was Spain's insistence that he had been responsible for the destruction of one of the Budapest legation's cars. Finally in 1990, Hungary, Spain, the United States, and Israel honored the courageous ersatz diplomat with medals for his incredible exploits. Now in his eighties, Perlasca remains unimpressed with his own bravery. "What would you have done in my place?" he asks. □

Chinese Trekkers

Innkeeper, foot inspector, and according to some accounts, a spy, Gladys Aylward played many different roles in her adventure-filled life. But all she ever really wanted was an opportunity to serve as a Christian missionary in China. She succeeded and became an exemplar of self-sacrifice by risking her life to save 100 Chinese children from the horrors of war.

From the first, the diminutive Cockney had to struggle to follow her vocation. The China Inland Mission began training her for service in Asia but soon decided that she would never make an acceptable missionary: Her theology was shaky, and they were sure the Chinese language would prove too much for her. But the officials failed to take into account Aylward's toughness and determination. Aylward learned from friends that a missionary in northern China, a widow named Jeannie Lawson, would take her on as an assistant if only she could pay her own way there. Then earning her living as a parlormaid, Aylward immediately began to save for her passage to China. In October of 1930, with nine pence in cash and a traveler's check for two pounds pinned inside her corset, she set out to realize her dream.

After a harrowing rail trip across Europe and Siberia, Aylward finally reached Beijing in China. Then, traveling by train, bus, and mule, she made her way to Yangquan in the northern province of Shanxi to meet Mrs. Lawson. Aylward's seventy-three-year-old mentor had not enjoyed much success. The inhabitants of Yangquan cursed the ▷

Giorgio Perlasca *(far left)* saved thousands from the fate suffered by these Hungarian Jews—identified by yellow Stars of David sewn to their clothing—who were rounded up by Nazi soldiers in October 1944 and sent to death camps in Germany.

missionaries as foreign devils and threw mud at them. Unfazed, the two intrepid women began learning the local dialect, and soon they hit upon a way to reach potential converts: They transformed their mission into a stopover for passing muleteers and called it the Inn of the Sixth Happiness.

Aylward behaved more like an aggressive business owner than a witness for the gospel. She literally dragged customers in off the street. When a mule train approached, Aylward would seize the lead mule by its bridle and pull it into the inn's courtyard. The other animals would follow, leaving the helpless muleteers with a choice between unsnarling the hopeless mess or accepting the missionaries' offer of food and free Gospel stories. As the two women had hoped, the mule skinners quickly spread word of the inn and its stories.

Jeannie Lawson died shortly after the inn opened, and Aylward carried on alone. The inn thrived and so did Aylward's reputation—so much so that the local mandarin offered her a job. The central government, hop-

ing to bring the vast nation into the twentieth century, had recently banned the age-old, crippling practice of binding young girls' feet. Aylward, the only woman in Shanxi whose feet had never been bound, was asked to enforce the government's decree.

The missionary accepted eagerly. This was a cause she could enthusiastically advance, and it enabled her to travel throughout the province. This she did, freeing girls from their crippling fetters and preaching Christianity along the way. Aylward also started a family of her own, buying unwanted children for small amounts of cash. The first child she adopted, a girl, she named Ninepence for her purchase price.

By 1936, when she had been working in Yangquan for six years, a thoroughly assimilated and accepted Aylward became a Chinese citizen. Her brood of adopted children grew and grew. But Aylward was more formidable than the typical do-gooder; she became a force to be reckoned

with, to be called upon in time of crisis. She was given a title that suited her perfectly—Ai-weh-deh, the "Virtuous One." But "virtue" implied more than mere goodness. The name was conferred after Aylward, largely by force of will, single-handedly quelled a prison riot.

Even as Aylward strengthened her position in China, however, a conflagration had begun to smolder. On July 7, 1937, a minor confrontation between Japanese and Chinese troops near Beijing erupted into all-out war. By 1938, Japanese forces had invaded China and pressed as far west as Yangquan; there the offensive stalled in a virtual stalemate. When the Japanese pushed near Yangquan, Ai-weh-deh took her children and fled, returning when the enemy was driven back. For two more years the tides of war ebbed and flowed in Shanxi. Victories on both sides were followed by defeats. Each change displaced more civilians, and Ai-weh-deh took in every refugee child who came her way. By April of 1940, they numbered 100.

Throughout this time, and despite the hazards brought about by

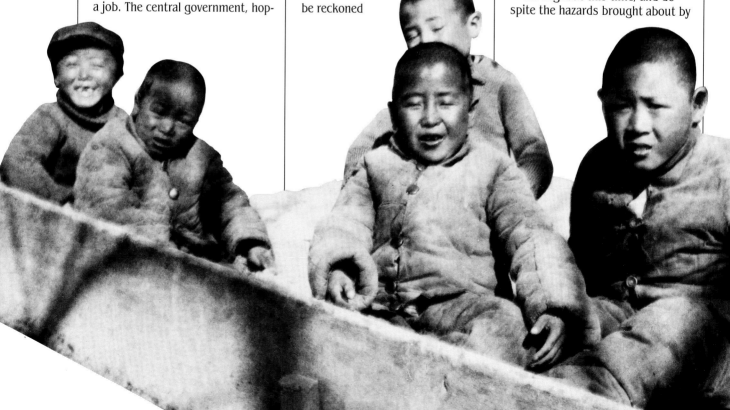

military operations and the presence of hostile forces, Aylward continued her travels to every corner of the province. She had her gospel to preach, her children to save; some writers have alleged that she also had intelligence to gather on behalf of the Nationalist Chinese Army and that the Japanese put a price on her head. But her central allegiance was unvaryingly to her beloved children.

Finally, seeing the Japanese once more about to take Yangquan, Ai-weh-deh decided to evacuate her brood to safety in the south. She nearly delayed her departure from the city too long, for enemy troops swept into Yangquan as she and her flock were leaving. According to legend, at least, Aylward was wounded by a Japanese bullet. Undeterred, the Virtuous One and her 100 children fled into the mountainous terrain of northern China—and, inadvertently, into a rare human epic of endurance and sacrifice.

Her charges ranged in age from four to fifteen. When the smaller ones became too tired to go on, Ai-weh-deh and the bigger children carried them. Two older boys served as scouts to mark the route ahead. The rest of the children followed, singing hymns. Ai-weh-deh told jokes to distract them from their fatigue and blisters. From time to time, like a stern drill sergeant, Aylward whistled the ragged column to a halt, so she could count their numbers to be sure that none had fallen by the way.

At night they slept outdoors on the ground or took shelter in roadside Buddhist temples. Their only provisions for the first week were two sacks of millet. On the seventh day of their flight, the scouts returned to warn that there were soldiers ahead. Fortunately, the troops were members of the Nationalist army and shared their rations with the children. After twelve days on the march, Ai-weh-deh and her children reached the Yellow River—and there the trek stalled. They had no means to cross the Huang He's wide, swift current. Aylward then took a form of action that was second nature to her missionary spirit: She had the children camp on the bank, and for three days they sang hymns and prayed for a miracle.

Indeed, the songs and prayers were heard by someone, for reports of a strange, wavering, high-pitched noise began to reach a Nationalist army unit headquartered in the vicinity. A scouting party identified the source as a band of hymn-singing children, and a sympathetic—and no doubt bemused—officer sent a boat to ferry the column across the river. Once more on their way, the weary youngsters soon arrived at a temporary refugee camp in Sian. From there, they were told, their journey would be easy. Instead of proceeding on foot, they would have the luxury of a train ride, which would take them to a major refugee settlement in Fufeng. In fact, the railroad leg of their journey was less luxurious than advertised. They rode huddled in open, high-sided coal trucks, often forced to lie down as the train ran a gauntlet of Japanese fire. "Mother," one coal-dusted ◊

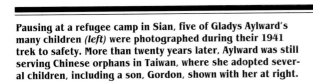

Pausing at a refugee camp in Sian, five of Gladys Aylward's many children *(left)* were photographed during their 1941 trek to safety. More than twenty years later, Aylward was still serving Chinese orphans in Taiwan, where she adopted several children, including a son, Gordon, shown with her at right.

child told Aylward, "we have all turned black." Four days after it began, the trip ended abruptly at a bombed-out bridge. Once more the children began to walk.

They trudged onward for nearly three more days over mountainous terrain before reaching a point where rail service resumed. They reboarded, and, at last, almost too exhausted to care, Ai-weh-deh's flock rolled into the refugee camp at Fufeng, where Madame Chiang Kaishek had established an orphanage for refugee children. The little band had covered more than 300 miles.

By then Ai-weh-deh was delirious, no longer certain of where she was or how long she had been on the march. Nevertheless, she attended to the needs of her children, and it was not until she was satisfied that they were truly safe that she let herself collapse. Doctors found that she had contracted typhus and pneumonia. She had kept going, however, until every one of her children reached safety.

Safety was a relative term in postwar China, however. After the Japanese surrender in 1945, the simmering Communist revolution came back to life. Ai-weh-deh continued her mission until 1949, when the Nationalist government was ousted by Communist forces and Ai-weh-deh returned to England and uncomfortable celebrity. Books celebrated her exploits, and one of them, a novel titled *The Inn of the Sixth Happiness,* was later made into a popular movie starring Ingrid Bergman. With typical modesty, Aylward refused to attend a screening. In 1957, she returned to what was left of her beloved China and opened an orphanage on Taiwan. There, in 1970, the Virtuous One died in her sleep. □

Flick of the Tail

As the limpid mountain sunlight streamed through the window of his laboratory in the mountains of New Mexico, physicist Louis Slotin prepared to tickle the dragon's tail, as he called it. In fact, he was about to condemn himself to a slow and painful death to save those who had gathered to observe his dangerous demonstration of how a nuclear chain reaction begins.

The nuclear age was still in its infancy. The first atomic bomb had been exploded in the New Mexico desert a little less than a year earlier by scientists at the top-secret Los Alamos National Laboratories. Two more bombs had destroyed the Japanese cities of Hiroshima and Nagasaki, forcing the surrender that ended World War II.

The first two bombs had drawn their explosive power from splitting atoms of U-235, a highly fissionable form of uranium. The third had split atoms of plutonium, a more fissionable element produced by altering the uranium atom. On May 21, 1946, Slotin was showing colleagues the onset of a chain reaction in two hemispheres of plutonium, a gray, leaden metal that is naturally warm to the touch.

Slotin, a tanned thirty-four-year-old native of Winnipeg, Canada, was one of the physicists brought into the wartime Manhattan Project, the secret, spare-nothing effort to build the world's first atomic bomb. Although plutonium had been used in the Nagasaki bomb, the new element's critical mass—the amount of plutonium in which a nuclear chain reaction would spontaneously occur—had not been well defined.

Slotin's job was to explore that unfamiliar territory. So secret and dangerous was this work that it was done in an isolated building shielded from the rest of Los Alamos by the steep walls of a canyon. The site was called Omega—the final letter of the Greek alphabet—because it was there that the critical last steps in bomb assembly were worked out. The name also hinted at the perilous nature of the work that was performed at Omega—the finality of death was seldom more than one misstep away.

Such research is done today with mathematical simulations, electronic computers, and robots designed to handle hazardous materials. But in 1946, none of these existed. Slotin's exploration was handwork. Complex calculations, delicate movements, and sensitive judgments were made by the most sophisticated—and most capricious—computer of all, the human mind and body.

The critical mass of a fissionable substance was determined by trial and error. Slotin, and others in the business of tickling the dragon's tail, maneuvered two hemispheres of plutonium toward each other, usually using an ordinary screwdriver as a lever, until the pieces almost met. As the hemispheres approached one another, instruments measured the rising level of radioactivity. When critical mass was reached—the "crit" in the argot of the nuclear trade—the instruments displayed a sudden, rapid rise in radiation levels. This was the experimenter's cue to push the pieces apart, and quickly. If they were not separated immediately, the chain reaction could accelerate, spewing massive bursts of invisible, but deadly, gamma radiation into the

crowd of observers. In September of 1945, the hemispheres had touched briefly, and the resulting spume of radiation had killed Slotin's lab assistant, Larry Daghlian.

Despite the hazard, however, Slotin was drawn to the demonstration. He had what a fellow scientist later termed "a positive hankering for danger." He had performed the procedure more than forty times; always, the dragon stirred but remained benign. Still, the young physicist's apparent nonchalance troubled some of his colleagues, and one of them had bluntly warned him: "I predict you won't last a year if you keep on doing that experiment."

That May, Slotin was about to leave Omega Site for a new assignment with Operation Crossroads, a series of atomic explosions carried out in the Pacific. On the fateful Tuesday he was tickling the dragon's tail for one last time to demonstrate the experiment to another Los Alamos scientist, Alvin Graves, who was visiting Slotin's laboratory. Six others—civilian and military lab assistants and technicians—stood around the room. Slotin, clad in the Los Alamos scientists' informal uniform of work clothes, gaudy Mexican silver belt buckle, and cowboy boots, nudged the two chunks of dark gray metal closer and closer with a screwdriver. A Geiger counter clicked more and more rapidly, signaling a growing level of gamma radiation. A second instrument, a

neutron monitor, silently confirmed the increasing production of subatomic particles by tracing a rising red line on a roll of paper. Closer. Faster. Higher.

Then the screwdriver slipped. The Geiger counter's clicks became a buzz, then ceased altogether as the sensitive instrument saturated with radiation. For a moment, an eerie blue light, softer but somehow brighter than the sunlight, filled the room. The hemispheres of plutonium had touched; the dragon was loose in the laboratory.

Louis Slotin lunged forward, grasped the pieces of plutonium with his bare hands, and pulled them apart. Then he stood back, his face a chalky white. Without speaking, he turned to a blackboard on the wall and drew a diagram of the room and each person's location at the time of the accident. The drawing would help medical personnel

calculate the dose of radiation each had received—and learn what amount would kill and what would not. Then, as the sour taste of radiation poisoning grew in their mouths, the eight men mutely filed from the laboratory.

Louis Slotin's action saved the others. Graves, who had been standing immediately behind Slotin, was most seriously affected, suffering nausea, fever, and hair loss for a month before finally recovering. The event left him with a small cataract on the lens of his left eye. Others suffered only slight effects. But the man who had tickled the dragon's tail so often suffered horribly from severe radiation burns on his hands and body and terrible damage within: His internal organs began to fail. Comatose a week after the accident, Louis Slotin died on the ninth day— Memorial Day, which celebrates America's military heroes. □

Gator Aid

As prelude to a fishing trip on a sultry September day in 1951, ten-year-old Parker Stratt of Coral Gables, Florida, and a nine-year-old girl, Jerry Gustafson, rode their bikes to an abandoned stone quarry to catch some minnows for bait. Descending a steep slope to the water's edge, Parker turned to pick up a bucket they used to dip minnows. Neither child was aware that they had become bait themselves.

Suddenly a seven-foot alligator burst from the water, sent Parker sprawling with a slap of its tail, and grasped Jerry's right arm in its jaws. Then the giant reptile backed into the water, dragging the terrified girl with it. Parker's first instinct was to reach for Jerry's hair and left arm to pull her away from the alligator, but he instantly realized that the girl's injured right arm might be torn off in such a gruesome tug of war. Even as he considered his options, both girl and alligator disappeared underwater. The boy waited.

Seconds later, the creature surfaced with Jerry, then rolled onto its back and momentarily lost its grip on the girl's arm. Parker was ready. Bracing his knees against the root of a tree, the boy stretched out over the water, seized Jerry by her injured right arm, and dragged the semiconscious girl out of the water. Then, as the alligator floated in the water, snapping its jaws at them, Parker pushed his companion up the pit's steep slope and out of danger.

Resting his friend in front of him on the frame of his bike, Parker rode a half mile to the Coral Gables municipal motor pool. The injured girl was put in a truck and driven to the nearest hospital, where doctors succeeded in saving her badly cut and broken arm.

Parker Stratt was immediately proclaimed a hero. A week after the fateful fishing trip, he was flown to New York to appear on national television. For months afterward, Miami area newspapers sang his praises, and he was honored by a host of organizations, including the Boy Scouts and Carnegie Hero Fund. President Harry S. Truman made Parker Stratt the recipient of the first Young American Medal for Bravery at a White House ceremony.

But to the ten-year-old boy, the title of hero became a burden as well as an honor, placing a weight of expectation that his young shoulders were not ready to bear. "My teachers and everyone looked at me differently after that," he said. "Every time we had a test in school I froze up. I made mediocre grades and I felt pretty bad about it." Thirteen years later, as a student at Dade Junior College, Stratt was still dogged by the feeling that he had not contributed anything since the day of the alligator.

Eventually he found his way into an occupation that allowed him to continue helping others in danger: Parker Stratt became a career lifeguard on a Florida beach. □

Flood Tide

Charlie Smith, a seventy-five-year-old retired coal miner, and his wife, Estella, fifty-eight, were entertaining an elderly guest, Oliver Dillard, when water first crossed the threshold of their home and invaded the living room. For two days in early March of 1963, a cold, drenching rain had soaked the hills and hollows of West Virginia's coal country. As night fell on March 11, streams throughout the area swelled into muddy rivers. In Logan, where the Smiths and Dillard lived, Island Creek and the Guyandotte River surged over their banks and took possession of the town's streets and buildings. For more than a day, the river rose at an unheard-of four feet per hour, trapping hundreds in homes and businesses.

Both of the Smiths were in poor health and neither could swim. Dillard was nearly blind. Had they ventured from the house, the fragile trio would no doubt have fared poorly in the floodwater coursing through town. They stayed inside and hoped for the best.

By dawn, the cold, clotted waters

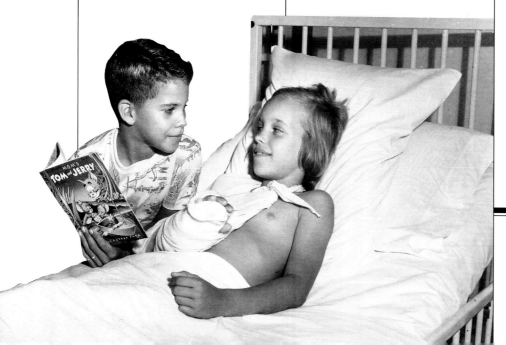

Hospitalized with injuries inflicted by an alligator, nine-year-old Jerry Gustafson smiles at Parker Stratt, ten, who rescued her from the creature's jaws.

lapped within fifteen inches of the ceiling of the Smith's tiny one-story home. The couple had spent the night standing on their bedroom furniture to keep from drowning; Dillard kept his footing on a parlor window sill. The tops of all the doors and windows were under water—and the river continued to rise.

William Neal, a local businessman, was in his small outboard-powered fishing boat, searching for stranded flood victims. The Smiths' home looked empty; but, hearing the cries of the trapped trio above the rush of water, he headed toward them. With Neal were Charles Stover, forty, a disabled veteran of World War II, and nineteen-year-old Stewart Miller, a carnival worker. They shouted encouragement to the people inside, then set about getting them out. The rescuers had brought an ax and an inflated inner tube; soon they also had a plan.

The window at which Dillard perched was covered by the porch roof; the roof and window, in turn, were covered by flood-water. To reach the blind man, the rescuers chopped a hole through the roof, and Stover, clad in a life jacket, slipped into the cold water, kicked out the window-panes, and grasped the blind man's hand, then led him underwater and out the shattered window to safety.

The Smiths presented a far more difficult problem. They stood in the bedroom, at the other end of the house. Because of their age and physical condition, the two of them could not make their own way to the submerged front window. The rescuers would have to go to the couple, swimming through the rooms and ducking underwater each time they had to pass through a doorway. Stover and Miller stripped down to their undershorts and went looking for the Smiths.

Speed was essential. The rooms were brightly lit by ceiling fixtures—a godsend, but only for the moment. The lights hung just fifteen inches from the rising water; when the flood reached them, the lights would short-circuit into the water—and electrocute everyone in the room. The prospect of electrocution was not the only hazard: The house itself was precarious. Because the structure rested on short timber pilings, it might shift and overturn at any time, trapping and drowning the people inside.

Pushing their inner-tube life preserver ahead of them, the two rescuers swam through the house past floating pillows, clothes, and furniture toward the stranded Smiths. They found the couple near exhaustion; the husband was about to give up. "Help him first," Estella Smith told Stover and Miller. They wrapped the old miner's exhausted arms around the inner tube and guided him to safety.

Thoroughly chilled, Stover and Miller swung their arms and rubbed their bodies for five minutes to warm up, then went back for Estella Smith. By now the water was only a foot from the ceiling, and the light bulb flickered ominously. But with a few more minutes of exhausting exertion, they had the woman safely outside, joining the other victims in Neal's boat.

Later that day, the floodwater rose another two feet, completely covering the Smiths' home. With little time to spare, Miller and Stover had managed to pull three strangers from what would have been their tomb. □

Charles Stover recalls the harrowing night in 1963 when he saved three elderly strangers from devastating spring floods *(above)* that struck Kentucky and West Virginia.

Ukrainian Crucible

Springtime in central Europe is a season of hope, a gradual release from the iron grip of winter. In April of 1986, as the days grew longer, the snow melted, and flowers raised their heads, citizens of the Ukrainian city of Kiev looked expectantly to the new season. In the countryside gardens bloomed, wheat fields greened, and fresh, bright leaves burst forth in the birch and aspen forests. Farmers prepared for the arduous but hopeful days of spring planting. But in the cities of Pripyat and Chernobyl, some eighty miles north of Kiev, quite another kind of harvest was being sown.

On the afternoon of April 25, technicians at Unit 4 of Chernobyl's nuclear-powered generating plant had begun to shut down the reactor for scheduled maintenance—and to test whether, during shutdown, enough electrical current remained to power emergency safety systems. Because the experiments took them into a regime of reactor operation that had not been much explored, the technicians first disconnected the emergency cooling system, to avoid destroying the hot reactor core with a sudden splash of cold water. With no margin for error in completing the rest of the steps, the team then let the reactor drift into a dangerously unstable low-power mode, where delays and a succession of bad decisions sealed Chernobyl's fate.

The 200-ton reactor core—a huge mosaic of uranium-packed fuel cylinders separated by layers of graphite—overheated; efforts to add cooling water only created explosive quantities of steam. As the

reactor sputtered out of control, the panicking technicians hit their emergency shutdown button, sending some 211 neutron-absorbing rods into the core to damp out the chain reaction. But before the rods could be fully inserted, at 1:24 a.m., the Number Four reactor core failed catastrophically.

At first, the building rumbled and shook. As a panic-stricken worker in the huge hall housing the reactor watched, 1,700 protective metal shields, each covering a fuel cylinder in the reactor and each weighing 770 pounds, began dancing like the lids of so many pots of boiling water. The massive pumps, which delivered sixteen million gallons of cooling water an hour to the reactor, shuddered and bucked. A series of explosions rocked the plant. A great fireball—a black cloud shot through with flames—rose into the air. Steel beams were wrenched and torn. The building's heavy reinforced concrete housing was shattered. Through a hole in the roof of the building were blasted chunks of red-hot nuclear fuel and graphite—fifty tons of radioactive material in all. The largest pieces fell back onto the surrounding buildings and grounds, starting numerous fires. The smallest particles blew away in the wind, creating a toxic plume that trailed across Europe. Another seventy tons of nuclear fuel from the heart of the reactor blew side-

ways out of the building, settling into heaps of lethally radioactive debris. The air was thick with radioactive dust and smoke. Tons of irradiated uranium—now unshielded—remained in the crater left by the explosion. The floor of the central hall housing Number Four reactor no longer existed.

For a few minutes after the rapid-fire explosions, a deep stillness enveloped the power plant. A freight train rumbled past. In the following silence, the crackling of flames

By November 1986, Chernobyl's Unit 4 reactor had been buried in a massive "sarcophagus" *(below)* composed of 300,000 tons of concrete and 6,000 tons of steel.

could be heard. Within minutes, firefighters swarmed over the buildings. The first to arrive climbed to the roof of the vast hall housing the generating turbines; the men were soon knee-deep in flaming, molten, radioactive tar. They stumbled over chunks of radioactive fuel from the reactor core and could barely find their way in the thick, acrid smoke. The next team tackled fires in the central hall, around the shattered reactor. Several firefighters were fatally irradiated when, to assess the situation, they climbed buildings next to the reactor and looked down into the core's barrage of neutrons and lethal radiation.

"We were told there was a high level of radiation," brigade commander Leonid Telyatnikov recalled a year later. "We knew about this. But we saw lots of flames—that was our main job. As we were

putting out the fires, you had the impression you could see the radiation. First a lot of the substances there were glowing, luminescent, a bit like sparklers. There were flashes of light springing from place to place as if they had been thrown." And yet the firefighters stayed, walking on lumps of ejected uranium, being showered with radioactive dust, working in relays until the fires were out or until the men collapsed. Seventeen were sent to Moscow that same day for radiation treatment. Telyatnikov himself underwent months of painful therapy and was still alive in 1992.

In the wrecked and burning turbine hall, technicians worked feverishly to pump stored fuel oil away to a safer place and managed to remove explosive hydrogen that could have caused yet another blast. More than one worker braved the thermonuclear hell of the shattered reactor hall to help injured comrades escape. Three men absorbed lethal doses when their bosses sent them to observe the damage. "I could feel the radiation going through my body," foreman Viktor Grigoryevich Smagin said later. ◊

In August, four months after its nuclear catastrophe, Chernobyl's reactor hall gapes wide as construction crews prepare to entomb the ruin in concrete.

Tragically, bureaucratic cowardice compounded the disaster, when the men in charge of the Number Four unit—whose mistakes had caused the explosion—could not accept the truth of what had happened. Engineers Aleksandr Akimov and Anatoly Dyatlov, denying the evidence of their own eyes, insisted even after the blasts that the reactor core itself must still be intact and needed only to be filled with cooling water. Akimov assured his superiors that the reactor had not been harmed and radiation levels were normal—in fact, radiation was estimated at 15,000 to 20,000 roentgens per hour, hundreds of times the lethal dose for humans.

Akimov and another engineer, Leonid Toptunov, gave their lives to that same delusion. Working in deadly radiation, they managed to get some water flowing, but their misguided sacrifice only made the situation worse. The radioactive water flooded other parts of the plant, threatened the remaining electrical service, and dangerously lowered the supply of cooling water available to keep Chernobyl's other reactors under control. In stark contrast to

his brave, but wrongheaded, colleagues, Yuri Bagdasarov, foreman at the neighboring Number Three unit, defied orders from above and shut down his water-starved reactor—averting a second meltdown.

At dawn on April 27, a macabre airlift began, as the military began trying to fill the still-burning reactor with sand and clay. Helicopter crews dropped some 5,000 tons of bagged sand into the glaring pit, flying as low as they dared, working until radiation made them too sick to continue.

Local coal miners volunteered their labor. They were sent onto the reactor roof to shovel graphite and fuel debris into the reactor for burial. Clad in bulky protective suits—useless at such radiation levels—they had time only to dash to the roof, make two ineffectual sweeps with their shovels, and flee. Radiation sickened them within an hour.

Anatoly Grishchenko, one of the Soviet Union's elite civilian helicopter test pilots, was called in to fly repeated missions over and around the damaged reactor, taking measurements and delivering supplies and equipment. By day Grish-

chenko flew; by night he gazed in awe at the luminous cone of radioactive gas projected upward by the infernal wreckage on the ground. More than once, he shuddered when he remembered that he had spent hours flying through that cone. Four times before his tour of duty ended, he flew directly over the open reactor. In mid-August, Grishchenko was called back to Chernobyl. Three more times he flew directly over the radioactive core. In September Anatoly Grishchenko was diagnosed with a bone-marrow disorder. Despite a marrow transplant, he fell ill again and died in 1990 after a hard-fought battle with cancer.

Thirty workers at the plant were killed in the initial explosion, and some experts have estimated that more than 5,000 workers died from their exposure at Chernobyl. No one yet knows the full impact of the world's worst nuclear reactor accident—only that it, like all disasters, summoned a legion of heroes. Twenty-six of them are buried in Moscow's Mitino Cemetery, their radioactive remains eternally isolated from the planet by sealed coffins shielded with lead. □

Potomac Nightmare

On Wednesday the thirteenth of January in 1982, one of the worst winter storms in recent history engulfed Washington, D.C. Within a few hours of the first flurries, a wet blanket of snow clogged roads, and lines of rush-hour

traffic stood steaming and still on the bridges that span the Potomac River and link the capital city with its southern suburbs. Just across the river at National Airport, within sight of the Washington Monument, seventy-nine passengers and crew members of Air Florida Flight 90 prepared for their escape from the Washington winter.

After long delays on the ground, they were finally cleared for departure shortly after 4:00 p.m. Engines

His heroism broadcast to the nation by television, congressional clerk Lenny Skutnik ferries Air Florida passenger Priscilla Tirado to safety in the ice-strewn Potomac River.

screaming, their Boeing 737 lumbered down the slushy runway, accelerating through the streaming blizzard. But snow, sleet, and ice coated the airplane's wings and clogged critical engine instruments. Ice-impaired and underpowered, the aircraft rose from the runway—but immediately faltered. Instead of climbing gracefully over the ice-choked Potomac River, it staggered along just above the ground, barely airborne. Less than thirty seconds after lifting off, Air Florida Flight 90 belly-flopped onto the twin Fourteenth Street bridges, crushed several cars, and careered into the frozen river with a sound like shattering glass.

From their cars on the bridges and roads lining the shore, an audience of thousands of commuters watched the plane's violent plunge. The river became the stage of a frozen amphitheater. As the broken fuselage settled into the icy water, the horror-stricken witnesses saw only six tiny figures emerge from the shattered aircraft and struggle toward floating debris. All six of the Air Florida survivors had suffered injuries. The water in which they found themselves was barely above freezing; the air tempera-

ture hovered just below that. Wind was driving the snow and propelling blocks of ice through the water. Under the storm clouds, the winter light was quickly fading.

Conditions severely hampered professional rescuers with the U.S. Park Police. A whiteout caused by blowing snow at first grounded Don Usher, who piloted a Park Police helicopter. Finally, twenty minutes after the crash, the chopper battled sleet, wind, and low visibility to reach the wreckage. Usher and his paramedic, Gene Windsor, hovered over the wreck, trailing a lifeline for the survivors to grab.

Before the incredulous eyes of the pedestrians and motorists—now joined by a television news crew—one man in the water twice passed the lifeline to others who were waiting next to him. The heli- ◊

Hovering over ice floes and bits of debris, a U.S. Park Police helicopter rescued four of the five survivors of a 1982 Air Florida crash in Washington. But firefighters *(inset)* could not save the occupants of an automobile crushed as the Boeing 737 caromed off a congested highway bridge into the frozen Potomac River.

copter lifted two men and two women to safety and would have retrieved their benefactor. But it was too late. Having heroically passed the lifeline to his companions, he had slipped beneath the surface, his name eternally unknown.

By now, nearly forty minutes had passed since the crash. Priscilla Tirado, the one woman remaining in the water, was too weakened by shock and cold to hold the helicopter's lifeline. Desperately, Tirado screamed, "Won't somebody please come out here and save me?"

Somebody did. For Lenny Skutnik, the suspense and frustration of waiting and watching from the Virginia shore had become unbearable. The twenty-eight-year-old Congressional Budget Office clerk shucked his coat and cowboy boots and, risking his own life, jumped into the freezing water, swam twenty feet through chunks of ice, and towed Priscilla Tirado to shore. Rescued and rescuer were quickly wrapped in blankets and rushed to a nearby hospital. Television cameras captured every moment of Skutnik's heroic act; he was the hero of that night's news because he had managed, alone, to retrieve one of the crash survivors from certain death, at great risk to himself.

Less visible to the nation—but no less heroic—was Roger Olian, sheet-metal foreman at St. Elizabeth's Hospital in Washington. Although he too braved the freezing water, Olian never reached the survivors—yet all five gave him credit for saving their lives. In fact, he had led the first attempt to save them.

Moments after the crash, Olian had stopped his car and run to the Virginia riverbank, where he found a group of people improvising a lifeline by connecting lengths of rope,

battery cables, diapers, and other materials. Olian grabbed one end and strode into the water. Swimming when he could, crawling over chunks of ice when he had to, breaking two toes in his haste, he headed for the people in the wreckage. No other help was in sight. Olian ran out of rope seventy-five feet from shore and fifteen feet from the crash victims. Still he struggled, waving and shouting encouragement. After Olian had spent twenty minutes in the water, the

helicopter arrived and began its airlift. Although Olian never reached the people clinging to the wreckage, they took courage and comfort from his dogged progress and his endurance. One of the rescued men said later, "I was fascinated by this man. He just kept coming. It was he who saved my life."

"I didn't think I would make it," Olian said later, "but I knew I wasn't going to spend the rest of my life wondering if I could have made a difference." □

Poetic Justice

Lucille Babcock, a sixtyish woman with white hair and glasses who walks with a cane, is the former poetry editor of Little Rock's now defunct *Arkansas Gazette* newspaper and a poet in her own right. She is also living proof that stereotypes can lie; that poets—supposed by some to be faint of heart—are ca-

pable of decisive action; and that white-haired ladies can be more than a match for violent men.

Babcock's epic actions began one warm summer morning in 1987, as she busied herself with chores in her second-floor apartment. Suddenly, a woman's scream pierced the tranquil air: "My God, help me!" From her window Babcock saw a man dragging her twenty-two-year-

Brandishing her cane and scowling, poet Lucille Babcock (above) exhibits the ferocity that drove off a would-be rapist in her neighborhood.

old neighbor across the yard. Grabbing her cane, Babcock raced downstairs. When she reached the yard, the attacker had pinned his victim to the ground. He was choking her and trying to rip off her clothes.

"I'm a policeman," shouted Babcock, adding a rough allusion to the intruder's parents. "Get off her!" Explaining the deception later, she said, "I was trying to impress on him I'm not some little old gray-haired woman." Her words had limited effect, however, for the man remained on top of the young woman. But Babcock's cane did get his attention. She whaled him on the back, and he jumped up and lunged for her. She swung again, landing another blow.

With that, the would-be rapist ran for his car with Babcock in pursuit, swatting him on the back. The attacker had no chance of escape. When the man opened his car door, Babcock kicked it shut. She smacked him in the knees. Again he opened the door; again she kicked it shut and smashed his knees. And again. He landed a punch on her shoulder. She hit him over and over with her cane.

"I won't say I wasn't scared, because I really thought I was going to get killed," Babcock said later. Nevertheless, "I had to get him so he couldn't get her and she could get away. I was a mad, screaming woman and a fighting woman."

By now escape, not rape, was the only thing that was on the man's mind, but as he fled on foot another neighbor, Max Duncan, gave chase. Duncan was joined by two other men, and the three of them soon had the assailant in hand. The police later discovered that the man had a record of theft, battery, drug use, and threatened rape spread across three states.

The victim of the attempted rape crawled into her home, where Babcock comforted and cared for her while awaiting police and a rape counselor. But when a Little Rock police official called Lucille Babcock a hero, she demured. "I am not a hero," the pugnacious poet declared. "I just can't stand to see people being hurt." □

High Dive

Unconscious and spinning uncontrollably more than a mile above the Arizona desert, skydiver Debbie Williams seemed doomed. Her parachute unopened, she plummeted earthward at 160 miles per hour; the ground was less than half a minute away. Such incidents are rare in the sport of skydiving, but when they occur they are almost invariably fatal. Ordinarily, no one is close enough to help, and the complex, split-second dynamics of midair rescues render them very dangerous—attempts usually end in the death of both victim and would-be rescuer.

Williams was one of more than 400 skydivers who had gathered for an Easter weekend meet near Coolidge, Arizona, in 1987. The thirty-one-year-old elementary school teacher was a relative novice at the sport, with a mere fifty jumps to her credit. She and six other skydivers, including parachute instructor Gregory Robertson, planned a group jump in which they would join hands to form a ring. After a brief free fall, the ring members would separate and veer off in different directions to pull their rip cords at a safe altitude above the ground. Robertson, a veteran of more than 1,700 free falls, would be the last to jump and would close the ring.

It was a routine skydiving exercise, albeit a demanding one, ◊

Six months after her near-fatal fall, Debbie Williams went skydiving again with rescuer Greg Robertson.

calling for caution and split-second timing. But in the scant moments that skydivers have at their disposal, the plan unraveled. All seven jumpers exited from the plane smoothly, and the first four linked up successfully. But the fifth hurtled into the ring too rapidly, breaking it into a line. The skydivers who had composed the circle were now, as Robertson put it later, "like a rope of stone people, rocketing toward the earth."

The parachutists managed to restore the figure briefly before they once more began to scatter across the sky. In the ensuing confusion Williams slammed head-on into the parachute pack of another skydiver, Guy Fitzwater, at a speed of fifty miles per hour. The impact knocked Williams out.

Greg Robertson watched the collision from his position above and some fifty feet away from Williams, and he saw that the unconscious woman was now "like a rag doll spinning in space." Unless someone went to help her, she was going to die. "I just couldn't let that happen," he said later. "I had to try to get to her somehow." His mind racing, Robertson chose to try a rescue—to many, the most daring rescue of its kind that has ever been attempted.

Robertson pressed his hands and arms against his sides, pointed his head toward the ground, and crossed his ankles, streamlining himself to accelerate his descent. His wind resistance thus reduced, gravity pulled Robertson earthward at 200 miles per hour—about forty miles per hour faster than Williams's floppy, "rag-doll" form.

When the instructor reached Williams he slowed his fall by spreading his limbs wide. Then with one hand he grasped the unconscious skydiver's harness to stop the spinning; with his other hand he yanked her parachute's rip cord. Williams's chute billowed open, the sudden deceleration ripping her away from Robertson, who now pulled his own rip cord. They had been only 2,000 feet—a scant seven seconds with unopened parachutes—from impact.

Williams, still unconscious, landed in a heap. Although she suffered a fractured skull, nine broken ribs, and a perforated kidney, she was alive and would recover. Six months later, accompanied by Robertson, she returned to skydiving. □

Skydiving instructor Greg Robertson (in black) frolics in free fall with fellow instructors high above their Coolidge, Arizona, parachute center a year before his dramatic rescue of skydiver Debbie Williams.

After the 1989 San Francisco earthquake, surgeon James Betts *(below)* visits six-year-old Julio Beruman in an Oakland, California, hospital. Betts had to amputate the boy's right leg to extricate the trapped youngster from the collapsed wreckage *(left)* of Oakland's double-decker Nimitz Freeway.

The Kindest Cut

The massive magnitude-seven earthquake that shook the San Francisco area on October 17, 1989, splintered and burned apartment houses, severed bridges, cracked streets, and terrified World Series baseball fans, among thousands of others. The temblor killed an estimated 270 people and injured about 1,400 more, and left widespread tragedy in its wake. Nowhere was its deadly impact more concentrated, however, than in the ruins of Interstate 880, Oakland's Nimitz Freeway.

There, flexed to destruction by intense seismic tremors, the upper level of the double-deck freeway collapsed, dropping tons of concrete onto the rush-hour traffic moving along the bottom level. Within seconds and without any kind of warning, thirty-nine persons were killed, pinned in their crushed vehicles.

Six-year-old Julio Beruman and his sister Cathy, eight, remained among the living—but not without a price.

As aftershocks sent ominous shivers through the debris, rescue workers converged on the freeway to hunt for the living. They were stunned by what they found: Cars and trucks were crushed "to the thickness of their license plates," said one emergency worker. Actually, the space between roadway and upper deck was about two feet; a perverse kind of luck had turned that narrow space into a tomb for some and a protective cocoon for others. As rescue workers probed, the injured living cried out to them.

Julio and Cathy Beruman were trapped in a car with the bodies of their mother, Petra Beruman, and a friend, Yolanda Orozco. Cathy, although suffering minor head injuries, was relatively unencumbered by debris and could be freed quickly. But the full weight of the concrete gripped Julio's right leg, where he lay beneath Yolanda Orozco, whose body blocked rescuers' access to the boy. For two hours, workers employed every weapon in their arsenal to move the debris—all the while hoping that their actions would not bring down a greater avalanche of concrete and steel. Nothing worked. There was only one way left to ex- ▷

tricate Julio: His trapped leg would have to be amputated.

James Betts, a pediatric surgeon and member of the California Medical Association's Earthquake Preparedness Committee, was called to do the job. Before he could operate on Julio, however, there was another grisly task to be done. The body of Yolanda Orozco had to be cut in half with a chain saw so that the surgeon could reach his patient. Then Betts got to work.

The conditions under which he labored were daunting: As aftershocks rumbled, the amalgam of concrete and steel rubble creaked, groaned, and threatened to collapse. Jamming himself into the space, Betts could barely see a few inches ahead and worked as much by feel as by sight. There was no room to attach clamps to stanch the bleeding from the boy's severed artery; Betts plugged the wound with his finger.

But the effort was successful. Julio was extricated, rushed to the hospital, and Betts joined the surgical team that saved Julio's mangled left leg. Extricated by a surgeon's calm courage, the boy had lost a limb, not a life, to the earthquake. □

Herd Instinct

Even for well-armed hunters, the charge of an angry elephant can be a frightening experience. For unarmed naturalists studying African wildlife, it is a nightmare. An adult male elephant may weigh seven tons, stand twelve feet tall, and wield as weapons tusks that are two to five feet long. Females are only slightly smaller—the heaviest weighs a mere five tons. The creatures can run at speeds up to twenty-five miles an hour over virtually any terrain; in a sprint they are faster than a fleeing human. And they possess a shrewd intelligence that makes them, on their own ground at least, the peer even of experienced wilderness hands.

In October 1990, British zoologist Christopher Thouless and his assistant, Alexandra Dixon, tracked a band of elephants across Kenya's Laikipia Plateau—and, inadvertently, into a confrontation with an angry pachyderm. The pair intended to immobilize one of the elephants with an anesthetic dart, then affix a collar containing a radio transmitter. By tracking the movements of the collared animal, they would be

able to monitor the entire herd's migrations. Such marking operations are dangerous when dealing with the larger, but solitary, males. Approaching a herd—and its apprehensive female leader—is a much more complex problem. This time, it quickly went wrong.

Without preliminaries, the herd's three-ton matriarch suddenly charged the scientists. As they retreated, Dixon fell, and the angry elephant was instantly upon her. She gored the woman with her tusks and tossed her like a rag doll. For a moment, Thouless watched in horror. Then, as the angry creature prepared to kneel upon—and crush—her helpless victim, he rushed back into the fray, hurling stones and finally punching the animal in the face to divert her attention from Dixon.

His ploy succeeded, and the animal fixed her eyes upon her new enemy. Fortunately for Thouless, the matriarch had no time to assault him, for a ranger accompanying the party fired his rifle over the animal's head, and the elephant broke off her attack. During that intermission, Thouless picked up his injured colleague and carried her several hundred yards to safety.

Queen Elizabeth II awarded Thouless the Queen's Gallantry Medal, but the scientist—who returned to the African bush as soon as possible after the ceremony in London—modestly dismissed his act of courage. "I was quite frightened," he recalled, echoing many instant heroes, "but there was nothing else I could do." □

Back in Africa after being decorated by Queen Elizabeth II for saving an injured colleague from a charging elephant, zoologist Christopher Thouless once more monitors a Kenyan elephant herd.

AGAINST ALL ODDS

The world is filled with heroes neither made nor born— men and women brought to remarkable fortitude and courage less by choice than by circumstance. Induction into the legion of the inadvertently brave may befall anyone, anywhere, but aircraft and ships are among the more promising venues for this brand of self-discovery, along with mountains, wilderness, and war. And, often, the road to survival is smoothed by something more than the impulse toward self-preservation: Rage, a wish for revenge, fear, and patriotism foster incredible endurance.

The astonishing few are generally part of a much larger, less fortunate host of passengers, prisoners, and refugees who did not survive. Somehow, a stalwart minority—and they alone—were able to summon the courage and physical strength to prevail against seemingly overwhelming adversity. It is as if, reading the part of victim, they rejected the role. Uncommon as they are, however, they are not unique: This tiny pantheon of heroes glitters with the unquenchable spark that hides in every human spirit.

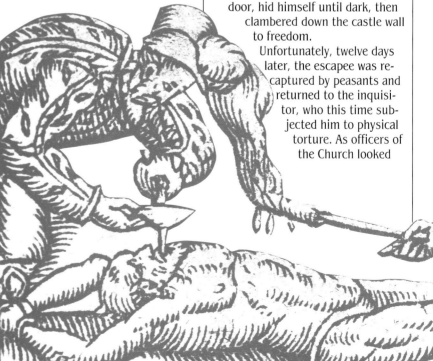

A contemporary artist depicted Richard Hasleton *(left)* before his misadventures began, including capture by the Spanish Inquisition and the water torture illustrated below.

Captive Audience

As a stranger in a number of strange lands, an Englishman named Richard Hasleton may have experienced the worst that the sixteenth-century world had to offer. In a span of ten years, according to his own colorful account, Hasleton was sold into slavery in Algiers, shipwrecked three times, tortured by the Spanish Inquisition, and imprisoned by Berber chieftans in the North African desert. Somehow, he lived to see the white cliffs of his homeland again and to tell his harrowing tale in *Strange and Wonderfull Things Happened to Richard Hasleton, borne at Braintree in Essex, In his ten yeares travailes in many forraine countries. Penned as he delivered it from his own mouth.* Published in 1595 by William Barley and dedicated to an adventurous London merchant named Richard Stapar, the trials of Richard Hasleton have become almost a handbook for survival.

Young Hasleton's misadventures began in 1582, when, leaving his family in England, he shipped out on a trading vessel that was bound for the Middle East. His luck quickly took a wrong turn. Shortly after reaching the Mediterranean Sea, the ship was set upon and captured by Turkish pirates, who sold Hasleton and other survivors into slavery.

The Englishman spent the next four miserable years shackled and chained to an oar, rowing a galley for an Algerian master. Pitiful rations, exposure to the elements, and rough labor took their toll of his comrades in slavery. But Hasleton himself somehow plumbed his physical reserves to survive forced labor

and repeated wrecks of the Algerian's ramshackle craft. During the third shipwreck, he managed to scramble ashore on the tiny island of Formentera off the east coast of Spain. There, with the aid of a fellow slave, Hasleton broke free of his detested iron fetters.

Freedom was fleeting, however. With the unerring instinct for trouble of all picaresque heroes, Hasleton had washed up in Spain at the time of its Inquisition, when the country's Catholic monarchs were consolidating their power by cracking down on heretics, Jews, Muslims, and others who did not follow the Church. Those tainted with real or imagined dissent were imprisoned, tortured, and sometimes put to death. Hasleton, a Protestant,

naively assumed that the Catholic Spanish would commiserate with him—a fellow Christian, if not a Catholic—who had been so ill-treated by the Moors. Instead, he and his partner were greeted with suspicion. Hasleton's comrade seemed immediately to grasp the situation: He promptly denounced Hasleton to the Catholic authorities.

Hasleton was brought before the chief inquisitor in Palma on the nearby island of Majorca and subjected to a month-long interrogation—evidently one of persuasion, not torture. Like so many victims of the Inquisition, the Briton was harangued for his heretical beliefs but stood firm, refusing to embrace Catholicism. The inquisitor consigned the refractory prisoner to the dungeon of Palma's castle. There Hasleton remained for a year, alone and barely sustained on a diet of bread and water—but, according to his own report, ever watchful for an opportunity to escape. One day, when the jailer's son failed to pull up the rope that was used to lower meals, Hasleton swarmed up the rope's length, heaved open a trapdoor, hid himself until dark, then clambered down the castle wall to freedom.

Unfortunately, twelve days later, the escapee was recaptured by peasants and returned to the inquisitor, who this time subjected him to physical torture. As officers of the Church looked on, a torturer tightened ropes binding Hasleton's arms and legs to a stretching rack, then poured water through a funnel in the prisoner's mouth until he was near drowning. Even brought within a hair of suffocation, Hasleton refused to recant. Eventually, he blacked out from the pain. Five days later, the Englishman was tied to a donkey and whipped as his captors paraded him through the streets.

Still, Hasleton did not succumb. Barely two days after his flogging, the remarkably resilient Briton broke from his cell. Eluding pursuers, he stole a small boat and slipped from Majorca's shores. Fortuitous storm swells carried him toward North Africa, where he landed in the Gulf of Bejaïa.

But once again Richard Hasleton found himself in the wrong place at the wrong time. He soon ran afoul of the Kabyle Berbers, a fierce and suspicious desert people who spared his life in order to exploit his skills as a metalworker

and carpenter. Although Hasleton was not physically abused, he was kept under lock and key when he was not working. Several times he escaped and several times he was recaptured. Finally, disguised in Arab mufti, the Englishman made it as far as Algiers.

Again, fate interceded. Hasleton encountered an old acquaintance: the galley master who had purchased him in 1582, who now reasserted his claims. The English consul, to whom Hasleton appealed for assistance, refused to intervene, and Hasleton spent three more grueling years behind the oar. Then, on Christmas Eve, 1592, a British merchant—possibly the Richard Stapar to whom Barley's publication was dedicated—rescued the brave and battered sailor. Richard Hasleton was taken aboard the ship *Cherubim* and brought home to London, liberty, and immortality. □

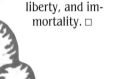

Heroic Villain

Captain William Bligh has come to personify the tyrannical commander, remembered for the cruelties that ignited a famous mutiny: the seizure of HMS *Bounty* by its crew in 1789. But to his contemporaries, Bligh was a hero—the courageous officer who had led his men through one of the most grueling ordeals in seafaring history.

Bounty, a 215-ton armed merchant vessel, had left England before Christmas in 1787, bound for Tahiti to pick up a cargo of sapling breadfruit trees. The starchy breadfruit was to be introduced into the West Indies, where plantation owners could use it as cheap food for slaves. Sailing what he described in a letter as "the completest ship I believe that ever swam," the thirty-three-year-old captain headed for Cape Horn, at the tip of South America, intending to round it into the Pacific. Cape Horn's infamous weather, however, defeated *Bounty;* after a month of futile trying, Captain Bligh turned the vessel to run eastward before the wind on a five-month voyage back across the Atlantic, past Africa, and into the Pacific from the west. The tired merchantman limped into Tahiti's anchorage on October 25, 1788, nearly a year after leaving its English port of Spithead.

Being now months behind schedule, Bligh elected to summer in Tahiti—the saplings could not be dug up until the Tahitian autumn. For five months, the crew enjoyed life on the beautiful island, where, as Bligh wrote later, "inclination seems to be the only binding law of marriage." Had Bligh been wiser, he might have foreseen how difficult it would be to impose the discipline ◊

of the sea on a ship's crew after a long sojourn in a tropical paradise. By the time *Bounty* was ready to sail, many of the crew had formed strong attachments with Tahitian women—indeed, three of the crew had already deserted. In April of 1789, the ship set sail for the West Indies with its breadfruit cargo, taking up a westward course for the Atlantic Ocean.

Bligh was evidently an able commander, and certainly he was highly qualified. He had joined the Royal Navy, as a captain's servant, when only seven; at twenty-two, he held the rank of full lieutenant under Captain James Cook, the great Pacific trailblazer. As a captain, Bligh had a reputation for fair dealing: He ran a healthy ship and was considerate of his crew's welfare. But he also ran a taut ship and could be ruthless, a liar, bully, miser, and cheat if he thought it would benefit the vessel and its owners. He was rigid and demanding, with a habit of greeting the smallest error with fierce, profane scorn. Most ordinary seamen—recruited or impressed from the ranks of England's many jobless poor—had little choice but to suffer Bligh's abuse, which, con-trary to myth, was mainly ver-bal. Such was not the case with twenty-four-year-old Fletcher Christian, who came from a good family and was unaccustomed to such rough handling. Though ranking on-ly as a seaman, Christian had officer's duties on the *Bounty*. Like his shipmates, he had en-joyed Tahiti and had left a woman there.

Serving under the abrasive Bligh wore at Christian's pride. Three weeks out of Tahiti, the cap-tain accused Christian of stealing coconuts from the ship's stores and cursed him in front of the crew. The consequences were borne by every man on board. Christian, seething, told a fellow crewman he would rather die 10,000 deaths than con-tinue to bear Bligh's abuse. Bligh apparently cooled quickly, however, and even invited Christian to join him for dinner the following night. But Christian, feigning illness, de-clined. Just before sunrise on the morning of April 28, Bligh woke to find Christian and three others in his cabin, armed with bayonets.

That day, Bligh was cast adrift on the open ocean, with eighteen sailors loyal to him, in a twenty-three-foot sailing launch. The boat was so overloaded that the waves lapped just eight inches below the gunwales. The men were panicked. But Bligh, behaving as though the launch were simply another chal-lenging command, soon calmed the castaways. The nearest island was then only about 30 miles away, but Bligh reasoned that, once there, they might wait in vain for a pass-ing ship to rescue them. Instead, he turned the launch toward Dutch Timor, 3,600 miles distant.

Bligh calculated the voyage to Timor would take eight weeks. To stretch their supplies, all agreed to live on a daily ration consisting of one ounce of bread and a quarter-pint of water. Bligh divided the men into watches so that some could sit and others half lie in the boat's crowded bottom. Under its small sail, the tiny boat headed slowly west, and Bligh began keeping a logbook in which he recorded in meticulous detail the events that befell the hapless band—a logbook that somehow survived the voyage.

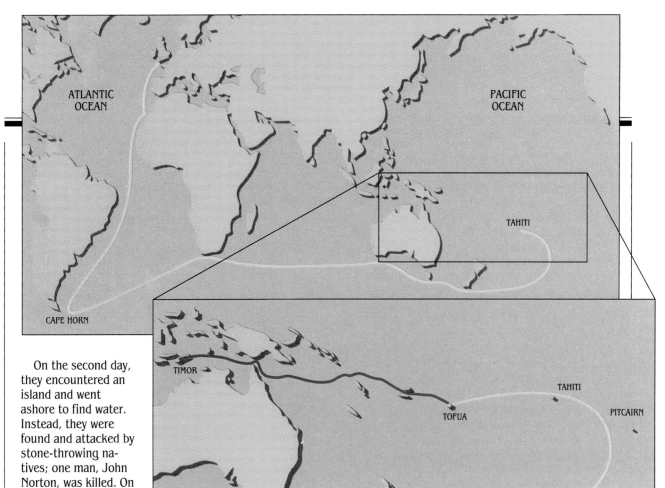

ATLANTIC
OCEAN

PACIFIC
OCEAN

TAHITI

CAPE HORN

TIMOR

TAHITI

TOFUA

PITCAIRN

On the second day, they encountered an island and went ashore to find water. Instead, they were found and attacked by stone-throwing natives; one man, John Norton, was killed. On May 3, the storms began. Green water poured over the transom. They jettisoned what they could to lighten the ship and then, freezing, numb, and stiff with cold and fatigue, began to bail. The rain was constant. Because the seawater was slightly warmer than the rain, the men wrung their clothes in it and put them on again. Their nights were miserably cold and cramped. When their bread rotted, they ate it anyway. Occasionally, Bligh would add a half-ounce of salt pork to the ration. To divide the food fairly, he improvised a scale of coconut shells with a pistol ball for a weight.

Remembering Norton's fate, they kept well offshore when passing islands. Once, two large canoes pursued them for most of a day before dropping back in the rain. At least the freezing downpour allowed the the castaways to drink their fill and

to capture thirty-four extra gallons of water. Bligh began teaching the men to navigate; they would need the skill if he did not survive.

Hope rose by day, only to vanish in violent storms and nights so wet, cold, and black that Bligh could not see the stars to navigate. He thought some of the men looked half-dead. He kept order as best he could, and when the men protested the short rations—"When our nights were particularly distressing," as Bligh put it in his journal— he offered a jot of rum.

Finally, a month after their ordeal began and for the first time in a fortnight, the sun emerged. The castaways had sufficient provisions to reach Timor, but, ever cautious, Bligh proposed further cuts to provide some margin for unanticipated delays. He was surprised when the

A yellow line traces the route of Captain William Bligh *(opposite)* and the *Bounty.* Prevented by storms from rounding Cape Horn into the Pacific, Bligh decided to approach the Far East by sailing across the South Atlantic and Indian oceans, rounding New Zealand, and summering in Tahiti. From there, *Bounty* followed a westward course for the West Indies. Mutineers set Bligh and his loyal crewmen adrift near Tofua, from which a blue line traces their arduous 3,600-mile journey to Timor.

men consented. By now, all of them were weak, constantly cold and wet, immobilized by crowding and hunger and suffering from severe stomach cramps.

The next day, they caught a small bird, which Bligh divided for dinner—entrails, feet, beak, and all. He reserved its blood for the sickest men. Soon the boat passed through a gap in Australia's Great Barrier ◊

Reef and landed on an island that the men thought was uninhabited. Ashore, they fed on wild berries and a stew of oysters, bread, and water. But the respite was short lived; spear-bearing natives appeared and drove them off. Once again, they were at sea, wet and cold and covered with sores. Their sunken, red-rimmed eyes were encrusted with salt. Threadbare rags hung in strips from their emaciated bodies. Bligh noted that many of his men seemed to be slipping into a coma. But they all still lived, and Bligh continued to push them to do their duty: survive.

Adversity of a different nature struck on May 31, as the sailors scavenged food on yet another island. One of the men challenged Bligh. The captain knew he must act decisively or face endless insubordination. "I determined either to preserve my command or die in the attempt," he wrote later. "Seizing a cutlass, I ordered him to lay hold of another and defend himself." The man backed down.

Bligh kept his crew together for two more weeks until finally reaching Timor, in what is now eastern Indonesia, on June 14. As they approached the Dutch colony, the wind failed and the men, looking like sticks draped in rags, sat up and rowed the last few miles into port. In forty-one days they had traveled 3,618 miles, beset by savages and brutal weather. Of the nineteen men who had been put off the *Bounty*, eighteen of them entered Timor alive, although six of these survivors did not live to see England again.

The men—sixteen mutineers and seven still loyal to Bligh—who had remained with the *Bounty* fared no better. Led by Fletcher Christian, they sailed for the island of Tupuai,

hoping to hide from any retribution. Trouble with the natives there drove them back to Tahiti, where most of them remained. But Christian and eight others, accompanied by kidnapped Tahitian women, sailed off in search of a more congenial home. They found it four months later at Pitcairn Island and burned and sank the *Bounty* in its bay—literally burning their bridge back to civilization. Within four years, Christian was dead, murdered by an islander whose wife he had stolen. Over the ensuing years of exile, the unequal distribution of females led to further murders, until only two of the original party remained: a midshipman by the name of Edward Young and seaman John Adams. The pair governed Pitcairn, and its score of mutineers' children, along strict Christian lines.

In March 1791, *Bounty* mutineers in Tahiti surrendered to the British man-of-war *Pandora*, sent from England to find them. Caged on deck, they started the long journey toward a trial. Crossing the Great Barrier Reef in August 1791, *Pandora* sank and took a handful of the prisoners with her. Of the ten finally tried in Portsmouth for the high crime of mutiny, seven were acquitted, and three were hanged.

Bligh, meanwhile, had become something of a celebrity, both for the infamous mutiny and his ordeal at sea. He was exonerated of blame for the loss of the *Bounty* and given a new command. Over the course of his long, stormy career, he weathered three more mutinies and five courts-martial and managed to retire as a vice-admiral. He died peacefully in bed at the age of sixty-three in 1817, twelve years before John Adams, Pitcairn's last surviving mutineer. □

Rafting

Few crew members survived the sinking of the British merchant ship *Benlomond*, torpedoed by a German U-boat off the coast of South America. Only one of them survived the sea: Poon Lim, a twenty-four-year-old second steward from Hainan, an island some 300 miles south of Hong Kong. Poon Lim did more than merely survive, however. Nearly fifty years after the *Benlomond* sinking, he still held the dubious distinction of surviving at sea in an open life raft longer than any other person known.

Poon Lim had first shipped out in 1936 as a "learn boy" aboard the SS *Tanda*. Finding the experience degrading, he returned to school in Hong Kong. As the Japanese army thrust toward the colony, however, Poon Lim took the second steward's berth aboard the Ben Line ship *Benlomond*. On November 10, 1942, as the *Benlomond* steamed eastward just north of the equator and about 750 miles off the mouth of the Amazon River, a stalking submarine sent two torpedoes into the vessel. The freighter shuddered, then swiftly rolled over and sank. Poon Lim was swept down with the ship in a great swirl of water but buoyed back from the depths by his life vest. Surfacing in the oily water, he saw only a few bubbles remaining from the maelstrom where the *Benlomond* had gone down and a few floating planks and fragments. A mere dog paddler of a swimmer, he clung to a shattered hatch cover and managed to rinse some of the oil from his eyes. Some distance away he now saw one of the ship's life rafts with five of his fellow crewmen on it.

He called out but got no response. Then, as he watched, the water near them was roiled by the surfacing of a German submarine.

All five were taken aboard the U-boat, and Poon Lim managed finally to attract the attention of German deck gunners. But, rather than aiding him, they jeered at the desperate steward and pantomimed a strafing with their gun. Soon the five *Benlomond* crewmen were restored to their raft, and the submarine submerged. When it was gone, so was the raft; Poon Lim never saw the men again and presumed them lost at sea.

Seeing a second, empty life raft in the distance, Poon Lim managed to swim through the oil to it.

The rude craft comprised a plank deck eight feet square with sides that rode three feet above the waves; only with great effort was the young sailor able to clamber aboard. The raft floated on six sealed steel drums lined with storage compartments containing canvas and wooden stakes for an awning, a flare pistol, water, and food. There was bottled lime juice, evaporated milk, chocolate, hard-tack, and pemmican, a high-energy mixture of meat, fat, flour, and molasses pressed into small bricks. Poon Lim decided that if he rationed the supplies, he could survive for fifty days—time enough, he believed, in which to be rescued.

The days dragged by, humid but dehydrating under the brutal equatorial sun. After a week, he sighted a ship and feverishly waved to it. The vessel turned toward him and passed close enough for its officers to inspect him through binocu- ◊

lars—then, perhaps fearing that the raft was a U-boat's decoy, they sailed on. It was as if Fortune had smiled upon the castaway, then spit in his face. For weeks afterward, waves of bitterness and anger would wash over Poon Lim when he thought of how the ship had left him alone on the ocean. He lost weight. Painful boils erupted on his feet, legs, and buttocks; he lanced them with a knife made from a pemmican can lid. And his rations ran dangerously low.

The incident of the ship had transformed Poon Lim, however. After a life of following other people's orders—a parent's, a teacher's, a superior's at sea—he realized that survival depended on how well he could act on his own. He recalled the furious activity with which his mother had met every difficulty in their family life and used her as his model. As a start, he began to collect rainwater in his awning and to fish as he had done on his home island. He fashioned a tiny hook from the spring of his flashlight. Sacrificing safety for food, he unbraided the lanyard that tied him to the raft and spun it into fishline. For bait, he tried hardtack, but the biscuits simply dissolved in seawater. Pemmican fell apart and merely fed the fish. But barnacles had attached themselves to the raft's hull, and when he dangled one on his improvised hook, he captured a small brown fish. He ate part and used the rest for bait.

Live fish were the best bait, and Poon Lim learned to hook the smaller ones through the tail and let them swim enticingly in a slick of chopped fish parts. He caught more and hung them in the sun to dry. But the effort involved in catching and processing dozens of small fish

daily was tiring and wasteful; he needed larger prey. With the metal water-tank key, Poon Lim began picking at the wood around one of the nails holding the raft together. He worked all night to expose four inches of steel. By dawn his arms were in spasm and his hands slick with blood and sweat. He pulled out the nail with his teeth, ignoring pain so excruciating that the roots of his teeth seemed on fire. When the nail abruptly came free, he almost lost it.

With the heavy water-tank key he beat the nail into a hook, which he attached to a longer fishing line made from rope. Soon Poon Lim was catching fish half his own size. He was well fed, and his hands healed. He had everything he needed. Poon Lim decorated his vessel with festoons of fish skeletons and felt almost content. By now he had been on his own for about 100 days.

Soon afterward, six airplanes droned overhead, spotted the raft, and dropped a dye marker to help a rescue vessel find him. Poon Lim's hopes rose. Rescue seemed at hand. But before help could arrive, a sudden storm drove him downwind and dispersed the dye. Lightning clawed the sky, and the seas rose to twenty feet. Seawater flooded his water tank and rotted his store of dried fish. His rescuers never came. The sea seemed to have gone barren, for he fished in vain. For five days he drifted under the sun without food or water. Desperately thirsty, he drank urine until his body produced no more. He wanted to cry but had no tears. Gripped by despair, Poon Lim felt that he was near death and thought he was dreaming when a small dark bird landed on the raft. He snatched at it, caught it, slit its breast, and

sucked the bird as if it were an orange. When the bird was dry, he bit into it. There was little left when he was finished.

When at last it rained again, Poon Lim filled his water tanks with fresh, sweet water. He drifted into fish-filled waters and caught all he needed. There were even more birds to eat. When the color of the sea turned a muddy brown, he suspected land might be near. Soon he could just discern the rough line of low, dark jungle on the horizon.

Then a boat appeared. As it approached, Poon Lim made out a man, woman, and young girl on board; they were a Brazilian fisherman and his family. After 133 days alone, he was saved. Remarkably fit after his ordeal, the young steward recuperated for 45 days in a Belém hospital and received a watch from the English colony there, engraved "To Poon Lim, bravest of the brave." The British consul and the Ben Line arranged to have him flown to the United States on an army plane. In New York, he performed a reenactment of his ordeal for the American navy, which used films and photographs of it to demonstrate survival at sea. By special act, he was given the U.S. Merchant Marine Combat Bar with One Star for his inspiring courage and fortitude. In war-torn London, King George VI invested Poon Lim with the British Empire Medal.

Despite his ordeal, Poon Lim eventually wished to go back to sea. Given permission to live in the United States by a special act of Congress, he tried to enlist in the U.S. Navy. But the celebrity steward was rejected as physically unfit. Courage and fortitude Poon Lim might have in abundance—but he also had flat feet. □

For a 1991 court hearing, Bob La-Gree reenacts the near-fatal accident that crushed him "like the cream in a cookie."

Rig Wrestler

A contest between a former professional wrestler and a 63,000-pound tractor-trailer sounds more like a made-for-television event than real life. But Bob LaGree—once known in the ring as Bobby DuPrey or the Bulldog—once did pit his strength against a runaway eighteen-wheeler. His reward for success was his life.

LaGree, a muscular 224-pounder, took up long-haul trucking when he quit wrestling. But he stayed in shape and entertained neighbors by pressing quarter-ton loads and hoisting the family Subaru a foot off the ground—with wife and daughter aboard. Near midnight on Halloween eve, 1985, LaGree had pulled his U.S. Postal Service rig into a New York State Thruway rest stop in Syracuse, intending to change vehicles there. But, as he walked from one rig to another, a driverless truck backed toward him down the slight incline of the parking area—evidently, none of its

three sets of brakes had been set. Before he could jump out of its path, LaGree was squeezed between the trailer and the frame of his tractor, "like the cream in a cookie," as he later put it. His bulk was compressed into a slender nine-inch cushion between the two vehicles. The impact shattered his pelvis, causing him to turn black from the waist down. He passed out briefly.

When he came to, LaGree gave a mighty heave and shoved the thirty-one-ton truck off his chest, against the incline. But the weight was too great for him to hold, and the truck rolled back. Belatedly, another driver spotted LaGree's predicament and helped LaGree move the truck's full weight off him. Given some slack, LaGree dropped to the ground and dragged himself clear.

Bob LaGree still works for the U.S. Postal Service in Austin, Texas. But he walks with a limp and avoids tractor-trailers. "If I see them coming down the road," he says, "I get in another lane." □

Dark Passage

At an early age, Frenchman Jacques Lusseyran learned that the spirit sees visions that are denied to the body's eyes. When he was only eight, the bespectacled Lusseyran was knocked off balance by a schoolmate and pitched into the corner of a desk face first. Doctors had to remove his right eye. The left was irreversibly maimed. The child accepted his sudden blindness with uncommon fortitude. Curious and plucky, supported by open-minded parents, Lusseyran explored a new world of sound and touch. He learned how to walk with confidence, quickly picked up the Braille alphabet, and resumed a life that was almost as active as before.

To his delight, he discovered that, while his eyes saw only darkness, his mind was bathed in dazzling hues. "I was aware," Lusseyran wrote in a 1963 memoir, "of a radiance emanating from a place I knew nothing about, a place that might as well have been outside me as within." He also developed an uncanny ability to feel the presence of objects, a skill dubbed "the sense of obstacles" by scientists who have studied the phenomenon.

Back at school, Lusseyran excelled, and by 1940, at sixteen, he was at the center of an energetic ◊

DÉFENSE DE LA FRANCE

ÉDITION DE PARIS
14 JUILLET 1943   N.36

JOURNAL FONDÉ LE 14 JUILLET 1941
NUMÉRO SPÉCIAL

— La France, avec nous ! —

CH. DE GAULLE

« Je ne crois que les histoires dont les témoins se feraient égorger. »
(PASCAL)

FÊTE DE LA LIBERTÉ

14 JUILLET

FRANÇAIS, LIBÉREZ-VOUS DE LA CRAINTE…

Jacques Lusseyran's last article for *Défense de la France (left)* appeared on July 14, 1943—Bastille Day—exhorting the French people to overthrow their German occupiers. In less turbulent times, the blind patriot *(below, highlighted)* posed with his classmates at lycée Louis-le-Grand in Paris.

circle of young men at the lycée Louis-le-Grand in Paris. These youths responded deeply to the fall of France to the German war machine in June of that year. The streets of their city, once vital, now seemed drained of spirit. To Lusseyran, the general anxiety was palpable, and the frightened silence nearly unbearable, for it smacked of complicity. Of the adults Lusseyran knew outside his family, only a history teacher at the lycée dared put himself at risk by discussing the war, the occupation, and the horrors of the Nazi regime.

In the spring of 1941, Lusseyran suffered an attack of measles. Gripped by fever—which the young patriot likened to the infection of Nazism in the body of France—he saw clearly what he needed to do. When he recovered, Lusseyran approached a handful of trusted friends and sketched out a plan to form a resistance movement to undermine the collaborationist Vichy government and the enemy.

So magnetic a personality was Lusseyran that within six months his comrades had recruited, and he had personally interviewed, 600 youths, most between sixteen and twenty-one. As the Volunteers of Liberty, they published an underground newspaper that aimed to fire public opinion and correct the lies of the official press. They also forged documents, monitored proscribed British and Swiss radio broadcasts, and aided downed Allied airmen. By January 1943, Lusseyran had affiliated his organization with a larger one, Défense de la France, and helped push the printing of its illicit newspaper to 250,000 copies per issue.

But his luck ran out that summer. One of Lusseyran's recruits betrayed him. He and more than twenty other DF leaders were arrested in a Gestapo sweep on July 20. Separated from friends, the blind man was cruelly interrogated for six weeks, then held at a Parisian jail with other political prisoners. In January 1944, anemic and shaky, he was deported to Germany. Lusseyran's pleasure at being reunited with several of his comrades along the way was tempered by the harsh realities of their transport. Packed into a railroad freight car, he and ninety-four others were forced to stand for three days; their only nourishment was one bowl of thin soup. Some went insane.

The freight-car doors opened upon the mean structures of Buchenwald, the dread concentration camp and execution ground established by the Nazis in central Germany. Torn from his friends, Lusseyran was sent to the work camp's invalid block. In this bedlam, 1,500 disabled, sick, and dysfunctional men lived in abject conditions. Lusseyran, now desperately ill, was reduced to crawling across a terrain of dying companions. As he did, his hands "traveled from the stump of a leg to a dead body, from a body to a wound." The stench was mitigated only by the horrible fumes from Buchenwald's crematoria.

Brutal cold, hunger, and anguish over the death of a close friend so enfeebled the Frenchman that he became consumed by disease. But, as he had following his youthful blinding, Lusseyran again experienced an epiphany. "Life had become a substance within me," he explained later. "It came toward me like a shimmering wave, like the caress of light."

Awed inmates took to calling him "the man who didn't die" and began coming to him for counsel. Lusseyran realized he had been given yet another mission: He would ferret out and report the true details of the war's progress in order to combat the dispiriting rumors that the Germans circulated through the camp. For nearly a year, he served as the voice of hope, carefully extracting the truth from his captors' lies and misinformation. For example, noting that Paris suddenly disappeared from Nazi reports in August 1944, he accurately reported to his fellow prisoners that the city had been liberated.

On April 10, 1945, as American general George C. Patton's Third Army fought toward Buchenwald, Lusseyran grappled with one final piece of disinformation. SS guards about to retreat offered the camp's remaining prisoners safe passage. On instinct, Lusseyran rejected the offer and tried to persuade others to do the same. Still, thousands of them chose to leave. Buchenwald was liberated the following day. Later, the news came that the SS guards had gunned down all the men who had left the camp on the eve of its surrender—only ten men survived the massacre.

On April 18, while working in the liberated camp, Lusseyran heard a voice cry out "Jacques!" and felt a warm embrace. A former comrade in arms—the chief of Défense de la France—had rushed all the way from Paris to find him and other DF survivors; only two besides Lusseyran survived Buchenwald. During his two-year ordeal, Lusseyran himself had lost nearly every one of his dearest friends. But his remarkable inner light had shone on, illuminating the path of those who journeyed with him through the long terror of the Nazi night. □

Out of Sight

Enos Mills snowshoed out of the stunted trees on the western slope of the Continental Divide, climbed above the timberline, and started east across a ridge some 12,000 feet above sea level. Around him, the high peaks of the Colorado Rockies glinted splendidly in the sun, and the snowfields blazed a perfectly brilliant white. He lingered in the dazzling glare of the treeless summit, photographing a flock of ptarmigan and admiring the mountain sheep silhouetted against the flaring backdrop of snow. Then Mills felt the first searing pain in his eyes that signaled the onset of snow blindness.

As a nature guide, Mills had known better. In fact, he had started the day wearing the protective goggles used at the turn of the twentieth century. But, as he was looking up into a tree, a mass of snow had dropped on him and sent his glasses spinning, burying them in the drifts. He had not bothered to blacken his face, which would have cut the glare, because he expected

his exposure to be brief. The beauty of the mountains had overwhelmed his judgment, however. Now, alone in a frozen wilderness, he was temporarily blinded, with no sense of how long he would be sightless. The surface of his eyeballs had been literally sunburned. When he squeezed them shut to mitigate the pain, they would not open—and a grim game of blindman's buff began.

Strangely, Mills felt no panic. He carried matches, a hatchet, and a staff, and he was in his element. In his mind's eye, he could visualize the pass that he had meant to cross and the eastern slope down which he would have to travel to reach the trail. He started downhill slowly, poking ahead of him with the staff so as not to stumble blindly off a cliff, swinging the stick back and forth, hoping he would hit a tree as he descended. Finally he found

one: He had reached the timberline.

But he did not know whether the trail lay to his left or right. The blazes cut into the bark to mark the way were invisible to his blind eyes and buried in snowdrifts besides. Digging down along their trunks, he felt tree after tree; finally, he brushed the rough splinters of a blaze cut in the bark. Confident once more, Mills headed down the mountain, shouting occasionally in hopes of attracting attention. Cooler air told him night was falling, but it made no difference. As he put it later, his lights had gone out at midday. When he tried to find more blazes, however, he found nothing—he had lost the trail. Suddenly, he found himself at the top of an unfamiliar cliff. His confidence drained away, and he feared that, like many lost hikers, he had traveled around in a circle. Worse, he

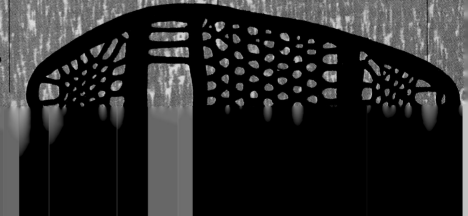

wondered whether he had inadvertently turned down the western slope, where there was no one for many miles, instead of the eastern slope, where there were cabins farther down the mountain.

Cautiously, Mills descended a rocky, snow-covered incline, listening to the echoes of his shouts, which told him that he had entered a canyon. The trees became both compass and altimeter. He knew that pines grow on south-facing slopes and spruce on hillsides facing north. The pines on his left informed him that he was indeed walking east.

Suddenly, the snow gave way and Mills plunged over a cliff—and landed on a ledge. Locating a dead tree with his staff, he climbed down its trunk and went on, only to be stopped by the deafening roar of an avalanche, so close that the outrush of air knocked him down. A mass of snow, earth, boulders, and splintered trees filled the canyon. Mills began clambering over it, but something gave way and dropped him into the icy stream at the canyon bottom. He lost a snowshoe; searching for that, he stumbled upon the warm carcass of a mountain sheep that had been killed by the avalanche. Mills rested and warmed his feet under the sheep's remains. Somehow he recovered the lost snowshoe and walked blindly on, hour after hour.

Groping through the forest for yet another night and into the next morning, Mills chanced upon a deserted cabin, where he was able to build a fire and break his sixty-hour fast with a handful of raisins he discovered in a pocket. Exhausted, he fell asleep on the cabin floor, leaving the fire to burn itself out. When he awoke, nearly frozen, he was still snow blind. Again, he forced himself back on the move, feeling his way with his staff. At last, there was the odor of smoke—a fire of aspen wood. Enos Mills stood still for a while, listening for any clues about his surroundings. Then a little girl's voice asked gently and curiously: "Are you going to stay here tonight?" □

Snow-blind Rocky Mountain guide Enos Mills *(left)* wandered sightless for three days in the rough, high-altitude terrain of Colorado's snowcapped Continental Divide.

Trojan Horse

To many of the 260,000 British and American soldiers captured by the Germans during World War II, escape was not only a sworn duty but an intellectually stimulating and physically invigorating hobby. In each camp, the prisoners pursued freedom with verve, imagination, and tunneling on a grand scale. They created escape committees to devise, approve, and organize breakout attempts. And they forged identity documents, manufactured civilian clothing, stole railroad schedules, and otherwise provided the logistical support that was needed to convert a breakout into what Allied prisoners of war called a home run—a successful escape to safety in Britain or a neutral country. The use of sports imagery was not idle bravado: Escape had become their national pastime, albeit a dangerous one.

Just how dangerous was shown at Stalag-Luft III, a large POW camp near the town of Sagan, about eighty miles southeast of Berlin. There, in a masterful but ultimately tragic attempt—the so-called Great Escape of March 1944—seventy-six prisoners tunneled their way to freedom. Their triumph was brief, however. Only three men scored home runs by reaching England. The rest were captured, and fifty men were shot by the Gestapo.

Even then, Stalag-Luft III had a history of such attempts, which had left a bitter aftertaste in the German garrison. One attempt in par-

ticular, executed five months earlier, must still have rankled. The scheme had been devised by British flight lieutenant Eric Williams and British lieutenant Michael Codner, who with one stroke solved two problems that had plagued all of Stalag-Luft III's escape tunnelers. The first problem was one of placement: where to locate the tunnel entrance so that it could be both close to the camp's fence—the closer to the fence, the shorter the shaft had to be—and concealed from guards. While it was a simple matter to hide a tunnel entrance in one of the camp's barracks, these were hundreds of feet inside the barbed wire. Putting the entrance close to the fence would leave it out in the open. A secondary problem, encountered by all secret diggers, was how to dispose of the soil from the tunnel. Each linear yard of a two-foot-by-two-foot burrow yielded three-quarters of a ton of bright yellow sand, which dried to a distinctive white aboveground, contrasting sharply with the dark gray topsoil.

The solution was suggested to Codner by his reading of ancient history—specifically, the Greek army's use of a hollow wooden horse to smuggle soldiers inside the walls of the besieged city of Troy. The modern-day variant was a horse of a different sort: a gym-

nast's vaulting dummy. The plan was both audacious and elegantly simple. The plotters would build a hollow horse and, each day, trundle it out of their barracks to a point near the barbed wire. Inside its base, the horse would carry one or two diggers and the purloined trowel they used for digging. As construction proceeded, the men on the surface would create a noisy distraction with their gymnastic exercises. When the day's work and play were done, the diggers would once more conceal themselves—bringing with them bags of sand—and be carried with the horse back into the barracks.

The German guards thought the prisoners were stupid to waste their energy with gymnastic exercise but permitted the inmates their pointless recreation. The horse that Eric Williams built of scrap wood was four and a half feet high, five feet long, and three feet wide. When it was ready, the POWs dressed in shorts and carried it outside, placing it close to the tripwire inside the twelve-foot fence. During the first week of use, one of the gymnasts was unbelievably clumsy, knocking the horse over again and again—and giving the guards a good view of its empty abdomen.

From then on, however, no one upset the horse. On July 8, beneath the amused eyes of their captors, the Britons began to dig. Every afternoon either Williams or Codner rode inside, and while one supervised the gymnasts in the daylight, the other tunneled in the dark, first straight down and then toward the wire, shoring up the first seven feet

of shaft to absorb the jolts from the gymnasts practicing overhead. The sweating digger worked for as much as two hours at a stretch while lying on his belly with his arms straight in front of him. When he and the sand—packed in sacks made from cutoff trouser legs—arrived back in the barracks, others distributed the spoil in inconspicuous spots throughout the camp compound.

Discovery never seemed more than a heartbeat away. One day in August 1943, Codner narrowly escaped being buried alive when the tunnel collapsed on top of him. A quick-thinking gymnast, seeing the ground sink, faked a fall onto the depression, concealing it from the guards. Codner made some temporary repairs to the tunnel, then exited as usual. The next day, Williams worked so hard making up for the cave-in setback that he was hospitalized for a week—as it turned out, a significant opportunity to rest and reflect upon their progress. In the hospital, Williams realized that they had dug just forty feet and had eighty more to go. Moreover, it occurred to him that getting through the tunnel was the beginning, not the end, of their escape.

Their aim was to emerge from the shaft, walk fifteen minutes through the forest, and step directly onto a departing train headed for Baltic ports, where they hoped to board a ship for neutral Sweden. Timing was everything, but their only railroad schedule expired October 31. After that, they might be forced to loiter near the railroad station—a surefire way to attract German attention. In order to speed things up the pair took in a third man, British flight lieutenant Oliver Philpot, who had been preparing himself for the first escape opportunity that came his way. The tunnel began to progress rapidly.

The war of nerves between German captors and Allied prisoners was heating up as the trio burrowed beneath the wire. New posters appeared warning that "escape from prison camps is no longer a sport" and that in the future escapees would be shot. Williams, Codner, and Philpot laughed off the threat as a bluff and kept digging. Nearby, a squad of German ferrets—guards so called because they specialized in exposing escape plans—discovered another tunnel and smashed it. But the horsemen's ruse continued undetected.

A few days before the end of October, they were ready, and at 6:00 p.m. on Friday, October 29, they crawled through their painfully constructed tunnel and emerged into a shallow ditch outside the wire, strode quickly through the woods, and stepped onto a waiting train. Camp guards discovered the hole after midnight, but by then the moles were on their way to Baltic Sea ports. Codner and Williams traveled as French workers and managed to have themselves smuggled aboard a Danish ship after a difficult fortnight on the road. Philpot, in the role of a Norwegian businessman, headed for the port of Danzig; by Sunday he had slipped aboard a Swedish ship. On November 13, the trio had its reunion in Stockholm—three home runs. □

Prison-camp forgers gave Oliver Philpot a passport identifying him as fictitious Norwegian businessman Jon Jörgensen.

Points of Honor

Late one summer night in 1951, United States Air Force captain Ward Millar hobbled out of a lightly guarded shack serving as a North Korean field hospital. That he could walk at all was, to Millar, a near miracle. But it would take several more miracles—all fervently prayed for and duly delivered—before the American pilot was able to make his way to freedom.

Two months earlier, Millar had broken both ankles when he parachuted from his crippled F-80 jet fighter. Lacking mobility, the pilot was easily captured and taken to a mud-floored hovel used as a hospital. The medical treatment he was accorded there only aggravated Millar's injuries: His feet were placed in casts that pointed them straight down, as if he stood on tiptoe.

Rather than despair, Millar experimented in secret, discovering that, with great effort and much pain, he was able to walk on his toes. Much of the pain was caused by the plaster casts, which cut into his insteps. He tied rags under his heels to absorb some of his weight and ease the pressure. Finally, as his healing progressed, Millar simply asked that the casts be removed. They were, and he was issued a comically oversize pair of galoshes. The floppy footwear was a godsend, for Millar could build up false heels inside them. With the help of two walking staffs, a kind of locomotion had become possible—locomotion and escape. On August 14, just after midnight, Captain Millar set out for freedom.

Like an eccentric mime on his points, the pilot tottered out of the hospital and tiptoed awkwardly across the darkened fields, where his clownish galoshes left unmistakable footprints, clearly embossing their American manufacturer's logo in the Korean soil. Millar carried a plastic canteen of water. He ate corn, apples, and peaches he found along the way. And he prayed, clutching the cross that he carried in his pocket.

He had hoped to limp westward to the coast, where he would inflate the yellow Mae West life vest he had kept and swim out into the Yellow Sea until he was rescued. But the coast was farther away than he had thought. Balancing on his blistered, crazily pointing feet, walking sticks flailing, he splashed across streams, poled his way up hills, and plunged down embankments.

At first, Millar tried to hide from the Korean workers he encountered by sleeping under bushes by day and traveling only at night. Progress was slow, so he resumed walking by daylight, passing himself off as a Russian so that he could purchase food—as if the Russians sent filthy, wild-eyed, six-foot-tall, bearded white men on tiptoes to buy groceries.

As he blundered through the countryside, dozens, then hundreds, of people must have become aware of his presence. Nevertheless, it was ten days before Millar was accosted by North Korean soldiers traveling in an army truck. His luck held. The truckdriver, whose name was Chai-Pill Kim, noted Millar's cross and said in English: "Jesus and Mary?" In all of Communist North Korea, the fugitive pilot had stumbled upon the rare soldier who was not only a Christian but an anti-Communist who wanted to flee to South Korea. Buying time, Kim covertly sabotaged his truck, delaying the American in the countryside until they were able to signal a passing American fighter plane with a mirror. The airborne attention they received also attracted North Korean soldiers, who assaulted the position where the pair waited anxiously to be rescued. Braving heavy fire, a rescue helicopter fluttered in long enough for Kim to piggyback Millar aboard. Moments later, it lifted the unlikely couple to safety in Seoul, where doctors began to put Captain Ward Millar back on his feet. □

Fighter pilot Ward Millar relaxes in Seoul after escaping from a North Korean prison hospital on two broken ankles.

Tanksgiving

Soon after World War II, Communist regimes came to power in the recently liberated countries of eastern Europe, creating a bloc isolated from the West by a 600-mile-long strip of walls, electrified fences, watchtowers, and minefields. "From Stettin in the Baltic to Trieste in the Adriatic," British leader Winston Churchill told an American audience in 1946, "an iron curtain has descended across the Continent." From the time that figurative curtain fell, thousands of people ran the gauntlet to freedom in the West, and hundreds died in the attempt. Vaclav Uhlik was one of the earliest—and cleverest—to try.

In fact, the Czechoslovakian mechanic had been training for such an exploit from an early age. As a teenager during World War II, Uhlik had fought in the underground resistance against the Nazis. There he honed skills in sabotage, caching supplies, repairing machinery, and planning that would later serve him well. He also learned the value of patience, of watching and waiting for the right opportunity to act. Arrested by the German Gestapo in 1942, Uhlik suffered two years in the brutal Buchenwald and Obacht concentration camps before escaping to join the Allied army as a tank corpsman in France.

After the Allied victory in 1945, Uhlik returned home with joy. He married, settled in the tiny village of Line, near the city of Pilsen in western Czechoslovakia, and fathered two children. A modest loan from friends and family helped him set up an auto-repair shop. When the Communist government began nationalizing businesses in 1948, Uhlik had six employees on his payroll. But in the economic panic that followed the government takeover, Vaclav Uhlik lost virtually everything. With just one diesel-powered truck to his name, he scraped out a living hauling firewood.

"That year," Uhlik recalled later, "the Communists announced a five-year plan. I had one of my own, but I did not announce it." Sure that a bleak future faced his family, Uhlik had made a bold and difficult decision: He would find a way to breach the iron curtain and leave his country for the West.

All of Uhlik's shrewdness, patience, and tactical acumen would be called upon. With the border growing tighter every day, he required a way of bypassing armed patrols, electrified fencing, and land mines. Reconnoitering on his wood-hauling forays, he found the fortified border impenetrable by any ordinary means. People who smashed through were blown up by mines ◊

on the far side of the fence or trapped by large concrete teeth set in the earth. Attempts to dig under the fence detonated mines, killing the diggers. But he also discovered a stretch of border about forty miles south of Line where the fence gave onto a marsh and so was less heavily defended. "What I need," he told confidante Walter Hora, a former employee then serving in the Czech army, "is a tank like the one I drove in France." With a vehicle armored against land mines, running on tractor treads, he thought he could safely cross that small rip he had found in the curtain.

Reeling with the audacity of this idea, Uhlik set about building the vehicle he needed. First he traded a large engine that he had put aside for the junked chassis of a self-propelled British cannon. Then, scavenging what they could, buying what they had to, Uhlik and Hora slowly assembled the necessary parts. Here they found tires, there treads and an engine. Their vehicle was designed to look like any other truck while in the shop but could be quickly converted into an armored vehicle with retractable treads. While they labored, they secretly listened to Radio Free Europe broadcasts to draw inspiration from others who had made it across the line.

There were a few close brushes with secret police and other authorities, but lies and bribes helped the pair protect the secret, and by 1953, the "tank" was ready—wildly improvised but surprisingly like the light armored vehicles used by the border patrol. At night, he thought, it might pass for the real thing. At 3:00 a.m. on July 24, Uhlik, his wife, Marta, and their children, Walter Hora, and three other friends squeezed into the vehicle's cramped passenger compartment. Wearing a stolen military cap on his head, Uhlik aimed south toward the soft place in the border with Bavaria. The tank's ungainly armor clanked unremittingly, but its engine moved it along at a remarkable sixty miles per hour. They hastened unchallenged along the narrow blacktop roads, past a military compound and its 500 sleeping border guards. Uhlik twice had to slow down and his passengers waited in terror for their capture and certain death. But the makeshift tank appeared convincing enough that guards waved the escapees on.

As the predawn sky began to lighten, Uhlik spotted the marsh where he planned to cross. He halted to lower the wide treads, but the lever was stuck—the treads would not descend. Without the traction they afforded, the tank would sink in the waterlogged ground beyond the fence. Near panic, Uhlik wrestled with the controls, sure that his bid for emancipation had come to an end. At any moment, he expected the border guards to begin strafing them. Then Hora added his weight to the effort, and the treads crunched into place.

Former tanker Uhlik spun his homemade juggernaut toward the electrified fence, opened the throttle, and charged. With a jolt, the tank ripped through the fence and skittered out into the marsh. Land mines detonated under its weight as it lumbered through the bog, but the steel belly plate withstood the blasts. A few thousand yards farther on, the doughty tank crawled out of Czechoslovakia and onto the free soil of the Federal Republic of Germany. Behind it, the iron curtain swung shut, sealing the border for another thirty-six years. □

Wheel Whelps

Physicians at Madrid's Gran Hospital de la Beneficencia were astonished that their patient, seventeen-year-old Armando Socarras Ramirez, was alive at all. The boy had been exposed to a temperature of forty degrees below zero Fahrenheit for more than eight hours, breathing air that contained only about a third of its sea-level oxygen content. But there he was, not merely alive, but smiling and alert in his hospital bed, giving the lie to conventional medical wisdom.

Socarras's survival was indeed a death-defying exploit. As he told his story to the astonished doctors, it became clear that cold and thin air had been only two of many perilous obstacles the young man had overcome. His tale began in Havana, Cuba, where Socarras lived with his parents. Like many other young Cubans chafing under the decade-old regime of dictator Fidel Castro, the boy yearned to live in the United States. Only there, he believed, could he fulfill his ambition to be an artist. The trouble was that Cubans customarily waited months or years for tickets on the daily flights to Spain or Miami—an eternity of waiting for a seventeen-year-old.

Jorge Pérez Blanco, a friend Socarras had met playing baseball, also wanted to escape Cuba for the United States. Putting their two adolescent heads together, they soon hatched an outlandish scheme. Like other youngsters, they had spent hours watching the jets at the Havana airport. They noticed that, just before its departure, each aircraft stopped at the head of the runway, where it remained motionless for a half-minute or so before hurtling down the runway and into

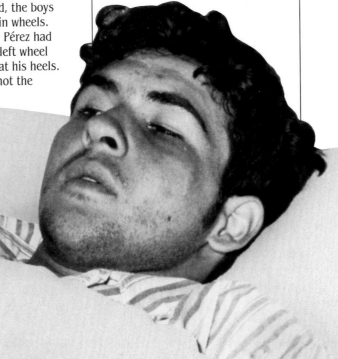

the sky.

If they could hide themselves somewhere close to the runway, they figured that it just might be possible to dash across the tarmac as a jet paused there, climb up the landing gear, and secrete themselves inside the wheel wells. It was a plot that required either great ignorance or a large dose of youthful overconfidence, for their plan ignored the dangers posed by the bitter cold and thin air at the high altitudes flown by jet airliners and the massive moving parts of a large aircraft's landing gear. To the two boys, the suicidal scheme had the look of salvation.

Telling no one about their plan, the pair settled on June 3, 1969, as the day of their escape. An Iberia Airlines DC-8 would be leaving that afternoon for Madrid. Forty-five minutes before flight time, Socarras and Pérez slipped through a hole they had found in the airport fence and made their way to a hiding place in the grass. They wore short-sleeved shirts and carried scraps of rope for harnessing themselves next to the plane's retracted wheels.

From their position prone in the grass near the runway, the boys watched as mechanics prepared the airplane and handlers loaded baggage far across the field. Before long, the passengers filed up the steps, the DC-8's doors were secured, and the aircraft taxied away from the terminal—toward the secret travelers. Socarras and his friend steeled their nerves as the great jet approached its takeoff position near them. The transport turned onto the runway and stopped. As the howl from the four jet engines mounted, the boys sprinted for the main wheels.

Within moments, Pérez had clambered into the left wheel well, with Socarras at his heels. But the space was not the empty aluminum cavern they had envisioned. Immediately, Socarras realized that the compartment was too jammed with wiring, plumbing, and machinery for both of them to fit. He ran for the right side and scrambled into place as the plane began to move. The cotton he had stuffed in his ears hardly dampened the roar of the engines.

Moments after liftoff, the massive four-wheeled assembly began to retract, hauled into its well by the ◊

complex motions of a powerful system of hydraulic struts. Socarras was burned when the tires—heated to hundreds of degrees by rolling friction—brushed against his skin; worse, he thought he would be squeezed by the huge, inward-pressing gear. Just when he thought he was doomed, the wheels locked in place. Then, before he could wriggle into a comfortable position, the wheel well opened again, and swirling winds once more buffeted the stowaway. A warning light in the cockpit had flashed, and the pilot was deploying and retracting the landing gear to see if that would extinguish the light. In the brief time that the bay doors were open, however, Socarras wedged himself into a better perch.

Jammed among the cables and piping, the teenager worried about his friend Pérez and contemplated the events of his short life. As the DC-8 climbed, the warm sea-level air of Havana was replaced by the thin, sub-zero air of the upper atmosphere; Socarras found breathing increasingly difficult. He shivered uncontrollably in the cold. At some point after the plane climbed to its cruising altitude of 30,000 feet, the youth passed out.

When he regained consciousness, it was just for a moment. The airplane was back on the ground and parked. The boy's frozen body thumped to the tarmac at Madrid's Baraja Airport, and he passed out again. When he next revived he was in a hospital. Aviation experts estimated that the odds for the teenager's survival were one in a million. Doctors thought he should have frozen to death and were surprised that Socarras suffered no apparent brain damage from the prolonged oxygen starvation. Aircraft engineers thought that he should have been crushed by the enormous landing gear as it folded tightly into the wheel well.

Socarras was the only one to reach Madrid, however. There was no trace of Jorge Pérez. For a time his fate remained a mystery; Cuba refused to tell what had happened to the boy. Then it came out that he had tumbled from his precarious wheel-well perch soon after the airplane started its takeoff roll, survived the fall, and was imprisoned for a short time as punishment.

Seven weeks after Armando Socarras Ramirez's ordeal by air, the International Rescue Committee and an uncle in New Jersey sponsored the rest of his dream. The young man finally boarded a flight for America, this time traveling inside the airplane, economy class. □

Walking Out

"I found myself outside the plane, flying apart from it, still strapped in my seat. I can remember turning over and over in the air. I remember thinking that the jungle trees below looked just like cauliflowers. Then I lost consciousness." So seventeen-year-old Juliane Koepcke described the tumultuous moments just after the breakup of the four-engine Lockheed Electra airliner in which she, her mother, and ninety other passengers were flying over the Peruvian jungle. One moment, they were cruising in bright sunlight; the next, their aircraft was being ripped apart by the turbulence of a tropical thunderstorm.

They had taken off from the coastal capital of Lima under clear skies, headed northeast for Pucallpa, a river port in the dense rain forest that covers the land east of the Peruvian Andes. It was Christmas Eve of 1971, and Marie Koepcke, an ornithologist and illustrator, had come to Lima on business and to fetch her daughter, who had just been graduated from a Lima high school, for the holidays. Juliane boarded the plane wearing her pretty Lutheran confirmation dress and high heels, happy to be returning home and eager to see her father, Hans, an ecologist.

About thirty minutes from the flight's destination, with the high ground of the cordillera behind him, the pilot made routine radio contact with the airfield at Pucallpa. Then he began the gradual descent through a field of thunderheads that sprouted over the jungle ahead. Suddenly, the plane was in the clouds, its windows streaked with rain, the sky blackened except for nearby flashes of lightning. Turbulence shook the craft. Flames sprang from its right wing. Marie Koepcke squeezed her daughter's hand and murmured, "This is the end of everything." The storm began to pull the Electra apart.

Wreckage from the disintegrating plane rained down along a ten-mile strip of foothill jungle. When she regained consciousness, Juliane found she was alone, belted into her upside-down seat. Her mother's seat, which was attached to Juliane's, was empty. The girl's shoul-

Bloodshot and battered, Juliane Koepcke *(inset)* tells rescuers about her nine days in the Peruvian jungle *(below)* that swallowed all traces of her shattered airliner except these metal scraps scattered in the treetops.

der hurt badly, and her right arm and foot had been gashed. She had lost her glasses and a shoe. Unfastening the safety belt that had saved her, the girl gingerly scouted the area, hoping to find other survivors. But there were only the scattered fragments of the Electra.

Juliane spent the night in the shelter of the inverted seat. In the morning, she crawled into the open and set out. Although she was by no means a seasoned jungle hand, Juliane had spent much of her life in and around the rain forest; it was not the terrifying wilderness to her that it might have been to someone less experienced. She knew, for example, that she must follow the water downhill as it fed from the foothills into the tangled tributaries of the Amazon. The wider the river became, her father had told her, the better the chances of there being settlements along it. Wearing one shoe, the pale, blonde girl began her trek out of the rough eastern foothills of the Andes.

Once, on the third day of her march, she heard the sound of search planes, but the dense forest canopy hid her from rescuers. The hot, humid twilight of the jungle floor was stifling, however, and she began traveling only in early morning or late afternoon to avoid being scorched. Insects stung her as she battled through the undergrowth. She lost her second shoe. Thorny plants tattered her clothes. As the jungle slashed her skin, flies laid eggs in the wounds. And there ◊

were grim mementos from the sky. Coming upon another inverted seat section from the Electra, she turned it over: Beneath a swarm of flies, three dead teenagers sat, still tethered in their chairs.

After several days of walking, Juliane encountered a stream and, wading and swimming, came to the broad Sheboya River. She contemplated catching toads for food but refrained, unsure which species were poisonous. For the same reason, she eschewed the fruit she found. Somehow she managed to push on through the thick growth along the water. On the tenth day, exhausted and plagued by the wriggling of maggots that had hatched in her wounds, Juliane spied an empty hut on the bank. Inside, she attempted to dig the larvae from the wounds in her arm and foot with a splinter dipped in kerosene. Then she slept.

She was awakened a short time later by three native hunters whose route took them to the cabin every three weeks. Overcoming their fear that the blonde wraith was an evil spirit, the hunters timorously approached, helped ease the discomfort of her infected cuts, and took her downriver in their boat to the jungle settlement of Tournavista. From there, a missionary pilot ferried her to Pucallpa, and home. Juliane was soon safely in the care of her father and a physician. "When I arrived," she said later, "I was a living nightmare." In fact, her physical health was remarkably good, considering what she had been through. But there was another nightmare that persisted long after her ordeal by rain forest. She had lived, while ninety-one others had died. "Why me?" she would ask. "And why not my mother?" □

Extremity in the Andes

When Daniel Fernandez returned safely to Uruguay, having survived seventy days high in the Andes Mountains after an airplane crash, people were awed at the resourcefulness and grit he and his fifteen companions had shown. They had endured cold, snow, and ice high in the cordillera; with few resources or supplies, they had lived for more than two months. But there was also talk about what they had done in order to survive—and the ugly term: *cannibalism.*

"Look now," his father instructed young Fernandez, "you must say that this isn't true." Replied the son, "It *is* true."

On October 13, 1972, forty passengers, most of them young rugby players and their friends and families, had been en route to a match in Chile aboard a chartered air force Fairchild F-227. Caught in severe mountain downdrafts, the aircraft was drawn closer and closer to the sharp teeth of the Andes until, finally, a wing clipped a rockface and the

airplane began to disintegrate, losing first one wing and engine, then the other. The fuselage hit the ground at some 200 miles per hour and tobogganed down the snow-covered slope, coming to rest in a steep valley.

Twenty-nine persons survived the impact, but two crew members died soon afterward. Most of the survivors were injured, however, and their chances of survival were slim. The aircraft's radio was destroyed, and the heavy snow blanket that had saved their lives also kept them near the wreckage. They were lightly dressed—October is springtime in the Southern Hemisphere. For provisions the group shared just eight chocolate bars, five nougat bars, a handful of candy and dried fruit, some crackers, two cans of mussels, and six bottles of wine and spirits. The survivors huddled inside the broken fuselage, hoping to stay warm until their rescuers arrived.

But there was no rescue. With alarm that increased daily, the stranded passengers monitored news reports of the search parties' progress on a transistor radio they had discovered in the wreckage. The news was not good; would-be rescuers could not find the downed Fairchild. Starvation had begun to stalk the desperate party, when, on the tenth day, nineteen-year-old medical student Roberto Canessa uttered the unspeakable. To survive, he said, they must eat the bodies of the dead. "It is meat," Canessa told his comrades. All were Roman Catholics, and Canessa added a theological justification to practical necessity: "The souls have left their bodies and are in Heaven with God." Canessa's words hung in the freezing air, but no one moved. The next day the radio told them that the search had been given up.

Finally, Canessa and three others crossed the snow to one of the partially exposed corpses. He cut away twenty matchstick-size slivers of frozen flesh with a piece of broken glass and placed them on the roof of the fuselage to dry in the sun. Hours later, finally overcoming his revulsion, Canessa picked up a piece of meat, pushed it into his mouth, and swallowed. As evening came, others followed his example.

Pedro Algorta elaborated on Canessa's theological argument. "It's like Holy Communion," he said. "When Christ died he gave his body to us so that we could have spiritual life. My friend has given us his body so that we can have physical life." Eventually, all of them accepted that devouring their deceased companions was the only way to survive. In this tiny society of survivors, some with broken bones and other serious injuries, the rigid human taboo against cannibalism had broken down.

The most difficult part of the act, the boys said later, was slicing flesh from the bodies. Once removed, the slabs were cut into slivers, and the meat ceased to be recognizably human. As weeks passed, they consumed every body part except skin, lungs, genitals, and head. Medical student Canessa preferred the liver, knowing it contained the greatest reserve of vitamins. Later, when even the supply of human flesh ran low, the survivors cracked skulls and ate the brains. Several bodies remained untouched, however— alive they had been too close to the survivors to be considered food, even in extremity. On the seventeenth day of the ordeal, a snow avalanche killed eight of the ◊

Stranded in the Andes, Uruguayan rugby team members and friends cluster by the plane's broken fuselage. Player Roy Harley (inset) and his mother had an emotional reunion after the rescue.

people still alive on the mountain. One of them was Liliana Methol, who had been traveling with her husband, Javier. Out of consideration for his feelings, Liliana's body was left as it was.

With the arrival of summer in late November, the snows thawed and the nineteen passengers who still survived realized that if they were going to be helped, they must do it themselves. Three more people died before Canessa and teammate Fernando Parrado set out across the snow. After ten days of difficult travel, they reached help in Chile. Soon, radio stations carried reports of the passengers' miraculous survival, and a helicopter was on its way from Santiago to fly the rest of the survivors to safety.

When they heard that rescue was at hand, the fourteen who had stayed with the airplane were jubilant. But one of them, Daniel Fernandez, intruded on their mood. Gesturing at the body parts and human bones scattered around the wreckage, Fernandez asked, "What about all that?"

Indeed, as word got out that they had survived by eating human flesh, the survivors were villified by an outraged public. Many of their parents were initially shocked that their sons had committed such an act—forgetting that cannibalism had kept them from dying on the mountain. If the survivors had offended, however, they had not sinned. In the view of the Catholic church, anthropophagy *in extremis* is permissible. □

Diehard

In December 1944, as their nation careened toward defeat in World War II, the Japanese army sent Lieutenant Hiroo Onoda to the small Philippine island of Lubang about eighty miles southwest of Manila. An intelligence officer, Onoda had been briefed on Lubang's importance: Its small Japanese garrison guarded the entrance to Manila harbor. Given a generous supply of explosives to destroy port and airfield facilities, he was ordered to conduct guerilla operations against the advancing Americans and Filipinos until further notice.

Although Onoda would be greatly outnumbered, he was cautioned against both surrender and the honorable alternative of ritual suicide; or hara-kiri. "You are absolutely forbidden to die by your own hand," General Akira Muto told the twenty-three-year-old officer. "It may take three years, it may take five, but whatever happens, we'll come back for you. Until then, so long as you have one soldier, you are to continue to lead him."

For most of the world, the war ended when Japan surrendered to the Allies the following August. But for Lieutenant Onoda, World War II had barely begun. Living on coconuts, bananas, and whatever they could steal, he and a handful of compatriots carried out a small reign of terror among the island's peaceful farmers and gathered intelligence to guide the Japanese counterattack that Onoda knew must

come. Staying nowhere for very long, they swept out of the mountains to attack farmers, burn houses, and destroy crops before melting back into the jungle. Farmers began refusing to work the land near the mountains.

After five years, in September of 1949, one of his men, Yuichi Akatsu, disappeared. A few months later, Onoda found a note in Akatsu's handwriting: "When I surrendered, the Philippine troops greeted me as a friend." But Onoda was convinced that this was a trick. He had been sent here by his division commander; if the war were over, the division commander would have come and told him so. He would wait for a countermanding order delivered just as his original orders had been: face to face.

In May of 1954, another of Onoda's men, Shoichi Shimada, was killed in a skirmish with the islanders. By now, the Japanese government knew about Onoda's war but did not know how to get him to surrender. It sent envoys who placed a Japanese flag bearing Onoda family names at the site of Shimada's death. But some of the names in the note were misspelled, and Onoda, who had been trained in deception by the Japanese army, considered this as evidence of yet another trick. He continued his personal war.

In 1959, Onoda's brother, Toshio, came to Lubang with a search party. For six months, they stalked the length and breadth of the island announcing through loudspeakers that the war had ended. Watching and listening from his hiding places in the jungle, Hiroo Onoda was convinced that the entreaties were spoken by an impostor who closely resembled his brother and could even

Even a hit-and-run driver could not overcome the spirit of Mugsy, Glen Maloney's pet terrier. The dog's battered, apparently lifeless body was buried one Saturday night. But on Sunday morning, after an adventure he never divulged, Mugsy appeared at the door, tail wagging, evidently none the worse for wear.

imitate his voice. Onoda's belief that his nation continued to fight World War II remained unshakable. After all, when he had left Japan in 1944, every citizen had seemed to agree that death was preferable to surrender. If Japan had lost the war, all Japanese would be dead. Likewise, if his side had won, Onoda's commanding officer would have informed him. Since he had seen living Japanese and had not been contacted by his commander, the once-young officer's hermetic, twisted logic proved that the war must still be in progress. The soldiers—by now reduced to just Onoda and one other man, Private First Class Kinshichi Kozuka—remained where they were.

Onoda pronounced the same judgment on the stacks of newspapers that were left by Toshio and the radio broadcasts he heard on a transistor set stolen from an is-

lander's hut. He was impressed by his enemies' cleverness, however, and the lengths to which they would go in order to deceive him. By 1972, when he and Kozuka managed to evade a 13,000-man army that swarmed over Lubang, Onoda's hit-and-run guerilla campaign had killed about thirty Filipinos.

Later that year, Kozuka died during a raid against farmers. Onoda became lonely. With no one left to convince of his cause's righteousness, self-doubt crept in. One day, after two years alone, Onoda was about to attack a man he found camped in a tent when the stranger spoke to him in Japanese. The newcomer was a good-natured twenty-four-year-old college dropout by the name of Norio Suzuki, who had actually come looking for Onoda as a lark. After a friendly campfire chat, Onoda said that he might be willing to consider a proper surrender after

all. Suzuki returned to Japan and tracked down one of Onoda's former superior officers, Yoshimi Taniguchi, now a mild book dealer in Tokyo, and persuaded him to go to Lubang and accept Hiroo Onoda's surrender.

On March 9, 1974, twenty-nine years after his guerilla war began, Lieutenant Hiroo Onoda marched out of the jungle. Taniguchi read the order to give up, and the next evening Onoda turned over his sword to a Philippine commander. The wayward soldier was freshly shaved, wore his ancient, patched uniform, and carried his obsolete rifle. On his return to Japan, Onoda received a hero's welcome.

But Japan was a different nation from the one that he had left. Hiroo Onoda soon emigrated to Brazil, where he became a farmer much like those he had spent most of his life terrorizing. □

Pin's Choice

Before the end of 1976 most of the lights of Pin Yathay's life had been extinguished, like stars obscured by a spreading cloud. His father and mother had died. Two of his sons were gone. His sister, three brothers, and a half-dozen other relatives were memories. Everyone he loved was dead, except his wife, Any, and one remaining son, six-year-old Nawath. And now Pin thought that he himself would be the next to go.

Pin and his family were inmates of a concentration camp at Don Ey, Cambodia, where they had been herded by the agents of the nation's Khmer Rouge revolution. Intent on instituting a Communist regime in record time, the Khmer Rouge emptied Cambodia's cities, driving millions of people into the countryside and setting them to work in the fields for the purpose of "reeducation." The resulting reign of terror aimed at extirpating all foreign and bourgeois influences. Anyone with a pair of glasses, a ballpoint pen, or a fancy wrist watch was the enemy. Education became a fatal liability. Doctors, teachers, lawyers, and former government officials were singled out, led away, and never seen again. People were killed by the tens of thousands; eventually more than a million died in Cambodia's work camps, hospitals, forests, and fields.

An engineer trained in Montreal, Pin had married into an upper-class Cambodian family and risen to be director of the Department of New Works and Equipment in Cambo-

dia's capital, Phnom Penh. In another time, Pin's credentials would have identified him as a valued citizen. But in the topsy-turvy world of the Khmer Rouge, where education was a sin and ignorance was more than bliss—it was life itself—Pin had become a marked man.

Pin had begun calling himself simply Thay to conceal his true identity. He tried to remain inconspicuous, claiming to be a mere technician. For a time he succeeded. Then, as he and his wife worked and starved in the Don Ey camp, one of the guards confronted Pin. He knew Pin's true identity, he said, but he would not waste a bullet to kill him now; the prisoner would die soon anyway. If he was alive next week, then they would kill him.

Pin Yathay felt helpless to fight back. He first thought that he would give himself up to the release of death. But he could not. He knew that his captors would not merely execute him—they would take him into the jungle and slaughter him like an animal. He cleaved to the last words of his father: "Stay alive, my son," the old man had said from the bamboo mat where he lay dying. "Stay alive to escape."

But Pin and Any were in no con-

dition to escape. They were weak with illness and their limbs were swollen with the characteristic edema of starvation. Simply to walk was almost impossibly laborious. The guard was right. They would die soon—unless they formed a plan. What emerged from their minds was a desperate scheme that bore an apalling price: To give themselves a chance to survive, Pin and his wife would leave behind their only surviving child, Nawath. A woman in the camp who had lost all six of her own children agreed to take him in. Pin Yathay gave the six-year-old the same advice his father had given him: Be careful. Pretend ignorance. Survive. He never saw the boy again.

Pin and Any slipped out of Don Ey camp, planning to escape across the border of Thailand, seventy miles to the west through heavily patrolled Khmer Rouge territory.

Pin forged false travel passes,

Khmer Rouge soldiers like these murdered one million Cambodians and dumped the bodies in mass graves *(right)*.

and the couple walked two days to another camp—beyond the eyes of the guard who knew them. They remained for seven months, accumulating supplies and recruiting ten others. The members of the escape group bartered clothes and jewels for rice and dried fish to eat on their journey. They questioned fellow inmates to learn as much as possible about the Cardamom Mountains, which lay between them and freedom. In late May of 1977, just before the start of the rainy season, they set off westward.

They traveled through a terrifying political landscape, gripped by fear that, at any moment, they would encounter a Khmer patrol. The physical landscape was no better—a trackless jungle through which they moved only with difficulty. The sun was their compass, leading them west. Two days out, Pin, Any, and another woman, Eng, became separated from the others. They rationed their rice so their meager supply would last until they reached Thailand. The jungle grew thicker, the mountains steeper. On the ninth night, their cooking fire leaped out of control and set the woods ablaze. They fled. When the fire subsided, Any returned to the campsite to retrieve the metal can they used as a cook pot. Pin and Eng waited for her in the total darkness. After a time, Pin went to search for her,

groping after her through the disorienting labyrinth of the nocturnal rain forest. He found the fire but not Any. He searched further without success. When he returned to tell Eng about Any's disappearance, that woman, too, was gone. Pin Yathay now was truly alone.

Like a robot, his mind fixed entirely on continuing his flight, Pin pressed on. His rice gone, he ate mushrooms and fruit. He caught animals: tortoises, snakes, and a bat he trapped in a hollow tree. These he ate raw because the rains had drowned the possibility of building a fire. Hunger also drove Pin to make dangerous mistakes. Once, a benign-looking green fruit seared his mouth like acid.

Leeches clung to his feet and ankles; he cut the creatures off. After three weeks, Pin felt he had walked twice the distance to Thailand, but still there was no sign of the Me Tuk River near the border. He only knew that he must be very close.

Then, one day, three teenage boys in black stepped from the jungle, waved guns, and took him to their camp on the banks of the Me Tuk, where they were joined by a score or more other Khmer Rouge soldiers. They fed Pin, but at night they tied him painfully in a tent. Most ominously, they spoke of Pin as "enemy"—a term reserved for those they intended to kill.

The camp food gave Pin diarrhea, and the illness saved his life. Late one night, after a trip to the latrine, Pin managed to force some slack in the rope when the guard retied his bonds. Working out of the fetters, Pin slipped from the tent, crept to the river, and hauled himself painfully hand over hand along a cable that was stretched across the swollen, rushing Me Tuk.

For that entire night, Pin struggled through the jungle, then fell into an exhausted twenty-four-hour sleep. When he awoke, Pin pressed on until, at last, he heard a distant rumble that he realized must be the noise of road traffic. He stepped quickly toward the sound, into a sloping meadow . . . and stopped. His foot had grazed a sharp object that instantly transformed the euphoria of imminent shelter into dread. The meadow was planted with sharpened bamboo stakes, so densely arrayed that he dared not try to walk between them.

For three hours, expecting to be shot at any minute, Pin traversed the open bamboo minefield by uprooting stake after stake to make way for his steps. Beyond the deadly meadow, he walked into Thailand until he reached the busy road whose noise had lured him. And there, heavy with the silences of many deaths, he lay down amid the rough sounds of the living. □

Swept Away

On Monday, June 5, 1989, William Lamm *(below)* and his brother-in-law, Richard Schoonmaker, were scuba diving in the Atlantic Ocean off Vero Beach, Florida. Not far from their boat, Lamm encountered a submerged concrete slab. This was, he thought, an artificial reef, put in place to attract and shelter fish and other marine life. Hundreds of similar man-made outcrops dot the shallow waters off the Florida coast.

Thinking that the structure might have attracted a succulent red snapper that he could catch for dinner, Lamm explored the slab further. He found a large lip of concrete that seemed to shelter a cavern and slipped over the edge, looking for a fish. Abruptly, Lamm himself was caught, grasped by a current that grew stronger and stronger, dragging him into the darkness faster than he had ever thought possible underwater. Later, his speed was estimated at fifty miles per hour. Unable to resist and barely able to control the movements of his own limbs, he was slammed repeatedly against the hard surface of the cavern. His diving gloves were torn away, and his wet suit was shredded.

Clasping his air supply's mouthpiece between his teeth, Lamm could still breathe—and think. He guessed that he had been sucked into an intake pipe of some sort, and his racing mind told him that he was probably doomed. Either the pipe would carry him directly into the whirling jaws of a turbine or pin him against a grate intended to screen out debris, where he would drown when his air ran out.

But before he could dwell on the grim certainty of death, the ordeal was over. Lamm popped to the surface of a pond on the grounds of the St. Lucie Nuclear Power Plant. As he had suspected, he had been sucked into an intake tunnel—one of the sixteen-foot-diameter intake pipes feeding the reactor. A small fraction of the water is diverted into the turbine through a debris screen; had Lamm been swept that way, he surely would have drowned as the torrent pinned him against the screen. Instead, he had been shunted into a quarter-mile-long bypass pipe that directed unneeded water away from the plant's pumps and turbines. A security guard relayed a message to Richard Schoonmaker that his vanished diving buddy, while shaken, was safe. □

Elmo Wortman and children Cindy, Jena, and Randy pose by the Alaskan waters that nearly killed them.

Home Wrecked

During the 1970s, Elmo Wortman, a divorced carpenter raising four children, decided to take his family back to the elements of land and sea. His decision was more than a faddish return to fundamentals, however. Finding himself unable to pursue his trade due to a debilitating form of rheumatism, Wortman concluded that he and his son and three daughters would do better on his minimal income in the coastal wilds of British Columbia and Alaska than in a city. Together, the family built a thirty-three-foot sailboat, which they eventually anchored at Suemez Island, a tiny, rocky outpost on the Pacific side of Prince of Wales Island. As the crow flies, Suemez is about 75 miles west of Ketchikan, Alaska. But in their boat, the Wortmans had to cross more than 150 miles of rough, open water in order to reach either Ketchikan or Prince Rupert, in British Columbia to the southeast.

The family fared well in the wild, however, fishing and digging clams to make a rugged subsistence existence. The three younger children—fifteen-year-old Randy and the two girls, Cindy, sixteen, and Jena, twelve—and their father lived aboard their boat, appropriately, christened *Home*, and in a floating log house that they also constructed and moored nearby. Periodically, they voyaged to the mainland or to Prince of Wales Island to buy supplies, receive medical and dental checkups, and visit the eldest daughter, seventeen-year-old

Margery, who lived with family friends and attended school in the island town of Craig.

Idyllic in some ways, their existence always contained a latent peril. Even the simplest errands were vastly complicated by distance and scores of rough islands, in a rugged land where any slip could be fatal. In that setting, a trip to the children's orthodontist was easily transformed into a month-long wilderness trial that put their survival skills and character to the test.

On February 13, 1979, they were making a nighttime run down the Dixon Entrance, a passage from Prince Rupert to the Pacific that is notorious for its swirling currents and rapid weather changes. Sailing with his three youngest children, Wortman encountered a wicked snowstorm, whose winds were later estimated to have topped ninety miles per hour. For two days, they battled to save the craft, but the fierce gale drove them onto the shoreline of Long Island, a rocky finger just south of Prince of Wales Island. As *Home* foundered, they jammed whatever food and supplies they could into plastic bags, sealed the bags and cast them adrift, hoping they would land on the nearby beach. The Wortmans cut loose their lightweight, six-foot plastic

dinghy and swam through the icy water for land. The surf slammed them into the rocks and badly battered Elmo's legs.

All four survived the pounding, and the tiny dinghy—so fragile they expected it to be destroyed—washed ashore intact. Soaked and only partly clad, they salvaged the remains of their boat from drift piles on the beach. Styrofoam pads, a rope ladder, plastic jars, two oars, a sail, assorted shoes, a handful of matches, white gasoline, six apples, and three onions made up the bulk of the provisions that the family had to work with. The Wortmans' last meal of hamburgers, eaten on board the *Home* the night before the wreck, a few dozen mussels and clams pried from rocks, and mouthfuls of seaweed would have to carry them through the next phase of their ordeal.

The children, versed in outdoor living, gathered firewood and set up shelter. For two nights, the family camped on the snow-swept beach as the father regained strength from a bout of intestinal flu. Wortman calculated that from their position on Long Island, they could reach safety by crossing a mile-wide portion of Kaigani Strait to the larger Dall Island, then making their way north along its shore to a ◊

cabin on Rose Inlet that was owned by friends. The total distance was about 25 miles—not great by the reckoning of a family that routinely voyaged 150 miles to buy groceries.

They were aware of the difficulties, however. Kaigani Strait is fraught with strong currents and high winds. And the flimsy dinghy—hardly a seaworthy vessel—was also too small to carry all four of them. They decided to build a raft for the journey.

Because construction required better protection from the weather, they shifted their rough camp. Randy and Jena paddled the dinghy along the shore, as Elmo and Cindy hiked through deep snow along the cliffs. Elmo's feet were numb with frostbite. Finally, they reached a quiet cove and began to incorporate the dinghy, several large driftwood logs, and a piece of plywood found on the beach into a seaworthy raft. The improvised vessel was lashed together with rope from their lost boat's ladder. Three days after being stranded, they were once more ready for the sea. On February 18, they paddled north for several hours across the strait, then continued paddling for the next six days, sustained only by the rare shellfish they could find. Their progress was laboriously slow, and they were often beached by strong winds.

At last, reaching a place on the coast that Elmo believed was only an hour or two away from the cabin, the father made a painful decision. Although their goal was so near, Cindy and Jena were listless with starvation and unable to paddle. Bundled against the damp and wind, they would stay behind on the beach as Elmo and Randy made a final dash for assistance. Elmo planned to radio for help from the

cabin, then return to his daughters with food from the supply always stored there. In the morning, as the girls slept, father and son dismantled the raft and set out in the dinghy. They expected to return by noon, but their plan soon unraveled. Strong winds slowed their progress. Ice forced them to abandon the dinghy. Walking on painfully frozen feet, Elmo and Randy reached the cabin as darkness fell.

The hike was crippling. Both father and son were forced to cut away portions of frozen, infected toes. Randy excised flesh down to the bone. Tormented by the thought of his daughters alone on the beach, yet physically unable to walk, Elmo instituted a regime of soaking their feet and smearing them with antibacterial soap to speed their healing. He sat at the CB radio for hours, flooding the airwaves with Mayday calls. No one answered.

On March 8, warming weather melted the snow and exposed a boat on shore near the cabin. The vessel was a ruin, however, and the pair had to spend the entire next day patching it before they could row back for the girls. By now, two weeks had elapsed since they had left the pair at the cove; expecting to find Cindy and Jena dead, the father and son sadly planned to retrieve the bodies, then row north to the town of Hydaburg. Elmo left a note explaining their situation and apologizing for taking supplies from

the cabin, and the two set out.

Randy rowed for six hours, until they reached the cove. Although badly wasted and too weak to move, Cindy and Jena had narrowly survived. The elder sister had been hallucinating about her father's arrival for several days; when she had first seen him, she believed that he was just another wraith of her fevered imagination.

Reunited once more, the four Wortmans climbed into the boat, and Randy, demonstrating astonishing stamina, rowed six hours back to the cabin. Stumbling into the shelter, Elmo saw, with a shock, bags of fresh groceries in the kitchen. Someone had been there. As it turned out, the cabin owners' business partner had arrived at the secluded house, found Elmo's note, and gone for help.

The next morning, March 11, a Coast Guard helicopter airlifted the family to safety. Doctors amputated half of Elmo's right foot and all the toes on his left. Randy and Cindy also lost parts of their feet. Jena, the youngest, fared best; somehow, her feet had never frozen.

But the experience turned the family back toward civilization. Elmo moved his household into Craig as soon as he was able, leaving the treacherous waters of Dixon Entrance to work their spell on other mariners. Within a year of the *Home*'s wreck, the waters had claimed forty lives. □

When Bill Waite collapsed at the controls of his Piper Comanche in 1974, Bob Corson, at an Atlantic City airport about fifteen miles away, heard a radio call from Waite's nonpilot wife, Martha. Corson took off in a Beechcraft Bonanza, approached the Comanche, and talked Martha through eighty minutes of flying lessons—and a safe landing at McGuire Air Force Base in New Jersey.

Icefall

On a vacation in the Alps in 1976, Romans Claudio and Maria Antonietta Turella were dazzled by the sublime crags that stood as a backdrop to the Italian ski resort of Cervinia. Claudio, an amateur photographer, took portraits of Cervino, the great massif that straddles the border with Switzerland, where the mountain is called the Matterhorn. But he yearned for even more spectacular views. On Sunday, February 29, after several days of skiing, the couple took a cable car to Plateau Rosa, a glacier field at an altitude of nearly 12,000 feet and an impressive vantage point for Alpine photography.

By noon, under the intense, high-altitude sun, Claudio was happily snapping photographs while Maria Antonietta, carrying a box lunch, scouted for a pleasant picnic spot. Claudio was putting his camera away when he heard Maria Antonietta cry his name. Turning, he glimpsed her form plunging into a hole in the snow. Acting instinctively, Claudio ran toward the spot—and he, too, plummeted into an icy declivity.

Maria Antonietta and Claudio had dropped into a crevasse in the glacial ice that had been disguised by a thin cover of snow. They slid sixty feet down before coming to rest a few feet apart on separate, narrow ice shelves. Below them, the frozen chasm fell away into unplumbed blue depths. Claudio's back and chest had been badly hurt in the fall. Maria Antonietta, unhurt but stunned, helped her husband edge from his tiny perch to her larger ledge. Still, they now shared a space less than two feet deep.

For a while, the couple shouted for help but ceased as the sky far above darkened. In the gloom of the frozen cavern, they shivered in walking clothes that provided scant protection from the frigid temperature in the chasm. They passed the hours praying and conversing, to keep each other from dropping into an unsteady sleep—which might send them toppling deeper into the crevasse.

They waited all day Monday, but no rescuers came. Their mood swung between hope and despair. They could not know a search had been organized on the very evening of their disappearance. But since there was confusion about whether the Turellas had intended to hike on the Plateau Rosa or in another area nearby, parties were sent to both places, dividing their effort.

By Monday night, Claudio raged with fever brought on by injuries. He hallucinated about elevators, which he insisted would carry him and his wife to safety. Maria Antonietta massaged his icy limbs and stuffed his boots with napkins from the picnic bag, which she emptied and placed on his head for warmth. On Tuesday night, she dreamed they were being saved. When she awoke to find herself still in the crevasse, she sobbed in anguish.

Meanwhile, Claudio's elder brother, Mario, had flown in from Rome to join the search. On Wednesday, he and the rescue parties scoured the slopes above Cervinia. By Thursday, few besides Mario Turella believed that the couple could still be alive. He pleaded for just one more day before giving up the hunt.

That night, Maria Antonietta herself became convinced that they could no longer stay where they were. Claudio could hardly stand, and his back muscles were locked in painful spasms. Peering about, she spotted a cavelike opening not far from the ledge and managed to coax Claudio into it. A serenity about their fate settled over her. Without anxiety, she abandoned them to God.

Friday morning, a three-man team headed for Plateau Rosa led by Germain Ottin, a sixty-three-year-old retired mountain guide. The trio began combing the steep slope above the cable-car depot but turned back when Ottin decided the Turellas would have sought out less challenging terrain. Retracing his steps, he noticed a flawed patch in the smooth perfection of the snow field's surface. There was a hole and, wafting from far below, an indistinct sound—a human voice.

Rescue had come just in time. Within hours a blizzard blanketed the region, and snow fell for two days without stopping, completely obscuring what had almost been their tomb. □

The Climb of a Lifetime

On a rare occasion when surefooted seventeen-year-old Hugh Herr stepped into unfamiliar terrain, it nearly killed him. As it was, Herr's life was irrevocably changed, and he discovered within himself a deep well of strength and ingenuity that has given a feeling of hope to all who hear his story.

An avid, skilled rock climber, Herr set out with a friend in January of 1982 for New Hampshire's Mount Washington, the site of some of North America's most severe weather. Although Hugh Herr possessed remarkable agility and superior skill in finding and exploiting tiny hand- and footholds on sheer rock cliffs, his experience in navigating ice and snow and surviving in bitter cold was limited.

The two climbers lost their way on the mountain, and three days passed before searchers were able to find them. Herr's feet were severely frostbitten, and when gangrene set in, doctors were forced to amputate both of his legs four inches below the knee.

For months after the operation, Herr struggled with despair and anger. He was wracked with phantom pains in his absent limbs. He was tortured by the symptoms of withdrawal from the morphine doctors used to control his ferocious pain. But gradually, he came to grips with his sorrow and rage and began to imagine himself regaining his strength—and even, one day, climbing again.

Herr's physical therapists told him that with prosthetic devices he would be able to walk, drive, and possibly navigate a bicycle. Climbing, they said, was out of the question. Herr almost believed them, even though he had already been clambering around his parents' house, trying some of his old climbing moves while using only his arms. The temporary prostheses caused excrutiating pain—so much that Herr found it easier to climb than to walk. With the help of his brother Tony, he spent the summer pushing himself through brutal workouts. Simultaneously, he improved his walking skills using newly fitted, less painful artificial limbs.

In the following year, Herr realized that his condition could be used to some advantage. As a rock climber, he was no longer limited by the size and shape of natural feet. Herr built prosthetic devices just for climbing, the feet shaped so they would wedge neatly into cracks and grip narrow ledges that his real feet could never have negotiated. He sought ever keener challenges in New York State's Shawan-gunk Mountains, his favorite climbing haunt. Before long he was scaling the most technically difficult routes, feats reserved to only the most proficient climbers. In July of 1985, Herr completed a very difficult ascent in New Hampshire called Stage Fright. For him, the accomplishment marked the high point of his recovery.

Stage Fright also marked a personal turning point for Herr. Applying the same single-mindedness that he had once reserved for climbing, he graduated summa cum laude from Millersville University, near his home in Lancaster, Pennsylvania. In 1991, he entered graduate school at the Massachusetts Institute of Technology, with the goal of learning to design ways for others to overcome physical losses. "Someday," he says, "when technology is advanced enough, people will no longer be physically disabled." The young man with a problem had become a solver of other people's problems. □

Amputee-climber Hugh Herr *(above)* attaches a "foot" he designed for gripping the tiniest holds, then demonstrates its effectiveness and his skill *(right)* on a sheer rock face in New York's Shawangunk Mountains.

ACKNOWLEDGMENTS

The editors wish to thank these individuals and institutions for their valuable assistance in the preparation of this volume:

Maître Robert Achalé, Paris; Janet Bord, Corwen, Clwyd, Wales; Terence Charman, Imperial War Museum, London; Sylvie Clair, Archives d'Outre-Mer, Aix-en-Provence, France; Jena Wortman Conrow, Florence, Oregon; Jef Dauber, *Baltimore Sun*, Baltimore, Maryland; Enrico Deaglio, Rome; Mark Dickens, UPS, Louisville, Kentucky; A. J. Dickinson, Royal Humane Society, London; Joe Distler, New York; Martyn Farr, Powys, Wales; Joseph Geraci, National Postal Museum, Smithsonian Institution, Washington, D.C.; Jo Giovannoni, *Harley Women Magazine*, Elgin, Illinois; Robert Hamilton, *Baltimore Sun*, Baltimore, Maryland; Curt Harker, Salem County Historical Society, Salem, New Jersey; Meg Harris, United States Postal Service, Washington, D.C.; Robert Headland, Scott Polar Research Institute, Cambridge, England; Don Herbert, UPS, Bowie, Maryland; Hugh Herr, Cambridge, Massachusetts; Maurice Herzog, Neuilly-sur-Seine, France; Verlen Kruger, Lansing, Michigan; Diane Latone, UPS, Atlanta, Georgia; Donald Loker, Niagara Falls Public Library, Niagara Falls, New York; Claire Lusseyran, Paris; Pascal Lusseyran, Châteauneuf-sur-Sarthe, France; Mrs. J. C. Neeve, Gladys Aylward Charitable Trust, Crawley, Sussex, England; Germain Ottin, Valtournanche, Aosta, Italy; Jacqueline Pardon, Bourg-la-Reine, France; Giorgio Perlasca, Padua, Italy; Arthur Pollack, *Boston Herald*, Boston, Massachusetts; Ron Rae, Pelikan Pictures, Ltd., Southfield, Michigan; Ken Shapero, UPS, Louisville, Kentucky; Robert Sinclair, Hull, England; Junko Tabei, Kawagoe, Japan; Claudio Turella, Rome; Geoff Yeadon, Cowling, Yorks, England.

PICTURE CREDITS

The sources for the illustrations that appear in this book are listed below. Credits from left to right are separated by semicolons; from top to bottom by dashes.

Cover: S. Peter Lewis, background, Royal Observatory, London. **3:** S. Peter Lewis. **7:** Martyn Farr/Allsport, London, background, Richard Fukuhara/West Light, Los Angeles. **8, 9:** *Memoirs of the Lady Hester Stanhope*, Vol. 1, Henry Colburn, London, 1845. **10:** By kind permission of the President and Council of The Royal Society, London. **11:** Mary Evans Picture Library, London. **12, 13:** From *The Life of Captain Sir Richard F. Burton*, Vol. 1, by Isabel Burton, Chapman and Hall, London, 1893. **14:** Courtesy The National History Museum, London—National Portrait Gallery, London. **16:** Library of Congress. **18, 19:** Norsk Telegrambyra, Oslo. **20:** UPI/Bettmann, New York. **21:** Art by Time-Life Books—from *Beyond Euphrates*, by Freya Stark, John Murray, London, 1951. **22:** Colin Luke, London. **23:** UPI/Bettmann, New York. **24:** Scan-Foto, Oslo. **25:** Keystone, Paris, inset, © Galen Rowell/Mountain Light, Albany, California. **26:** Keystone, Paris. **27-29:** AP/Wide World Photos, New York. **30, 31:** Peter Marlow/Sygma, New York, background, art by Fred Holz. **32:** Alain Dejean/Sygma, New York (3)—art by Fred Holz; Alain Keller/Sygma, New York. **33:** Martyn Farr/Allsport, London. **34:** Lindsey Dodd/Geoff Yeadon, Keighley; Martyn Farr, Crickhowell, Powys, Wales. **35:** Yorkshire Television, Leeds. **36:** Art by Time-Life Books. **37:** © John Fairfax Group Pty. Ltd., Sydney. **38, 39:** *People Weekly,* © 1987 Steve Kagan (2); © Galen Rowell/Mountain Light, photo by Ron Kauk, Albany, California. **40:** Valerie Fons Kruger. **41:** F. Rickard/MGA, Chamonix, France, background, Bill Ross/West Light, Los Angeles. **42, 43:** Courtesy Salem County Historical Society, Salem, New Jersey (2)—Michael Latil (3). **44, 45:** Al LeClaire Photography, courtesy Local History Department, Niagara Falls Public Library, Niagara Falls (2), background, Library of Congress LC 208023. **46, 47:** Al LeClaire Photography, courtesy Local History Department, Niagara Falls Public Library, Niagara Falls—Mary Evans Picture Library, London. **48:** Evan Sheppard, courtesy National Postal Museum, National Museum of American History, Smithsonian Institution, Washington, D.C., background, courtesy United States Postal Service, Washington, D.C. **49:** Bibliothèque Nationale, Paris. **50-52:** Roger-Viollet, Paris. **53, 54:** AP/Wide World Photos, New York. **55:** *The Texaco Star*, White Plains, New York. **56, 57:** Courtesy Princeton University Library, Department of Rare Books and Special Collections, Princeton, New

Jersey; satellite image provided by Environmental Research Institute of Michigan (ERIM), Ann Arbor. **58:** AP/Wide World Photos, New York; UPI/Bettmann, New York. **59:** Photo by Hermann Schuschke, © Friedrich M. Öttinger, Gaimersheim, Germany. **60, 61:** Sygma, New York; Vlastimir Shone/Gamma Liaison, New York. **62:** Courtesy David Boehm Productions, Inc. **63:** Greg Riffi/Gamma Liaison, New York. **65:** Zoltan Ovari, Augsburg—art by Time-Life Books. **66:** Sygma, New York. **67:** Produced by ARC Pictures Inc., photography by Ruggero Gabbai—courtesy Raul Garcia. **68:** Elyse Lewin/The Image Bank, New York. **69:** Leo Tierney/*Boston Herald*, Boston. **70:** F. Rickard/MGA, Chamonix, France. **71:** Royal National Lifeboat Institution, London, background, H. D. Thoreau/West Light, Los Angeles. **72:** Robert Sinclair, Cottingham, Hull. **73, 74:** Royal National Lifeboat Institution, London. **75:** Photos courtesy the Hinckley Fire Museum, Hinckley, Minnesota. **77:** United States Coast Guard, Washington, D.C. **78, 79:** Times Printing Company, Inc., Manteo, North Carolina; Royal Geographic Society, London, inset, The

Hulton Picture Company, London. **80, 81:** The Hulton Picture Company, London—Royal Geographic Society, London (2). **82:** Brian Brown. **84, 85:** Nina Gladitz Film Production; Bundesarchiv, Koblenz, Germany, courtesy the United States Holocaust Memorial Museum, Washington, D.C. **86, 87:** The Gladys Aylward Trust, Crawley, Sussex. **89:** AP/Wide World Photos, New York. **90:** UPI/Bettmann, New York. **91:** AP/Wide World Photos, New York—Charles H. Stover. **92, 93:** Sipa Press, New York; Igor Kostin/Sygma, New York; Sipa Press, New York—Sovfoto, New York. **94:** AP/Wide World Photos, New York. **95:** UPI/Bettmann, New York. **96:** Art Meripol. **97:** Neal Slavin. **98:** Photo by Bill Will, courtesy Gregory Robertson. **99:** Mark Downey/Gamma Liaison, New York—*People Weekly*, © 1989 John Storey. **100:** Carolyn Clark. **101:** S. Peter Lewis © 1985, background, W. Cody/West Light, Los Angeles. **102, 103:** The Henry E. Huntington Library and Gallery, San Marino, California—Roger-Viollet, Paris. **104:** Mary Evans Picture Library, London—Roger-Viollet, Paris. **105:** Art by Time-Life Books. **106:** AP/Wide World Pho-

tos, New York. **107:** United States Navy. **109:** Robert L. La Gree. **110:** Jean-Loup Charmet, courtesy Madame J. Pardon—courtesy Pascal Lusseyran. **112, 113:** Art by Time-Life Books; Library of Congress LC 24732, background, Todd Powell/Profiles West, Buena Vista, Colorado. **114:** Popperfoto, London. **115:** Art by Fred Holz, based on a sketch by Eric Williams from *The Wooden Horse*, revised and expanded edition, published by Collins, London, 1979—Popperfoto, London. **116:** Smithsonian Institution 85359AC. **117:** UPI/Bettmann, New York. **119:** Photos by Evan Sheppard (2)—UPI/Bettmann, New York. **121:** Stern, Heidemann, Hamburg; Harold Sells, Jr. **122, 123:** Jean-Pierre Laffont/Sygma, New York. **125:** Photo by Norio Suzuki, Kyodo News Service, Tokyo. **126, 127:** From *Stay Alive My Son*, by Pin Yathay with John Man, The Free Press, New York, 1987—AP/Wide World Photos, New York; Jon Swain/Sipa Press, New York. **128:** Courtesy Bill Lamm. **129:** Photo by Kirk Petersen, courtesy Margery Wortman Mathes. **131:** Claudio Turella, Rome. **132, 133:** © 1985 S. Peter Lewis.

BIBLIOGRAPHY

Books

Anderson, Antone A., and Clara Anderson McDermott. *The Hinckley Fire.* New York: Comet Press Books, 1955.

Andrews, Allen. *The Mad Motorists.* Philadelphia: J. B. Lippincott, 1965.

Bonington, Chris. *Quest for Adventure.* New York: Clarkson N. Potter, 1981.

Brodie, Fawn M. *The Devil Drives: A Life of Sir Richard Burton.* New York: W. W. Norton, 1967.

Brown, Walter R., and Norman D. Anderson. *Rescue! True Stories of the Winners of the Young American Medal for Bravery.* New York: Walker, 1983.

Burton, Richard F. *Personal Narrative of a Pilgrimage to El Medinah and Meccah* (2nd ed., Vol. 1). London: Longman, Brown, Green, Longmans & Roberts, 1857.

Canning, John (Ed.). *100 Great Adventures.* New York: Taplinger, 1969.

Clark, Ronald W. *Great Moments in Escaping.* New York: Roy, 1958.

Cochrane, John Dundas. *Narrative of a Pedestrian Journey through Russia and Siberian Tartary.* New York: Arno Press & New York Times, 1970 (reprint of 1825 edition).

Crone, G. R. (Comp. and Ed.). *The Explorers: Great Adventurers Tell Their Own Stories of Discovery.* New York: Thomas Y. Crowell, 1962.

Cronkhite, Daniel. *Death Valley's Victims: A Descriptive Chronology, 1849-1980.* Morongo Valley, Calif.: Sagebrush

Press, 1981.

Devine, Elizabeth (Ed.). *The Annual Obituary 1983.* Chicago: St. James Press, 1984.

Farr, Martyn. *The Darkness Beckons: The History and Development of Cave Diving.* St. Louis: Cave Books, 1991.

Farwell, Byron. *Burton: A Biography of Sir Richard Francis Burton.* New York: Viking, 1963.

Fiennes, Ranulph. *To the Ends of the Earth.* New York: Arbor House, 1983.

Fraser, Antonia (Ed.). *Heroes & Heroines.* New York: A & W, 1980.

Fuller, Edmund (Ed.). *Mutiny! Being Accounts of Insurrections, Famous and Infamous, on Land and Sea, from the Days of the Caesars to Modern Times.* New York: Crown Publishers, 1953.

Garrett, Richard. *Cross-Channel.* London: Hutchinson, 1972.

The Girl Book of Modern Adventurers. London: Hulton Press, 1957.

Great Adventures That Changed Our World. Pleasantville, N.Y.: Reader's Digest Association, 1978.

Gunning, Thomas G. *Amazing Escapes.* New York: Dodd, Mead, 1984.

Gwynn, Stephen. *The Life of Mary Kingsley.* London: Macmillan, 1932.

Halliburton, Richard. *Complete Book of Marvels.* Indianapolis: Bobbs-Merrill, 1960.

Hamalian, Leo (Ed.). *Ladies on the Loose.* New York: Dodd, Mead, 1981.

Haslip, Joan. *Lady Hester Stanhope.* Heron Books, 1970.

Heatter, Basil. *Against Odds.* New York: Farrar, Straus & Giroux, 1970.

Hendrickson, Robert. *The Great American Tomato Book.* Garden City, N.Y.: Doubleday, 1977.

Herzog, Maurice. *Annapurna: Conquest of the First 8000-Metre Peak.* Translated by Nea Morin and Janet Adam Smith. London: Jonathan Cape, 1952.

Heyerdahl, Thor. *Kon-Tiki: Across the Pacific by Raft.* Translated by F. H. Lyon. Chicago: Rand McNally, 1950.

Hogg, James (Ed.). *Travels of Lady Hester Stanhope* (Vol. 1 & 2). Salzburg: Institut für Anglistik und Amerikanistik, 1983.

Holman, James. *A Voyage Round the World, Including Travels in Africa, Asia, Australia, America* (Vol. 1 & 2). London: Smith, Elder, 1834.

Horder, Mervyn. *On Their Own: Shipwrecks & Survivals.* London: Gerald Duckworth, 1988.

Hough, Richard. *The Bounty.* New York: Penguin Books, 1984.

Israel, Elaine. *Up, Over, Under, and Around: The New Explorers.* New York: Julian Messner, 1980.

Jackson, Donald Dale, and the Editors of Time-Life Books. *The Aeronauts* (Epic of Flight series). Alexandria, Va.: Time-Life Books, 1980.

Jerdan, William. *Men I Have Known.* London: George Routledge & Sons, 1866.

Jones, Tristan:
Outward Leg. New York: Hearst Marine Books, 1985.
Somewheres East of Suez. New York: Hearst Marine Books, 1988.
To Venture Further. New York: Hearst Marine Books, 1991.

Keay, John. *Eccentric Travellers.* Los Angeles: Jeremy P. Tarcher, 1982.

Kingsley, Mary H.:
Travels in West Africa (3rd ed.). London: Frank Cass, 1965.
West African Studies (3rd ed.). New York: Barnes & Noble, 1964.

Lamont, Lansing. *Day of Trinity.* New York: Atheneum, 1965.

Leslie, Edward E. *Desperate Journeys, Abandoned Souls.* Boston: Houghton Mifflin, 1988.

Lewis, David. *Ice Bird: The First Single-Handed Voyage to Antarctica.* New York: W. W. Norton, 1975.

Lusseyran, Jacques. *And There Was Light.* Translated by Elizabeth R. Cameron. Boston: Little, Brown, 1963.

McCormick, Donald. *The Master Book of Escapes.* New York: Franklin Watts, 1975.

McCunn, Ruthanne Lum. *Sole Survivor.* San Francisco: Design Enterprises of S.F., 1985.

Markowitz, Jack. *A Walk on the Crust of Hell.* Brattleboro, Vt.: Stephen Greene Press, 1973.

Medvedev, Grigori. *The Truth about Chernobyl.* Translated by Evelyn Rossiter. Moscow: HarperCollins, 1991.

Meegan, George. *The Longest Walk: An Odyssey of the Human Spirit.* New York: Paragon House, 1989.

Michener, James A., and A. Grove Day. *Rascals in Paradise.* New York: Random House, 1957.

Millar, Ward M. *Valley of the Shadow.* New York: David McKay, 1955.

Mills, Enos A. *The Adventures of a Nature Guide.* Garden City, N.Y.: Doubleday, Page, 1920.

Neider, Charles (Ed.). *Man against Nature: Tales of Adventure and Exploration.* New York: Harper & Brothers, 1954.

Newman, Steven M. *Worldwalk.* New York: William Morrow, 1989.

O'Brien, Andy. *Daredevils of Niagara.* Toronto: Ryerson Press, 1964.

Onoda, Hiroo. *No Surrender: My Thirty-Year War.* Translated by Charles S. Terry. Tokyo: Kodansha International, 1974.

Osius, Alison. *Second Ascent: The Story of Hugh Herr.* Harrisburg, Pa.: Stackpole Books, 1991.

Palmer, T. S. *Chronology of the Death Valley Region in California, 1849-1949.* Hollywood: Borgo Press, 1989.

People in Peril and How They Survived.

Pleasantville, N.Y.: Reader's Digest Association, 1983.

Philpot, Oliver. *Stolen Journey.* New York: E. P. Dutton, 1952.

Pin Yathay, and John Man. *Stay Alive, My Son.* New York: Macmillan, Free Press, 1987.

Prejevalsky, N. *Mongolia, the Tangut Country and the Solitudes of Northern Tibet* (Vol. 1). Translated by E. Delmar Morgan. London: Sampson Low, Marston, Searle, & Rivington, 1876.

Read, Piers Paul. *Alive: The Story of the Andes Survivors.* Philadelphia: J. B. Lippincott, 1974.

Rice, Edward. *Captain Sir Richard Francis Burton.* New York: Charles Scribner's Sons, 1990.

Schachtel, Roger. *Fantastic Flight to Freedom.* Milwaukee, Wis.: Raintree, 1980.

Scotland, Andrew (Comp.):
Courage and Adventure. London: Odhams Books, 1964.
Discovery and Achievement. London: Odhams Books, 1963.

Snow, Edward Rowe. *Astounding Tales of the Sea.* London: Alvin Redman, 1966.

Strange and Wonderfull Things Happened to Richard Hasleton, Borne at Braintree in Essex, in His Ten Years Travailes in Many Forraine Countries. Penned as He Delivered It from His Own Mouth. London: William Barley, 1595.

Swenson, Grace Stageberg. *From the Ashes: The Story of the Hinckley Fire of 1894.* Stillwater, Minn.: Croixside Press, 1979.

Thomas, Lowell:
Great True Adventures. New York: Hawthorn Books, 1955.
The Untold Story of Exploration. New York: Dodd, Mead, 1935.

Tripp, Jenny. *One Was Left Alive.* Milwaukee, Wis.: Raintree, 1980.

True Stories of Great Escapes. Pleasantville, N.Y.: Reader's Digest Association, 1977.

Tschiffely, A. F. *Southern Cross to Pole Star: Tschiffely's Ride.* Los Angeles: J. P. Tarcher, 1983 (reprint of 1933 ed.).

Walter, David. *Great Adventurers.* Morristown, N.J.: Silver Burdett, 1979.

Westman, Paul. *Thor Heyerdahl: Across the Seas of Time.* Minneapolis, Minn.: Dillon Press, 1982.

Whittingham, Richard. *The Rand McNally Almanac of Adventure.* Chicago: Rand McNally, 1982.

Wilcox, Desmond. *Ten Who Dared.* Boston: Time-Life Television Book, Little, Brown, 1977.

Williams, Eric. *The Wooden Horse* (rev. ed.). London: Collins, 1979.

Williams, Gurney, III. *True Escape and Survival Stories.* New York, Franklin Watts, 1977.

Wortman, Elmo. *Four against the Wilderness.* Edna Bay, Alaska: Top Notch, 1992.

Wulffson, Don L. *More Incredible True Adventures.* New York: Penguin Books, E. P. Dutton, 1989.

Periodicals

Abruzzo, Ben L., Maxie L. Anderson, and Larry Newman. " 'Double Eagle II' Has Landed!" *National Geographic,* December 1978.

"Almost Could See the Radiation, a 'Hero of Chernobyl' Recalls." *Atlanta Constitution,* April 9, 1987.

"Articles Tell about Area Scouts." *Miami Herald,* January 4, 1953.

"Blondin." *Daily Gazette* (Niagara Falls, N.Y.), June 27, 1859.

"Blondin." *Lockport Advertiser & Democrat,* July 1, 1859.

"Blondin at the Falls." *Buffalo Daily Courier,* August 17, 1859.

"Blondin's Crossing at the Falls with a Man upon His Back." *Globe* (Toronto), August 19, 1859.

Brooks, Barbara. "Diver Gets Sucked through Underwater Pipeline." *Scuba Times,* November-December 1989.

Browne, Malcolm W.:
"Around the World with Ballon and Gizmos." *New York Times,* January 28, 1992.
"Round-the-World Balloon Flight Put Off, This Time Till November." *New York Times,* February 23, 1992.

Burton, Roger. "Murder Suspect Denied Bond." *Index-Journal* (Greenwood, S.C.), September 27, 1988.

"Canadian Scientist Dies of Exposure to Radiation." *New York Times,* May 30, 1946.

"Captain Boyton." *Times,* May 29, 1875.

"Caving International Interview." *Caving International,* October 1979.

"A City Trembled, Its People Held." *People,* October 30, 1989.

Cooper, Nancy, Joyce Barnathan, and Andrew Nagorse. "A Folk Hero in the Slammer." *Newsweek,* June 15, 1987.

Cote, Elizabeth. "Hanover High Students Hop to It." *Boston Globe,* June 17, 1988.

"Crossing Niagara Falls on a Tight-Rope." *Press* (Philadelphia), June 28, 1859.

Doerner, William R. "Kremlin Prop Wash." *Time,* June 15, 1987.

Dougherty, Margot. "Photographer Galen Rowell Seeks Peak Experiences." *People,* December 8, 1986.

"Driving to the Four Corners of the Earth: Peking to Paris 1907." *Special Historia 449,* April 1984.

Dunn, Elisabeth. "A Dangerous Liaison." *Country Living,* November 1991.

"Gables Boy to Get U.S. Medal." *Miami News,* June 1, 1952.

Gillette, Ned. "Rowing Antarctica's 'Most Mad Seas.' " *National Geographic,* January 1989.

"The Greatest Modern Adventures." *Backpacker*, January 1988.

Hamilton, Alan. "Elephant Attack Hero Honored." *London Times*, October 30, 1991.

Harby, Samuel F. "They Survived at Sea." *National Geographic*, May 1945.

"The Indomitable Tristan Jones." *Cruising World*, January 1992.

Jones, Tristan. "Fifty Years at Sea." *Cruising World*, October 1988.

"Jumper Dives to Rescue Colleague in Coolidge Event." *Casa Grande Dispatch*, April 22, 1987.

Kelso, John. "After Bench Pressing His Car, Tractor-Trailer Rigs Were Easy." *Austin American Statesman*, June 22, 1991.

Kernan, Michael. "Richard Burton, a Man for All Ages except His Own." *Smithsonian*, February 1990.

Lane, Teresa. "Vero Diver Prepared 'to Die Fast.' " *Palm Beach Post*, June 8, 1989.

Lewis, David. "Alone to Antarctica." *National Geographic*, December 1973.

"Lieut. Holman, the Blind Traveller." *Gentleman's Magazine and Historical Review*, September 1857.

" 'Like Walking on Dark Side of Moon,' Say Cave Victors." *Observer* (London), August 4, 1991.

"A Loving Father Eases the Recovery of Julio Berumen, the Quake's Littlest Survivor." *People*, December 4, 1989.

Matthiessen, Peter. "The 'Madman' of Chernobyl." *New York Times*, October 14, 1991.

"Mayor Cudden Lauds Response to Area's Call for Assistance." *Logan Banner* (Logan, W.Va.), March 13, 1963.

Mills, Judy. "The Longest Honeymoon." *Women's Sports & Fitness*, March 1987.

"A Miraculous Sky Rescue." *Time*, May 4, 1987.

"Mons. Blondin's Great Feat." *Buffalo Daily Courier*, July 1, 1859.

"Monsieur Blondin Walks the Tight Rope Across Niagara River." *Daily Spectator* (Toronto), July 1, 1859.

Moritz, Rob. "Attacker Chased off with Cane." *Arkansas Gazette*, July 30, 1987.

Moses, Sam. "The Only Way to Go Is Up." *Sports Illustrated*, June 6, 1977.

Neill, Michael. "From Sea to Shining Sea." *People*, September 21, 1987.

Oliver, Peter. " 'It Had to Be Done.' " *Backpacker*, January 1989.

Ottinger, Fritz. "Nepal-Gipfel Rad!" *Rad Magazine*, August 8, 1987.

Peck, Douglas L. "View Finder." *Runner's World*, April 1991.

Plummer, William, and Vickie Bane. "Never Say Grounded." *People*, October 7, 1991.

Plummer, William, and Mary Huzinec. "Amazing Inspirations." *People*, Fall 1991.

"Radiation from Accident Hits 8 at Los Alamos." *New York Times*, May 24, 1946.

Randall, Glenn. "Galen Rowell." *Backpacker*, February 1990.

Reed, Susan. "19,000 Miles Later, George Meegan Says His Way Is No Longer the Highway." *People*, October 10, 1983.

"Ringing the Globe for Adventure." *Insight*, November 5, 1990.

Roberts, David. "Galen Rowell." *American Photographer*, November 1983.

Ryan, Michael. "This Quiet Man Saved Thousands." *Parade*, August 19, 1990.

Schneider, Richard C., M.D., Michael Papo, M.D., and Carlos Soto Alvarez, M.D. "The Effects of Chronic Recurrent Spinal Trauma in High-Diving." *Journal of Bone and Joint Surgery*, June 1962.

Schwartz, David M. "On the Royal Road to Adventures with 'Daring Dick.' " *Smithsonian*, March 1989.

Sullivan, Robert. "A Big Dreamer—and Doer, Too." *Sports Illustrated*, December 10, 1990.

"Survivors and Heroes of an Icy Crash." *Life*, January 1983.

"Thor Heyerdahl: Sailing against the Current." *U.S. News & World Report*, April 2, 1990.

Trimble, Jeff. "Gorbachev Takes On the Generals." *U.S. News & World Report*, June 15, 1987.

"Tristan Jones." *Cruising World*, January 1989.

Van Dyne, Larry. "The Crash of Flight 90." *Washingtonian*, December 1986.

"Voyager and Naturalist: David Lewis, M.D." *Cruising World*, January 1989.

Waddington, Richard. "The 'Last' Japanese Soldier Fights the War for Nature." *Asahi Evening News*, December 27, 1985.

Watson, Russell, John Barry, and Joyce Barnathan. "Marching Orders." *Newsweek*, June 15, 1987.

Wood, John. "Galen Rowell's Motto: In Focus and in Jeopardy." *Modern Maturity*, April-May 1991.

"World-Girdler Steve Newman Sets a Record by Walking in a Very, Very Big Circle." *People*, March 30, 1987.

Wyrick, Bob. "It's Tough to Be a Hero." *Miami Herald*, September 20, 1964.

Other

Boy Scouts of America. Announcement of award to Parker Stratt of the Gold Medal for Life Saving. New York: December 13, 1951.

"Katherine Finkbeiner Attempted to Save an Indeterminate Number of Persons from Being Shot, Greenwood, South Carolina, September 26, 1988." Annual Report. Carnegie Hero Fund Commission, 1988.

"Richard Rathiby Hoodless." Award. Royal Humane Society, January 6, 1834.

INDEX

Numerals in italics indicate an illustration of the subject mentioned.

A

Abruzzo, Ben, 30-*31*, 32
Acapulco cliff divers, 67-69, *68*
Adams, John, 106
Aerialists, *44*
Air Florida Flight 90, *94-96, 95*
Airline disasters: Air Florida Flight 90, *94-96, 95*; crash in Andes Mountains, 122-124, *122-123*; emergency landing at McGuire Air Force Base, 130; Northwest Airlines crash, 76; Peruvian jungle crash, 120-122, *121*
Ai-weh-deh (Gladys Aylward), 85-88, *87*
Akimov, Aleksandr, 94
Algorta, Pedro, *123*
Alligator rescue, 90
Amputee-climber, *101, 132-133*
Anderson, Maxie, 30-32, *31*
Andes Mountains airplane crash, 122-124, *122-123*
Annapurna expedition, 24-26, *25*
Antarctica: Lewis's voyage, 36-37, *map 36*; Shackleton's expedition, 78-81, *79, 80*
Arabian Nights, 13
Argentina: journey from Buenos Aires to Washington, D.C., on pampas pony, *20-21, map 21*
Arkansas Gazette, 96
Atlantis Society, 28
Atomic bomb, 88
Auto stunts: driving across America in reverse, *55*; race from Beijing to Paris, *49-51, 50*
Aylward, Gladys, 85-88, *87*

B

Babcock, Lucille, *96-97*
Back-Up Boys, *55*
Bagdasarov, Yuri, 94
Balloon flight, 30-32, *31, maps 30-32*
Bamboo stakes, 127
"Barefooting," *63*

Barry, Edward, *75, 76*
BBC, 22
Beame, Abraham, *58*
Beard: of bees, *62*
Beaujard, Michel, 63
Bedlam, 8
Bedouins, 9
Bee beard, *62*
Beijing to Paris auto race, *49-51, 50*
Bends, 35
Benlomond (ship), 106, *107*
Bergman, Ingrid, 88
Beruman, Cathy, 99
Beruman, Julio, *99*-100
Beruman, Petra, 99
Best, William, *75, 76*
Betts, James, *99*-100
Beyond the Euphrates (Stark), 21
Bicycling through the Himalayas, *59-60*
Blanco, Jorge Pérez, 118-120
Bligh, William, 103-106, *104*
Blind traveler, *10*
Blondin, Charles, 43-44
Boer War, 15
Boreham Cave, *33*
Borghese, Scipione, 49-51
Bounty (ship): mutiny on, 103-106, *104*
Bouquet, Laurent, *41, 70*
Boyton, Paul, 46-47
British East India Company, 11
British Museum, 15
Brothers, Richard, 8
Bruce, Michael, 9
Buchenwald, 111, 117
Bungee jumping, *63*-64
Burton, Isabel, 12, 13
Burton, Richard Francis, 7, 10, *11*-13
Byron, Lord (George Gordon), 9

C

Cambodia: escape from, 126-127
Canessa, Roberto, 123, 124
Cannibalism, 122, 123, 124
Canoeing expedition from Canada to Cape Horn, *40*
Cape Hatteras, 77

Castro, Fidel, 118
Catholicism, 123, 124
Cave diving, *7, 33-35, 34*
Chai-Pill Kim, 116
Chernobyl, 92-94, *92-93*
Chiang Kai-shek, Madame, 88
Chicamacomico Station, 77, 78
Chichan, Cecilia, 76
Chichan family, 76
China: auto race from Beijing to Paris, *49-51, 50*; Communist revolution, 88; Japanese invasion of, 86-88; orphans' trek to safety, *86,* 87-88; Russian expedition to, 15-17, *map 16*
Chinese orphans' escape to freedom, *86,* 87-88
Christian, Fletcher, 104, 106
Churchill, Winston, 117
Civil war: Chinese, 88; Spanish, 83
Cliff divers of Acapulco, 67-69, *68*
Club de Clavadistas, 67-69, *68*
Codd, Michael J., 58
Codner, Michael, *114*-115
Colcord, Henry M., 43-44
Collignon, Victor, *49, 50, 51*
Communism: Cuban regime, 118; postwar takeover of Eastern Europe, 117; revolution in China, 88
Concentration camps: Nazi, 83, 84, 85, 111, 117; Khmer Rouge, 126-127
Continental Divide, *112-113*
Cook, James, 104
Cooke, Don, *62*
Coolidge, Calvin, 21
Cormier, Georges, *49, 51*
Corson, Bob, 130
Creighton, Charles, *55*
Crimean War, 12
Cuba: escape from, 118-120
Cycling: in Himalayas, *59-60*
Czechoslovakia: escape from, *117*-118

D

Daghlian, Larry, 89
Dangerous Sports Club, 64
Daring Dick, *56-57*

Darling, Grace Horsley, *71, 73-74*
Darling, William (brother of Grace), 73-74
Darling, William (father of Grace), *73*, 74
Darwin, Charles, 14
Dead Man's Handshake, 35
Dead Sea, 27
Death Valley, *82-83*
de Dion-Bouton (French auto), 49, *51*
Défense de la France, *110*, 111
Desert rescue, 82-83
Dillard, Oliver, 90-91
Divers: cave divers, *7, 33-35, 34;* cliff
    divers of Acapulco, *67-69, 68;* trapped
    scuba diver, *128*
Dixon, Alexandra, 100
Dobson, Joseph, 72
Double Eagle (helium balloon), 30-31, 32
Double Eagle II (helium balloon), 30, 31-
    32; maps 30-32
"Dragon's tail," 88-89
Driving across America in reverse, *55*
Duncan, Max, 97
Dyatlov, Anatoly, 94

E
Earthwinds (balloon), 32
Easter Island, *24*
Egyptians, 24
Eichmann, Adolf, 84
Elephant: charge, 100; used in Kra expe-
    dition, *28-29*
Elephant Island, *80-81*
Elizabeth II, 100
Emergency landing at McGuire Air Force
    Base, 130
Endurance (ship), 79-80
English Channel: motorcycle crossing,
    52; test of India-rubber floating suit,
    46-47
Escapes: Cambodian concentration camp,
    126-127; Chinese orphans, *86,* 87-88;
    Cuba, 118-120; Czechoslovakia, *117-*
    118; German POW camp, 114-*115;*
    Haslecon's, 102-103; North Korean
    prison hospital, 116; trapped scuba
    diver, *128*

Ettenhuber, Thomas, 28, 29
Euphrates River, 22
Everest, Mount, 24, 59, 66

F
Fairbanks, R. J. (Dad), *82*-83
Fang (African tribe), 15
Fascists, 83
Fernandez, Daniel, 122, 124
Fitzwater, Guy, 98
Flagpole sitting, *53-54*
Flood rescue, 90-*91*
Forest fire: Hinckley, Minnesota, 75-76
Forfarshire (paddle steamer): wreck of,
    73-74
Fram (ship), *18, 19*
Franco, Francisco, 83
Franz Josef Land, 18, 19
French resistance, 111
Frostbite, 26, 37, 130, 132
Fruit catcher, *69*

G
Garcia, Raul, *67,* 69
Genet, Ray (Pirate), 66
Genet, Taras, *66*
George VI, 108
Gillette, Ned, 17
Gobi Desert, *16*-17, 50, *51*
Godard, Charles, *49,* 51
Gordon, George (Lord Byron), 9
Gouvy, Bruno, 70
Grand tour, 10
Grape catching, *69*
Graves, Alvin, 89
Great Escape of March 1944, 114
Greenland, 18
Grishchenko, Anatoly, 94
Guinness Book of Records, The, 69
Gustafson, Gerry, *90*

H
Halliburton, Richard, *56-57*
Hang glider, motorized: from Germany to
    Australia, 64-*65, map* 65
Hara-kiri, 124

Harar, 11
Hargis, James, *55*
Harley, Roy, *123*
Hasenmayer, Jochen, 34-35
Hasleton, Richard, *102*-103
Henry Wagner (boat), *28*-29
Hermoine (coal brig), 72
Herr, Hugh, *101, 132-133*
Herzog, Maurice, 24, *25, 26*
Heyerdahl, Thor, 23-*24*
Hillary, Edmund, 24
Himalayas, 24, *25,* 26, *59-60,* 66
Hinckley, Minnesota: forest fire, 75-
    76
Holman, James, *10*
Home (sailboat), 129, 130
Honeymoon canoers, *40*
Hoodless, Richard, *72*
Horses: Przhevalsky's, *16;* rescue at sea
    by, 72; trek from Argentina to Wash-
    ington, D.C., on pampas pony, *20-21,*
    map 21
Horseshoe Fall, *45,* 46
"Human Fly," 57-*58*
Hungarian deportation of Jews, 83, *84-*
    85
Hussey, L. D. A., *79*
Huxley, Thomas, 14

I
Ice Bird (boat), 36-37
Ichac, Marcel, 24, *25,* 26
India-rubber floating suit, *46-47*
Inn of the Sixth Happiness, 86
Inn of the Sixth Happiness, The (novel),
    88
International Rescue Committee, 120
Iron Curtain, 117

J
Jackson, Frederick, 18
James Caird (lifeboat), *80-81*
Japanese World War II soldiers, 124-
    125
Johansen, Hjalmar, *18,* 19
Johnson, Robert Gibbon, *42-43*

Jones, Tristan, 27-29

K

Kama Sutra, 13
Keld Head-Kingsdale link, 34-35
Kelly, Alvin (Shipwreck), 53-54
Khmer Rouge, 126-127
Kingsley, Charles, 14
Kingsley, George, 14
Kingsley, Mary, 14-15
Koepcke, Juliane, 120-122, 121
Koepcke, Marie, 120
Koldunov, Alexander, 61
Koller, Hans, 59
Kon-Tiki (ship), 23-24
Korean War: escape from prison hospital,
    116
Kra expedition, 28-29
Kruger, Valerie, 40
Kruger, Verien, 40

L

Lachenal, Louis, 24, 25, 26
Lady of the Outer Banks (surf boat), 77
LaGree, Bob, 109
Lamm, William, 128
Land diving, 64
La Quebrada cliffs, 67, 68
Lawson, Jeannie, 85, 86
Lewis, Barry, 36
Lewis, David, 36-37
Life raft: survival at sea on, 106-108, 107
Lifesaving Service, 78
Lindbergh, Charles, 30
Lockheed Electra: crash in Peruvian jun-
    gle, 120-122, 121
Longstone lighthouse saga, 73-74
Los Alamos, 88
Lubang, Philippines, 124-125
Lusseyran, Jacques, 109-111, 110

M

McKenna, Tim, 63
McKinley, Mount, 66
Maloney, Glen, 124
Manhattan Project, 88

Marconi, Guglielmo, 46
Massachusetts Institute of Technology,
    132
Le Matin, 49, 51
Mecca, 12
Medina, 12
Merriman, C. S., 47
Meryon, Charles, 9
Methol, Javier, 124
Methol, Lilliana, 124
Middle East travels, 10-13, 21-22
Midgett, John Allen, Jr., 77-78
Migration theories: South Pacific, 23-24
Millar, Ward, 116
Miller, Stewart, 91
Mills, Enos, 112-113
Mirio (British tanker), 77-78
Mongolia: Russian expedition, 15-17,
    map 16
Mormons, 12
Moscow: flight into Red Square, 60-61;
    Mitino Cemetery, 94
Motorcycles: crossing English Channel
    on, 52; "First Lady" of, 64
Mountain rescues: Alps crevasse, 131;
    Andes Mountains plane crash, 122-
    124, 122-123
Mugsy (terrier), 124
Mussolini, Benito, 83
Mutiny on the *Bounty,* 103-106; map 105

N

Nansen, Fridtjof, 18-19
National Geographic Society, 21, 39
Nationalist Chinese Army, 87, 88
Nazis: concentration camps, 83, 84, 85,
    111, 117; deportation of Hungarian
    Jews, 83, 84-85; occupation of France,
    109-111; resistance movements
    against, 111, 117; U-boats, 106, 107
Neal, William, 91
Newman, Larry, 31, 32
Newman, Steven, 38-39
Niagara Falls: going over in a barrel, 45-
    46; tightrope crossing, 43-44
Nile River, 12

Nimitz Freeway, 99
Nobel Prize, 19
Norgay, Tenzing, 24
North Pole, 18-19
Northwest Airlines 1987 crash, 76
Norton, John, 105
Nuclear radiation accident at Los Alamos,
    88-89
Nuclear reactor meltdown at Chernobyl,
    92-94, 92-93

O

Olian, Roger, 96
Onoda, Hiroo, 124-125
Orozco, Yolanda, 99, 100
Ottin, Germain, 131
Öttinger, Fritz, 59-60
Oudot, Jacques, 26
Our Desert Camp (Tyrwhitt-Drake), 12-13
Outer Banks, North Carolina: shipwrecks,
    77-78
Outward Leg (trimaran), 27-28
Ovari, Zoltan, 64-65

P

Pahlavi dynasty, 22
Palmyra, 9, 12-13
Pampas pony: ridden by Tschiffely from
    Argentina to Washington, D.C., 20-21,
    map 21
Panama Canal: swim through, 56-57
Pandora (ship), 106
Parachute jump: from World Trade Cen-
    ter, 67
Parachute rescue, 97-98
Parcel post: shipment of four-year-old
    child by, 48
Parrado, Fernando, 124
Patton, George C., 111
Pentecost Island, 64
Perfumed Garden, The (Burton), 13
Perlasca, Giorgio, 83-85, 84
Perrey, H. S., 52
Peru: airplane crash, 120-122, 121; mi-
    gration theories about, 23-24
Philpot, Oliver, 114-115

Pierstorff, May, 48
Pilgrimage to Holy Lands, *8-9*
Pin Any, 126-127
Pin Yathay, *126*-127
Pitcairn Island, 106
Pitt, William (the Younger), 8, 9
Polar expeditions: Nansen's trek to North
    Pole, *18-19;* Shackleton's expedition to
    Antarctica, 78-81, *78-79, 80-81*
Polo, Marco, 17
Pons, Auguste, *49,* 50
Pons, Lily, 49
Poon Lim, *106*-108
Potomac River airplane crash, *94-96, 95*
Powers, Harry, 75, 76
Pripyat, Ukraine, 92
Prisoners of war (POWs): German POW
    camp escape, 114-*115*
Przhevalsky, Nikolay Mikhaylovich, 15-17,
    16
Przhevalsky's horse, *16*
Publicity stunts: crossing U.S. in reverse,
    55; flagpole sitting, *53-54;* India-
    rubber floating suit, *46-47*

R
Ra I (papyrus boat), 24
Ra II (papyrus boat), 24
Radioactivity: Chernobyl nuclear reactor
    meltdown, 92-94, *92-93;* Los Alamos
    nuclear accident, 88-89
Radio Free Europe, 118
Ramirez, Armando Socarras, 118-120,
    119
Rape: thwarted attempt, 96-97
Rébuffat, Gaston, 24, *25,* 26
Red Square: Rust's flight into, *60*-61
Resistance movement in France, 111,
    117
Riffi, Gregg, *63*-64
Roaring Twenties, 53
Robertson, Gregory, *97-98*
Robinson, Dot, 64
Root, James, 75, 76
Rowell, Galen, *39*
Royal Geographic Society of London, 12,
22
Royal Humane Society, 72
Royal National Lifeboat Institution, 74
Rubber-suit test across English Channel,
    46-47
Rugby team: stranded in Andes, 122-124,
    122-123
Rust, Mathias, *60-61*

S
Salem, New Jersey, *42,* 43
San Francisco 1989 earthquake, *99*-100
Sanz-Briz, Angel, 83, 84, 85
Schoonmaker, Richard, 128
Schuschke, Hermann, 59-60
Scott, Robert Falcon, 78, 79
Screaming Sixties, 36
Scuba diver's escape from an intake pipe,
    128
Sea Dragon (Chinese junk), 57
Shackleton, Ernest, 78-81, *79*
Shackleton's transantarctic expedition,
    78-81, *78-79, 80-81*
Sherpas, 26, 59, 60
Shipwrecks: British merchant ship *Ben-
    lomond,* 106, 107; Longstone light-
    house saga, *73-74;* rescue on horse-
    back, 72; torpedoed British tanker,
    77-78
Skutnik, Lenny, *94,* 96
Skydiving rescue, 97-98
Sky surfing, *41, 70*
Slotin, Louis, 88-*89*
Smagin, Viktor Grigoryevich, 94
Smith, Charlie, 90-91
Smith, Estella, 90-91
Snow-blind Rocky Mountain guide, 112-
    113
Sokolov, Sergei, 61
South Pacific: migration theories, 23-24;
    origin of bungee jumping, 64
Spanish Civil War, 83
Spanish Inquisition, 102
Speke, John Hanning, 12
Speleology, 33
Spijker, Jacobus, 49, 51
Spyker (auto), 49, 51
Stalag-Luft III, 114-*115*
Stanhope, Hester, *8-9*
Stapar, Richard, 102, 103
Stark, Freya, *21-22*
Statham, Oliver, 33-*34, 35*
Stover, Charles, *91*
*Strange and Wonderfull Things Happened
    to Richard Hasleton* (Hasleton), 102
Stratt, Parker, *90*
Suez Canal, 28
Sufi sect, 11
Sullivan, Kathy, 66
Swimming: through Panama Canal, *56-
    57*

T
Tanganyika, Lake, 12
Tank escape out of Czechoslovakia, *117*-
    118
Tavilla, Paul, *69*
Taylor, Anna Edson, *45-46*
Telyatnikov, Leonid, 93
Terray, Lionel, 24, *25, 26*
Texaco, 55
Thacker, Harry, *52*
Thong Chai (elephant), *28-29*
Thouless, Christopher, *100*
Tightrope walker: crossing Niagara Falls,
    43-44
Tirado, Priscilla, *94,* 96
Titicaca, Lake, 27
Tomato-eating stunt, 42-43
Toptunov, Leonid, 94
Torpedoed tanker *Mirio,* 77-78
Tractor-trailer accident, *109*
Train rescue from forest fire, 75-76
Travels in West Africa (Kingsley), 15
Truman, Harry S., 90
Tschiffely, Aimé Felix, *20-21*
Tunneling out of POW camp, 114-*115*
Turella, Claudio, *131*
Turella, Maria Antonietta, *131*

U
U-boats: torpedoed *Benlomond* in World

War II, 106, 107; in World War I, off
American coast, 77
Uhlik, Vaclav, *117*-118
Ukraine: Chernobyl power-plant accident,
92-94, *92-93*
United States Atlantic Life-saving Service,
46
United States Coast Guard, 77
United States Congress, 77, 108
United States Park Police, 95
Uruguayan rugby team: stranded in An-
des, 122-124, *122-123*
Usher, Don, 95

V

Vaulting horse: used in German POW
camp escape, 114-*115*
Verrazano, Giovanni da, 77
Vestris (ship), 21
Vichy government, 111
Victoria, Lake, 12
"Vincent, John," 67

Volunteers of Liberty, 111
Voyage Round the World (Holman),
10

W

Waite, Bill, 130
Waite, Martha, 130
Walk around the world, *38*-39
Walker, Jimmy, *20*
Walker, Meriwether L., 56-57
Wallenberg, Raoul, 83
Washington, Mount, 132
Weir, Mike, 69
West African Studies (Kingsley), 15
Wilderness photographer, *39*
Williams, Debbie, 97-*98*
Williams, Eric, *114*-115
Willig, George (Human Fly), 57-*58*
Windsor, Gene, 95
Wisener, Lloyd A., 48
World Trade Center: human ascent of, 57-
58; parachute jump from, *67*

World War I, 19, 77
World War II: atomic bomb, 88; escape
from German POW camp, 114-*115;*
French resistance, 109-111; German U-
boats, 106, 107; Japanese soldiers on
Philippine Island, 124-*125;* Japanese
invasion of China, 86-88; Perlasca's
rescues of Hungarian Jews, 83-85, *84-
85;* surrender of Japan, 88. *See also*
Concentration camps
Worsley, Frank, 81
Wortman family, *129*-130
Wrestler crushed between tractor-trailers,
109
Wright brothers, 46

Y

Yangtze River, 17
Yeadon, Geoff, 33, *34, 35*
Yost, Edwin, 30, 31
Young, Edward, 106
Young American Medal for Bravery, 90

Time-Life Books is a division of Time Life Inc.,
a wholly owned subsidiary of
THE TIME INC. BOOK COMPANY

TIME-LIFE BOOKS

PRESIDENT: Mary N. Davis

MANAGING EDITOR: Thomas H. Flaherty
Director of Editorial Resources: Elise D. Ritter-Clough
Executive Art Director: Ellen Robling
Director of Photography and Research:
John Conrad Weiser
Editorial Board: Dale M. Brown, Janet Cave, Roberta
Conlan, Laura Foreman, Lee Hassig, Jim Hicks, Blaine
Marshall, Rita Thievon Mullin, Henry Woodhead
*Assistant Director of Editorial Resources/Training
Manager:* Norma E. Shaw

PUBLISHER: Robert H. Smith

Associate Publisher: Sandra Lafe Smith
Editorial Director: Russell B. Adams, Jr.
Marketing Director: Anne C. Everhart
Director of Production Services: Robert N. Carr
Production Manager: Prudence G. Harris
Supervisor of Quality Control: James King

Editorial Operations
Production: Celia Beattie
Library: Louise D. Forstall
Computer Composition: Deborah G. Tait (Manager),
Monika D. Thayer, Janet Barnes Syring, Lillian Daniels
Interactive Media Specialist: Patti H. Cass

**Library of Congress
Cataloging-in-Publication Data**
Above and Beyond / by the editors of Time-Life Books.
p.   cm.   (Library of curious and unusual facts)
Includes bibliographical references.
ISBN 0-8094-7735-1
ISBN 0-8094-7736-X (lib. bdg.)
1. Heroes—Biography. 2. Adventures and
adventurers—Biography. 3. Courage.
4. Curiosities and wonders.
I. Time-Life Books. II. Series.
Ct105.A26 1992
920.02—dc20   92-7151 CIP

LIBRARY OF CURIOUS AND UNUSUAL FACTS

SERIES EDITOR: Carl A. Posey
Series Administrator: Roxie France-Nuriddin
Art Director: Cynthia Richardson
Picture Editor: Sally Collins

Editorial Staff for *Above and Beyond*
Text Editor: John R. Sullivan
Senior Writer: Stephanie A. Lewis
Associate Editor/Research: Vicki Warren
Assistant Editors/Research: Michael E. Howard,
Ruth J. Moss
Assistant Art Director: Alan Pitts
Senior Copy Coordinator: Jarelle S. Stein
Copy Coordinator: Juli Duncan
Picture Coordinator: Jennifer Iker
Editorial Assistant: Terry Ann Paredes

Special Contributors: William Barnhill, John Clausen,
Marge Dumond, Jack McClintock, Gina Maranto, An-
thony K. Pordes (text); Catherine B. Hackett, Maureen
McHugh, Tanya Nádas-Taylor, Robin S. H. Tunnicliff
(research); Louise Wile Hedberg (index)

Correspondents: Elisabeth Kraemer-Singh (Bonn),
Christine Hinze (London), Christina Lieberman (New
York), Maria Vincenza Aloisi (Paris), Ann Natanson
(Rome). Valuable assistance was also provided by An-
gelika Lemmer (Bonn); Caroline Alcock, Judy Aspinall
(London); Trini Bandrés (Madrid); Nelly Sindayen
(Manila); John Dunn (Melbourne); Libby Williams
(Mexico City); Juan Sosa (Moscow); Elizabeth Brown,
Katheryn White (New York); Leonora Dodsworth
(Rome); Dick Berry, Mieko Ikeda (Tokyo).

The Consultant:
Don L. Wulffson is the author of *Incredible True Adventures, The Upside-Down Ship, The Invention of
Ordinary Things, How Sports Came to Be,* and *Point-
Blank,* as well as numerous educational programs
and more than 300 stories, poems, and nonfiction
pieces. He is the recipient of the Distinguished
Achievement Award for his educational writing and
the Leather Medal Award for his poetry.

Other Publications:

LOST CIVILIZATIONS
ECHOES OF GLORY
THE NEW FACE OF WAR
HOW THINGS WORK
WINGS OF WAR
CREATIVE EVERYDAY COOKING
COLLECTOR'S LIBRARY OF THE UNKNOWN
CLASSICS OF WORLD WAR II
AMERICAN COUNTRY
VOYAGE THROUGH THE UNIVERSE
THE THIRD REICH
THE TIME-LIFE GARDENER'S GUIDE
MYSTERIES OF THE UNKNOWN
TIME FRAME
FIX IT YOURSELF
FITNESS, HEALTH & NUTRITION
SUCCESSFUL PARENTING
HEALTHY HOME COOKING
UNDERSTANDING COMPUTERS
LIBRARY OF NATIONS
THE ENCHANTED WORLD
THE KODAK LIBRARY OF CREATIVE PHOTOGRAPHY
GREAT MEALS IN MINUTES
THE CIVIL WAR
PLANET EARTH
COLLECTOR'S LIBRARY OF THE CIVIL WAR
THE EPIC OF FLIGHT
THE GOOD COOK
WORLD WAR II
HOME REPAIR AND IMPROVEMENT
THE OLD WEST

*For information on and a full description of any of
the Time-Life Books series listed above, please call
1-800-621-7026 or write:*
Reader Information
Time-Life Customer Service
P.O. Box C-32068
Richmond, Virginia 23261-2068

This volume is one in a series that explores astounding but surprisingly true events in history, science,
nature, and human conduct. Other books in the series include:

*Feats and Wisdom of the Ancients
Mysteries of the Human Body
Forces of Nature
Vanishings
Amazing Animals
Inventive Genius
Lost Treasure
The Mystifying Mind
A World of Luck
Hoaxes and Deceptions
Crimes and Punishments
Odd and Eccentric People
Shadows of Death
Manias and Delusions*